# First World War
## and Army of Occupation
# War Diary
## France, Belgium and Germany

24 DIVISION
17 Infantry Brigade
Buffs (East Kent Regiment)
8th Battalion
21 August 1915 - 31 January 1918

WO95/2207/1

The Naval & Military Press Ltd
www.nmarchive.com
Published in association with The National Archives

Published by

## The Naval & Military Press Ltd

Unit 10 Ridgewood Industrial Park,

Uckfield, East Sussex,

TN22 5QE England

Tel: +44 (0) 1825 749494

www.naval-military-press.com

www.nmarchive.com

*This diary has been reprinted in facsimile from the original. Any imperfections are inevitably reproduced and the quality may fall short of modern type and cartographic standards.*

© **Crown Copyright**
**Images reproduced by permission of The National Archives, London, England, 2015.**

# Contents

| Document type | Place/Title | Date From | Date To |
|---|---|---|---|
| Heading | WO95/2207/1 | | |
| Heading | 8th Bn East Kent Regt (Buffs) 1915 Aug-1918 Jan | | |
| Heading | 8th Bn East Kent Regt (Buffs) Aug 1915-Oct 1915 | | |
| Heading | 8th Battn. The Buffs (East Kent Regiment). August And September (21.8.15 to 30.9.15) 1915 | | |
| War Diary | Blackdown | 21/08/1915 | 31/08/1915 |
| War Diary | Boulogne | 01/09/1915 | 02/09/1915 |
| War Diary | Maninghem | 03/09/1915 | 21/09/1915 |
| War Diary | Nouveauville 10-35 54. Map | 22/09/1915 | 22/09/1915 |
| War Diary | Guarbecque | 23/09/1915 | 24/09/1915 |
| War Diary | Bethune | 25/09/1915 | 25/09/1915 |
| War Diary | Noeux-Les-Mines | 27/09/1915 | 28/09/1915 |
| War Diary | Molinghem | 29/09/1915 | 30/09/1915 |
| Heading | 24th Division 8th E. Kent Vol I Oct 15 | | |
| War Diary | Molinghem | 01/10/1915 | 01/10/1915 |
| War Diary | Houtkerque | 02/10/1915 | 05/10/1915 |
| War Diary | Reninghelst | 06/10/1915 | 17/10/1915 |
| War Diary | Reserve Dugouts | 20/10/1915 | 26/10/1915 |
| War Diary | Reninghelst Camp D | 26/10/1915 | 31/10/1915 |
| Heading | 24th Division 8th E. Kent Vol. 2 Nov 15 | | |
| Heading | War Diary Of 8th (Service) Batn The Buffs From 1st November 1915 to 30th November 1915 | | |
| War Diary | Camp A Near Ouderdon | 01/11/1915 | 01/11/1915 |
| War Diary | H.Q. Dugouts | 03/11/1915 | 07/11/1915 |
| War Diary | Reninghelst Camp A | 09/11/1915 | 13/11/1915 |
| War Diary | H.Q. Dugouts | 15/11/1915 | 20/11/1915 |
| War Diary | Reninghelst Camp G | 22/11/1915 | 22/11/1915 |
| War Diary | Eecke | 23/11/1915 | 24/11/1915 |
| War Diary | Arneke | 24/11/1915 | 24/11/1915 |
| War Diary | Houlle | 25/11/1915 | 25/11/1915 |
| War Diary | Bayenghem Les-Eperlecques | 26/11/1915 | 27/11/1915 |
| War Diary | Bayenghem | 28/11/1915 | 28/11/1915 |
| War Diary | La Panne | 29/11/1915 | 30/11/1915 |
| Heading | 24th Division 8th E. Kent Vol. 3 December 1915 | | |
| Heading | War Diary of 8th (Service) Batn The Buffs from 1.12.15 to 31.12.15 | | |
| War Diary | La Panne | 01/12/1915 | 31/12/1915 |
| Heading | 8th Battalion "Buffs" East Kent Regiment. January 1916 Dec 17 | | |
| Heading | War Diary of 8th (Service) Bn The Buffs.from 1.1.16 to 31.1.16 Volume 4 | | |
| War Diary | La Panne | 01/01/1916 | 05/01/1916 |
| War Diary | Poperinghe | 06/01/1916 | 07/01/1916 |
| War Diary | Camp E H 19.b.4 6 Sheet 28 B Series | 08/01/1916 | 13/01/1916 |
| War Diary | Ramparts Ypres | 14/01/1916 | 17/01/1916 |
| War Diary | Bn H.Q. in Ramparts Ypres | 18/01/1916 | 22/01/1916 |
| War Diary | Camp B | 24/01/1916 | 29/01/1916 |
| War Diary | Bn H.Q. Belgian Chateau | 30/01/1916 | 31/01/1916 |
| Heading | 8th Battalion "Buffs" East Kent Regiment. February 1916 | | |

| | | | |
|---|---|---|---|
| Heading | War Diary of 8th (Service) Batn The Buffs from 1st February 1916 to 29th February 1916 Volume 7 | | |
| War Diary | Bn. H.Q. Belgian Chateau | 01/02/1916 | 05/02/1916 |
| War Diary | Bn. H.Q. Dugouts | 06/02/1916 | 11/02/1916 |
| War Diary | Bn. H.Q. Dugouts At Belgium Chateau | 12/02/1916 | 15/02/1916 |
| War Diary | Bn. H.Q. Camp C | 16/02/1916 | 18/02/1916 |
| War Diary | Camp C | 19/02/1916 | 29/02/1916 |
| Heading | 8th Battalion "Buffs" East Kent Regiment. March 1916 | | |
| Heading | War Diary of 8th (Service) Batn The Buffs from 1st March 1916 to 31st March 1916 | | |
| War Diary | Camp C G 11 C5 5 Sheet 28 | 01/03/1916 | 06/03/1916 |
| War Diary | Camp C | 07/03/1916 | 07/03/1916 |
| War Diary | Bn. H.Q. I24a2.1 Sheet 28 | 08/03/1916 | 20/03/1916 |
| War Diary | Camp A G 11 c 5.5 Sheet 28 | 22/03/1916 | 22/03/1916 |
| War Diary | Fletre | 22/03/1916 | 30/03/1916 |
| War Diary | Bulford Camp T26a 3.8 Sheet 28 | 31/03/1916 | 31/03/1916 |
| Heading | 8th Battalion "Buffs" East Kent Regiment. April 1916 | | |
| Heading | War Diary of 8th (Service) Batn The Buffs from 1st April 1916 to 30th April 1916 Volume 9 | | |
| War Diary | Bulford Camp T 26 a.3.8 Sheet 28 | 01/04/1916 | 04/04/1916 |
| War Diary | Bn. H.Q. Ash House V14 a 4.5 Sheet 28 | 06/04/1916 | 06/04/1916 |
| War Diary | Bn H.Q. Ash Hse | 07/04/1916 | 11/04/1916 |
| War Diary | Bn. H.Q. Grand Munque Farm | 12/04/1916 | 17/04/1916 |
| War Diary | Bn. H.Q. U.13 c.6.3 | 18/04/1916 | 23/04/1916 |
| War Diary | Bulford Camp | 24/04/1916 | 29/04/1916 |
| War Diary | Bn H.Q. U.13.c.6.3 | 30/04/1916 | 30/04/1916 |
| Heading | 8th Battalion "Buffs" East Kent Regiment May 1916 | | |
| Heading | War Diary of 8th Batn The Buffs From 1st May 1916 To 31st May 1916 Volume 10 | | |
| War Diary | Bn. H.Q. | 01/05/1916 | 06/05/1916 |
| War Diary | Grand Manque | 07/05/1916 | 10/05/1916 |
| War Diary | Bn HQ U 13 c 6.3 Sheet 28 | 11/05/1916 | 16/05/1916 |
| War Diary | Bulford | 17/05/1916 | 17/05/1916 |
| War Diary | Bn. H.Q. Bulford Camp | 18/05/1916 | 24/05/1916 |
| War Diary | Bn. H Q U.13. C.6.3 Sheet 28 | 25/05/1916 | 31/05/1916 |
| Heading | 8th Battalion "Buffs" East Kent Regiment. June 1916 | | |
| Heading | War Diary of 8th Batn The Buffs From 1st June 1916 to 30th June 1916 Volume 11 | | |
| War Diary | Bn. H.Q. U13 C6.3 | 01/06/1916 | 02/06/1916 |
| War Diary | Grande Munque Farm | 03/06/1916 | 09/06/1916 |
| War Diary | Bn HQ U.13.c.6.3 | 10/06/1916 | 18/06/1916 |
| War Diary | Bulford Camp | 19/06/1916 | 22/06/1916 |
| War Diary | St Jans Capelle | 23/06/1916 | 29/06/1916 |
| War Diary | Locre | 30/06/1916 | 30/06/1916 |
| Miscellaneous | Report On Raid Carried Out By A Party Of 8th Buffs On 2nd Australian Brigade Front On Night Of 28th/29th June. | 29/06/1916 | 29/06/1916 |
| Miscellaneous | Report on Raid carried out by 8th Batn The Buffs. | 30/06/1916 | 30/06/1916 |
| Heading | 8th Battn. The Buffs (East Kent Regiment). July 1916 | | |
| War Diary | Bn HQ Cookers Fm Sheet 28 N.35.c.4.9 | 01/07/1916 | 05/07/1916 |
| War Diary | Bn HQ Cookers Fm | 06/07/1916 | 07/07/1916 |
| War Diary | Aircraft Fm | 08/07/1916 | 16/07/1916 |
| War Diary | Cookers Farm | 18/07/1916 | 19/07/1916 |
| War Diary | Locre | 20/07/1916 | 20/07/1916 |
| War Diary | Sheet 27 | 21/07/1916 | 21/07/1916 |
| War Diary | Belcroix Farm | 22/07/1916 | 24/07/1916 |

| | | | |
|---|---|---|---|
| War Diary | Breuilly | | |
| War Diary | Le Mesge | 25/07/1916 | 31/07/1916 |
| Heading | 8th Battalion "Buffs" East Kent Regiment. August 1916 | | |
| Heading | War Diary 8th (Service) Battalion The Buffs for the month of August 1916 Volume 12 | | |
| War Diary | Bn HQ France Sheet 62D E.18 D | 01/08/1916 | 03/08/1916 |
| War Diary | The Sandpits | 04/08/1916 | 07/08/1916 |
| War Diary | Bn HQ Sheet 62C A7 B27 | 08/08/1916 | 10/08/1916 |
| War Diary | T.24.b. Central | 11/08/1916 | 15/08/1916 |
| War Diary | Bn HQ. Cookers Carnoy | 16/08/1916 | 16/08/1916 |
| War Diary | Bn. HQ Sheet 57 S.W. S.24. B26 | 17/08/1916 | 22/08/1916 |
| War Diary | Hapry Valley Nr Bray | 23/08/1916 | 24/08/1916 |
| War Diary | Sheet 57D E15 | 25/08/1916 | 30/08/1916 |
| War Diary | F8d. | 31/08/1916 | 31/08/1916 |
| Heading | 8th Battalion "Buffs" East Kent Regiment. September 1916 | | |
| Heading | War Diary of 8th Battalion The Buffs.for the month of September 1916 Volume 13 | | |
| War Diary | Bn. HQ Montauban Alley 57 C. S.W. S.26. D.3.5 | 01/09/1916 | 01/09/1916 |
| War Diary | Carlton Tr. S.16.B.0.3. | 02/09/1916 | 03/09/1916 |
| War Diary | Carlton Tr | 03/09/1916 | 03/09/1916 |
| War Diary | Carlton Trench | 03/09/1916 | 03/09/1916 |
| War Diary | F.8.D | 04/09/1916 | 04/09/1916 |
| War Diary | Area "A" E.14 57 D.SE | 05/09/1916 | 05/09/1916 |
| War Diary | Yaucourt | 06/09/1916 | 30/09/1916 |
| Heading | 8th Battalion "Buffs" East Kent Regiment October 1916 | | |
| Heading | War Diary of 8th Service Battalion The Buffs October 1916 Volume 14 | | |
| War Diary | Bn. HQ. Zouave Valley | 01/10/1916 | 01/10/1916 |
| War Diary | Gouy Servins | 02/10/1916 | 08/10/1916 |
| War Diary | Dalys X17. C.1.0 | 10/10/1916 | 24/10/1916 |
| War Diary | Gouy Servins | 25/10/1916 | 25/10/1916 |
| War Diary | Noeux Les Mines | 26/10/1916 | 26/10/1916 |
| War Diary | Mazingarbe | 27/10/1916 | 27/10/1916 |
| War Diary | Mazingarbe | 28/10/1916 | 31/10/1916 |
| Heading | 8th Battalion "Buffs" East Kent Regiment November 1916 | | |
| Heading | War Diary of 8th (Service) Battalion The Buffs for the month of November Volume 15. | | |
| War Diary | Mazingarbe | 01/11/1916 | 01/11/1916 |
| War Diary | Bn. HQ Loos G.36.a.5.4 | 02/11/1916 | 05/11/1916 |
| War Diary | Bn HQ Loos | 06/11/1916 | 09/11/1916 |
| War Diary | Quality Street | 10/11/1916 | 16/11/1916 |
| War Diary | 14 Bis Section | 16/11/1916 | 21/11/1916 |
| War Diary | Mazingarbe | 22/11/1916 | 27/11/1916 |
| War Diary | 14 Bis Section | 28/11/1916 | 30/11/1916 |
| Heading | 8th Battalion "Buffs" East Kent Regiment December 1916 | | |
| Heading | War Diary of 8th Battalion The Buffs for the month of December 1916 Volume 16 | | |
| War Diary | | 01/12/1916 | 04/12/1916 |
| War Diary | 14 Bis Section | 04/12/1916 | 04/12/1916 |
| War Diary | Quality Street | 05/12/1916 | 10/12/1916 |
| War Diary | 14 Bis Right Sub Section | 11/12/1916 | 12/12/1916 |
| War Diary | 14 Bis Section | 13/12/1916 | 16/12/1916 |
| War Diary | Mazingarbe | 17/12/1916 | 21/12/1916 |

| | | | |
|---|---|---|---|
| War Diary | 14 Bis Section | 22/12/1916 | 26/12/1916 |
| War Diary | 14 Bis Right Sub Section | 27/12/1916 | 28/12/1916 |
| War Diary | Village Line | 29/12/1916 | 31/12/1916 |
| Heading | War Diary of 8th Battalion The Buffs Month Of January 1917 Volume 17 | | |
| War Diary | Village Line | 01/01/1917 | 03/01/1917 |
| War Diary | 14 Bis Right Sub Section | 04/01/1917 | 07/01/1917 |
| War Diary | Loos | 07/01/1917 | 07/01/1917 |
| War Diary | Mazingarbe Div Reserve | 08/01/1917 | 13/01/1917 |
| War Diary | Mazingarbe | 14/01/1917 | 18/01/1917 |
| War Diary | Loos | 19/01/1917 | 22/01/1917 |
| War Diary | Village Line | 23/01/1917 | 29/01/1917 |
| War Diary | Loos | 30/01/1917 | 31/01/1917 |
| Heading | War Diary of 8th Battalion The Buffs Month Of February 1917 | | |
| War Diary | Loos | 01/02/1917 | 05/02/1917 |
| War Diary | Mazingarbe | 06/02/1917 | 12/02/1917 |
| War Diary | Noeux Les Mines | 13/02/1917 | 28/02/1917 |
| Heading | War Diary of 8th Battalion The Buffs for the month of March 1917 Volume 19 | | |
| War Diary | Noeux Les Mines | 01/03/1917 | 01/03/1917 |
| War Diary | Cite de Forse 10 | 02/03/1917 | 03/03/1917 |
| War Diary | Right Sub Sector | 03/03/1917 | 08/03/1917 |
| War Diary | Bully Grenay | 09/03/1917 | 14/03/1917 |
| War Diary | Rt Sub Sector | 15/03/1917 | 21/03/1917 |
| War Diary | Fosse 10 | 22/03/1917 | 27/03/1917 |
| War Diary | Right Subsection | 27/03/1917 | 31/03/1917 |
| Heading | 8th Battn. E. Kent Regiment 17th Infantry Brigade 24th Division April 1917 | | |
| War Diary | Right Sub Sector | 01/04/1917 | 04/04/1917 |
| War Diary | Bully Grenay | 05/04/1917 | 06/04/1917 |
| War Diary | Angres II Right Sub Sector | 07/04/1917 | 09/04/1917 |
| War Diary | Angres II | 10/04/1917 | 19/04/1917 |
| War Diary | Les Brebis | 20/04/1917 | 20/04/1917 |
| War Diary | Hesdigneuil | 21/04/1917 | 21/04/1917 |
| War Diary | Bourecq | 22/04/1917 | 24/04/1917 |
| War Diary | Erny St Julien | 25/04/1917 | 26/04/1917 |
| War Diary | Bourecq | 27/04/1917 | 27/04/1917 |
| War Diary | Annezin | 28/04/1917 | 28/04/1917 |
| War Diary | La Bourse | 29/04/1917 | 30/04/1917 |
| Heading | War Diary of 8th Battalion The Buffs Month Of May 1917 Volume 21 | | |
| War Diary | La Bourse | 01/05/1917 | 08/05/1917 |
| War Diary | Robecq | 09/05/1917 | 10/05/1917 |
| War Diary | Morbecque | 11/05/1917 | 11/05/1917 |
| War Diary | Steenvoorde | 12/05/1917 | 17/05/1917 |
| War Diary | Steenvoorde Area | 18/05/1917 | 22/05/1917 |
| War Diary | Steenvoorde K 15.d.5.6 Sheet 27 | 23/05/1917 | 25/05/1917 |
| War Diary | G.19.d.2.8. | 26/05/1917 | 31/05/1917 |
| Heading | War Diary of 8th Battalion The Buffs Month Of June 1917 Volume 22 | | |
| War Diary | G.19.d.2.8. | 01/06/1917 | 01/06/1917 |
| War Diary | Steenvoorde | 02/06/1917 | 04/06/1917 |
| War Diary | Heksken | 04/06/1917 | 06/06/1917 |
| War Diary | M5.d Central Sheet 28 | 06/06/1917 | 10/06/1917 |
| War Diary | Middle Camp West | 11/06/1917 | 12/06/1917 |

| | | | | |
|---|---|---|---|---|
| War Diary | M.5.d. Central Sheet 28 | | 13/06/1917 | 16/06/1917 |
| War Diary | Micmac Camp | | 17/06/1917 | 18/06/1917 |
| War Diary | Dickebusch | | 19/06/1917 | 28/06/1917 |
| War Diary | Micmac Camp | | 29/06/1917 | 29/06/1917 |
| War Diary | Lumbres | | 30/06/1917 | 30/06/1917 |
| War Diary | Escoeuilles | | 30/06/1917 | 30/06/1917 |
| Miscellaneous | Operations 14/16th June 1917 | | 17/06/1917 | 17/06/1917 |
| Heading | War Diary of 8th Battalion The Buffs Month Of July 1917 Volume 23 | | | |
| War Diary | Escoeuilles | | 01/07/1917 | 08/07/1917 |
| War Diary | Ecault | | 09/07/1917 | 11/07/1917 |
| War Diary | Escoeuilles | | 12/07/1917 | 15/07/1917 |
| War Diary | Lumbres | | 16/07/1917 | 16/07/1917 |
| War Diary | Renescure | | 17/07/1917 | 17/07/1917 |
| War Diary | Caestre V.11.d.6.4. Sheet 27 | | 18/07/1917 | 18/07/1917 |
| War Diary | Eecke Area | | 19/07/1917 | 19/07/1917 |
| War Diary | Micmac Camp G32.c.8.8 | | 20/07/1917 | 20/07/1917 |
| War Diary | Micmac Camp | | 21/07/1917 | 22/07/1917 |
| War Diary | Line | | 23/07/1917 | 28/07/1917 |
| War Diary | Micmac | | 29/07/1917 | 30/07/1917 |
| War Diary | Ecluse | | 31/07/1917 | 31/07/1917 |
| War Diary | Line | | 31/07/1917 | 31/07/1917 |
| Heading | War Diary of 8th Battalion The Buffs Month Of August 1917 Volume 24 | | | |
| War Diary | Line | | 01/08/1917 | 03/08/1917 |
| War Diary | Micmac | | 04/08/1917 | 05/08/1917 |
| War Diary | Dickebusch Line | | 06/08/1917 | 09/08/1917 |
| War Diary | Line | | 09/08/1917 | 11/08/1917 |
| War Diary | Micmac | | 11/08/1917 | 15/08/1917 |
| War Diary | Dickebusch | | 16/08/1917 | 18/08/1917 |
| War Diary | Line | | 19/08/1917 | 23/08/1917 |
| War Diary | Micmac | | 24/08/1917 | 26/08/1917 |
| War Diary | Dickebusch | | 27/08/1917 | 27/08/1917 |
| War Diary | Line | | 31/08/1917 | 31/08/1917 |
| Heading | War Diary Of 8th Batn The Buffs Month Of September 1917 Vol. No. 25 | | | |
| War Diary | Line | | 01/09/1917 | 02/09/1917 |
| War Diary | Westoutre | | | |
| War Diary | Micmac | | 03/09/1917 | 06/09/1917 |
| War Diary | Dickebusch | | 07/09/1917 | 10/09/1917 |
| War Diary | Line | | 11/09/1917 | 15/09/1917 |
| War Diary | Dickebusch | | 15/09/1917 | 16/09/1917 |
| War Diary | Outtersteene | | 16/09/1917 | 21/09/1917 |
| War Diary | Ytres | | 22/09/1917 | 22/09/1917 |
| War Diary | Map 62c Ytres | | 22/09/1917 | 22/09/1917 |
| War Diary | Ytres | | 23/09/1917 | 25/09/1917 |
| War Diary | Map 62C Ytres | | 26/09/1917 | 26/09/1917 |
| War Diary | Haut-Allaines | | 27/09/1917 | 28/09/1917 |
| War Diary | Hervilly | | 29/09/1917 | 29/09/1917 |
| War Diary | Line | | 30/09/1917 | 30/09/1917 |
| Heading | War Diary of 8th Battalion The Buffs Month Of October 1917 Volume 26 | | | |
| War Diary | Line | | 01/10/1917 | 07/10/1917 |
| War Diary | Bernes | | 08/10/1917 | 14/10/1917 |
| War Diary | Line | | 15/10/1917 | 23/10/1917 |
| War Diary | Vadencourt | | 24/10/1917 | 31/10/1917 |

| | | | |
|---|---|---|---|
| Miscellaneous | Relief Orders by Lieut-Colonel F.C.R. Studd. Commanding 8th Battalion The Buffs. | 06/10/1917 | 06/10/1917 |
| Miscellaneous | Relief Orders by Lieut-Colonel F.C.R. Studd. Commanding 8th Battalion The Buffs. | 14/10/1917 | 14/10/1917 |
| Miscellaneous | Relief Orders by Lieut-Colonel F.C.R. Studd. Commanding 8th. Battalion The Buffs. | 22/10/1917 | 22/10/1917 |
| Miscellaneous | Relief Orders by Lieut-Colonel F.C.R. Studd. Commanding 8th Battalion The Buffs. | 30/10/1917 | 30/10/1917 |
| Heading | War Diary for November 1917 Volume 27 | | |
| War Diary | Line Map Ref, Nauroy L32. | 01/11/1917 | 06/11/1917 |
| War Diary | Line Map Sheet Nauroy Ed 2a About L31b | 07/11/1917 | 08/11/1917 |
| War Diary | Bernes | 09/11/1917 | 16/11/1917 |
| War Diary | Line | 17/11/1917 | 24/11/1917 |
| War Diary | Vadencourt | 25/11/1917 | 30/11/1917 |
| Miscellaneous | 8th Bn The Buffs Training Programme from 9th Nov-to 16th Nov 1917 | | |
| Miscellaneous | Instructions For Covering Party furnished by 8th Battalion The Buffs on Y/Z. night. | 19/11/1917 | 19/11/1917 |
| Miscellaneous | Tactical Scheme No. 6 | | |
| Heading | War Diary For Month Of December 1917 | | |
| War Diary | Vadencourt | 01/12/1917 | 03/12/1917 |
| War Diary | Line Map Sheet Naurdy 28b | 04/12/1917 | 06/12/1917 |
| War Diary | Line | 07/12/1917 | 07/12/1917 |
| War Diary | Hancourt | 08/12/1917 | 10/12/1917 |
| War Diary | Montigny | 11/12/1917 | 21/12/1917 |
| War Diary | Line Map Sheet Nauray Ed. 26 L.10a 6,11 & G.1 | 22/12/1917 | 28/12/1917 |
| War Diary | Montigny | 29/12/1917 | 31/12/1917 |
| Miscellaneous | Relief Orders by Major W.R. Corroll. M.C. Commanding 8th. Battalion The Buffs. | | |
| Miscellaneous | 8th Bn The Buffs Training Programme | | |
| Miscellaneous | Relief Orders. by Major W.R. Corrall M.C. Commanding 8th Battalion The Buffs. | 03/12/1917 | 03/12/1917 |
| Miscellaneous | Operation Order. by Major W.R. Corrall M.C. Commanding 8th Battalion The Buffs. | 05/12/1917 | 05/12/1917 |
| Operation(al) Order(s) | Operation Orders. 23 by Major W.R. Corrall M.C. Commanding 8th Battalion The Buffs. | 06/12/1917 | 06/12/1917 |
| Miscellaneous | 17th Infantry Brigade. | 24/12/1917 | 24/12/1917 |
| Miscellaneous | Relief Orders. by Major W.R. Corrall M.C. Commanding 8th Battalion The Buffs. | 26/12/1917 | 26/12/1917 |
| Heading | War Diary For Month Of January 1918 | | |
| War Diary | Montigny | 01/01/1918 | 02/01/1918 |
| War Diary | Vraignes | 03/01/1918 | 08/01/1918 |
| War Diary | Montigny | 09/01/1916 | 12/01/1916 |
| War Diary | Line | 13/01/1918 | 21/01/1918 |
| War Diary | Hancourt | 23/01/1918 | 31/01/1918 |
| Miscellaneous | Relief Orders by Major W.R. Corrall M.C. Commanding 8th Battalion The Buffs. | 01/01/1918 | 01/01/1918 |
| Miscellaneous | Addendum | 01/01/1918 | 01/01/1918 |
| Miscellaneous | 8th Battalion The Buffs. | 02/01/1918 | 02/01/1918 |
| Miscellaneous | Relief Orders by Lieut-Colonel F.C.R. Studd. Commanding 8th, Battalion The Buffs | 06/01/1918 | 06/01/1918 |
| Miscellaneous | Relief Orders by Lieut-Colonel F.C.R. Studd. D.S.O.Commanding 8th Battalion The Buffs | 11/01/1918 | 11/01/1918 |
| Miscellaneous | Relief Orders by Lieut-Colonel F.C.R. Studd. D.S.O.Commanding 8th Battalion The Buffs. | 17/01/1918 | 17/01/1918 |

| | | | |
|---|---|---|---|
| Operation(al) Order(s) | Operation Orders No.1. by Lieut-Colonel F.C.R. Studd. D.S.O. Commanding 8th. Battalion The Buffs | 18/01/1918 | 18/01/1918 |
| Miscellaneous | Relief Orders by Lieut-Colonel F.C.R. Studd. D.S.O. Commanding 8th Battalion The Buffs | 19/01/1918 | 19/01/1918 |
| Miscellaneous | Training Programme Jan 22nd to Jan 27th 1918 | 20/01/1918 | 20/01/1918 |

WO 95/2207/1

24TH DIVISION
17TH INFY BDE

8TH BN EAST KENT REGT (BUFFS)

~~NOV 1915 - DEC 1917~~

1915 AUG — 1918 JAN

(1917)

DISBANDED

24TH DIVISION
ATTACHED 72ND INFY BDE

8TH BN EAST KENT REGT (BUFFS)
AUG 1915 — OCT 1915

72nd Inf.Bde.
24th Div.

Battn. disembarked
Boulogne from
England 1.9.15.

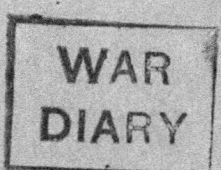

8th BATTN. THE BUFFS (EAST KENT REGIMENT).

AUGUST AND SEPTEMBER

(21.8.15 to 30.9.15)

1915

# WAR DIARY
## or
## INTELLIGENCE SUMMARY.
*(Erase heading not required.)*

Army Form C. 2118.

**8TH (SERVICE) BATTN**
**THE BUFFS.**

Instructions regarding War Diaries and Intelligence Summaries are contained in F.S. Regs., Part II and the Staff Manual respectively. Title pages will be prepared in manuscript.

| Place | Date 1915 | Hour | Summary of Events and Information | Remarks and references to Appendices |
|---|---|---|---|---|
| Blackdown Pl8 | 2.8 | — | 8th Buffs ordered to be prepared forthwith for embarkation to France with 24th Division. | |
| " | 29.8 | | Mobilisation proceeding | |
| " | 30.8 | 12.20 | 3 Off 106 OR advance party left Farnborough for Southampton. | |
| " | 31.9 | 6.52 am | 15 Offrs & 51 OR left 5 miles under Lt Col Romer C.B. C.M.G. arrived at Frensham & embarked on SS St Pionist | |
| | | 7.25 pm | 12 — Major Robinson 2i/c | |
| | | | Left at 11.15 pm | |
| Boulogne | 1.9 | 1.30 am | Arrived. Disembarked and proceeded by Route March to OSTROHOVE large rest camp & accommodated in tents. | |
| " | 2.9 | 11.55 am | Proceeded by route march to Railway Station & entrained, detrained at MONTREUIL transport joined us having arrived by rail from HAVRE. marched to MANINGHEM. and went into billets. Road good, marching heavy owing to heavy rain | |
| MANINGHEM 3.9 | | | In billets very wet day | |
| MANINGHEM 4.9 | | | Company parade. 1st draft arrived from England 3 pm | |
| " | 5.9 | | to march to await forbell & all Non Commwlofs | |
| " | 1.9 | | Company machine & ammn. Co & schws & Grenade officers interviewed by Lieut Hankin Comdy 114 Coys at HUCQUELIERS | |
| " | 7.9 | | Medical exercises under Senior Medical in vicinity of CLENLUE. 3 Lewis & Pistols by 4 & un 3/- Bomb L/Sgt Gamlin Bantr Corps to come to & return to & to & to relieve School at WISQUES | |

Army Form C. 2118.

# WAR DIARY
## or
## INTELLIGENCE SUMMARY

8TH (SERVICE) BATTN
THE B.FFS.

(Erase heading not required.)

Instructions regarding War Diaries and Intelligence Summaries are contained in F. S. Regs., Part II. and the Staff Manual respectively. Title pages will be prepared in manuscript.

| Place | Date | Hour | Summary of Events and Information | Remarks and references to Appendices |
|---|---|---|---|---|
| MANINGHEM | 1915 Sept 8th | 8.30 | Parade under Coy Arrangements. Major Robinson, Capt Howard, Capt Pherrington left on inspection to trenches at front. | |
| | 9th | | Parade under Coy arrangements. Digging 2 Schemes trenches. 1 officer went to gas & musketry range. 2.10 p.m. had a Bde alarm to practice turn out. no transport available being in use at SEMPY. | |
| | 10th | | Route march about 12 miles returned 1.30 p.m Brigade order MOVE and all arrangements made when orders to cancel. All officers attended practice lecture on G.M. & saw gas used practically in trench previously enclosed. | |
| | 11th | | Divisional exercise. Had breakfast while field and operations enclosed about 2 p.m. near MANINGHEM. | |
| | 12th | | Church parade for C of E, and also for all non conformists & men present sent by Brigade. | |
| | 13th | | Parade Coy Arrangement. Musketry & Coy range. French peasants cut by Brigade of French pulies & discharge in charge of shift. | |
| | 14th | 6.45 AM | Divisional Exercise breakfast on ground damp morning ie returned to billets after breakfast. | |
| | | | 2 N.C.Os reassembled for 2.9.C.M | |
| | 15th | 8.30 | Battalion parade & practice an attack and afterwards recovery who covered platoons an advance of enemy. 5 p.m. Stan return by Major Kay & S. 24 Div in Trenches returned " "Lt E T Smith on return to Trenches | |
| | 16th | | Battalion Coy drill. Musketry. Lt E T Smith returned from Trenches | |

# WAR DIARY

## 8TH (SERVICE) BATTN THE BUFFS

### INTELLIGENCE SUMMARY
*(Erase heading not required.)*

Army Form C. 2118.

Instructions regarding War Diaries and Intelligence Summaries are contained in F.S. Regs., Part II. and the Staff Manual respectively. Title pages will be prepared in manuscript.

| Place | Date | Hour | Summary of Events and Information | Remarks and references to Appendices |
|---|---|---|---|---|
| MANINGHEM | 17.9.15 | 8.30 | Battalion route march. F.G.C.M. on HERQUELERS. m. Sgt Full Cpl Plummidge. COs | |
| | | | Cos of Bn conference at Bn q It Ons | |
| " | 18.9 | 2am | Paraded & marched to rendezvous at ST DENEUX had breakfast. Moved off for Div. Exercise in support of 75" I Bng towards SEMPY. Operation terminated about 11 A.M. reached MANINGHEM about 1pm. very hot day but only 1 casualty | |
| " | 19.9 | | Sunday Church parade for all personnel. R.C. in village Church. 3.8.C.M on Cpl Plummidge promulgated. Received 2 day mails. About 6.30 pm news of accident at QUILEN. Lt Stewart Royal Sussex killed Pt HART injured. Thro accident to bomb. Ambulance French peasant on own farm at Strying. Case investigated by French Police & the maine. | |
| " | 20.9 | | Coy drills Musketry etc | |
| " | 21.9 | | Preparation for march. Left MANINGHEM 6.30 jm via Pt St MICHEL BELLEVUE. RIMEUX DENNEBROEUCQ NOUVERVILLE about 1 minute arrived 10am rather warmed. Part billets. H.Q. in Chateau 1705. | |
| NOUVEAUV -ILLE 10-35 BY.MAP | 22.9 | | Rest. marched 6.15 pm via PONCHE BASSE BOULOGNE AIRE. LA HAMEL ISBERQUES MOLINGAM Station to CUARBECQUE. Arrived about 2.30AM. Heavy march about 18 Miles. Men marched very well | |
| | | | Several men would help but all managed to get to billets except one picked up by ambulance. good billets. very wise night to march. moonlight & clear road. Buffs led Brigade. | |
| CUARBECQUE | 23.9 | | Rested in billets. men day but turned wet at night | |
| " | 24 | | Resting. Marched at 6.30 to Bellaine very bad roads. | |

Army Form C. 2118.

# WAR DIARY
## or
## INTELLIGENCE SUMMARY.
*(Erase heading not required.)*

Instructions regarding War Diaries and Intelligence Summaries are contained in F. S. Regs., Part II. and the Staff Manual respectively. Title pages will be prepared in manuscript.

| Place | Date | Hour | Summary of Events and Information | Remarks and references to Appendices |
|---|---|---|---|---|
| Bethune. | 25.9.15 | 11 a.m. | The Battalion received of this morning a Colonel Romer asked the following words. "Dear, I am not going to say very much to you this morning, only that you remain where you are the "Buffs". We then moved forward, afterwards the firing line via Vermelles. | |
| Noeux-les-Mines | 27.9.15 | 10 p.m. | On Saturday evening Sept 25th 1915 on a village VENDIN-LE-VIEIL. At 12.30 A.M. on the 26th the battalion moved forward to the attack. We first came under fire, the enemys artillery opening a heavy fire on us at Sailly-la-Bourse. The attack was withdrawn, by verbal orders from Brigadier-General B.M. Bulfin C.B., D.S.O. We remained for the night in readiness Night very cold, & ground very heavy. 1 officer casualty, 2/Lt H.E.T. Robinson. On Sunday Sept. 26th 1915 we were aroused during the early morning by gunfire who however did no damage. At 10.30 a.m. verbal orders arrived to prepare for an attack at 11 o'clock a.m. Almost at once the enemy commenced a heavy bombardment of our trenches. The objective being a German position about a mile away. Artillery formation was adopted on leaving the trenches, but long distance rifle fire caused us to extend our lines almost immediately. The B.M. were suffering the West Kents. The advance was carried forward rapidly & by 11.30 a.m. the leading lines of the Buffs had arrived within 25 yards of the German barbed wire. No gaps could be | |

Army Form C. 2118.

# WAR DIARY
## or
## INTELLIGENCE SUMMARY.
*(Erase heading not required.)*

Instructions regarding War Diaries and Intelligence Summaries are contained in F.S. Regs., Part II. and the Staff Manual respectively. Title pages will be prepared in manuscript.

| Place | Date | Hour | Summary of Events and Information | Remarks and references to Appendices |
|---|---|---|---|---|
| | | | observed in the wire entering towards. During the advance towards the machine guns on both flanks were encountered. At 11.30 a.m. an order came down the line from the right, to withdraw. The enemy's fire especially from our left flank became heavier & very considerable losses occurred. The Bn. were relieved during the night 26/27.9.1915 & rested in a field close by [illeg.] This evening Sept 27/9/15, when we are ordered to NOEUX-LES-MINES, & we are now in bivouac. Weather very wet. Here we remained until 6.7 p.m. Sept 27/9/15. We were informed this morning that our attack yesterday morning broke off the sixties Battalion of the enemy, who have to have reinforced the German Line opposite the French, this considerably helping the later to capture Souchez. + 14,000 prisoners, 26 guns, C.C.H. & F.C. Ronald Capt H. Tolman. officers and rifles at 4 a.m. today numbered 24. [bracket] Major G. Warghton Capt G.H. Cross, Capt H. Hills Capt A.H.G. Keehnal. [/bracket] | 245. Montgomery Capt Waterfall 26/ J. Kimbell R/Clt. Boradle & Capt R. Jones = 215 Courage = P.J.K. Saunders = S Vaughan = B. Pickering = H Taylor = 2 S. Skeff = E Wanstall x Lt R Evans |
| NOEUX-LES-MINES. | 28.9.15 | 5.30 p.m. | We have remained in bivouac all day, but orders [illeg] arrived to prepare to move. | |
| MOLINGHEM | 29.9.15 | 8.30 p.m. | We entrained at NOEUX-LES-MINES last night at 11 p.m. & arrived at BERGUETTE Station at 1.30 a.m. this morning. Men very tired, but were in good billets. Casualties church parade in these in known at 12 noon today 530. Rifle & Kit inspection this evening. Weather for a short burst (4 miles) this afternoon. Weather fair. | |
| MOLINGHEM | 30.9.15 | | Resting. | |

34th Kiowin.

121/7608

S/O E. Keas
Vol I

Sub B
1.9.15

Aug Sept / Oct 15

Volunt 2 17s Bale 23.10.15. 18'

# WAR DIARY
## or
## INTELLIGENCE SUMMARY.
(Erase heading not required.)

Army Form C. 2118.

Instructions regarding War Diaries and Intelligence Summaries are contained in F. S. Regs., Part II. and the Staff Manual respectively. Title pages will be prepared in manuscript.

| Place | Date | Hour | Summary | Appendices |
|---|---|---|---|---|
| MOLINGHEM | 1.10.15 | | Resting. Orders received today that we entrain tomorrow evening. Destination unknown. Transport left by road this morning at noon. | |
| HOUTKERQUE | 2.10.15 | 9.30 p.m. | We entrained at BERGUETTE this morning at 7.20 & arrived in the area of GODEWAERSVELDE at 8.15 a.m. We then marched here, having crossed into BELGIUM on the way. We are in billets, but not as comfortable as at MOLINGHEM. The four companies are spread out over a very large area. | |
| HOUTKERQUE | 3.10.15 | 9.30 p.m. | This morning we had a memorial service for those who fell on the 26th Sept 1915. The whole Brigade attended. | |
| HOUTKERQUE | 4.10.15 | 9.30 p.m. | This morning the 8th R. Buffs were inspected by Major General T.E. Capper C.B., the G.O.C. 24th Division. He delivered us an address & enforced his appreciation of the manner in which the men had maintained the traditions of the Regiment. | |
| HOUTKERQUE | 5.10.15 | 9.30 p.m. | At 1 p.m. today A & B Coys marched from HOUTKERQUE to the trenches around HILL 60, being attached to the 9th Hussars for instruction in Trench warfare. The march was a very hard one of 20 miles. Weather not so bad. C & D companies remained at HOUTKERQUE. | |
| RENINGHELST | 6.10.15 | 9.30 p.m. | A & B companies remain in trenches. 1 man killed & 3 men wounded in A Co. by a French mortar bomb. C & D companies marched from HOUTKERQUE to a small wood close to RENINGHELST, occupying huts. The huts were found in a very dirty condition. | |
| RENINGHELST | 7.10.15 | 9.30 p.m. | A & B companies were relieved this evening by C & D companies. Weather fine. Major A.P.H. Trueman joined the battalion this evening & took command. | |
| RENINGHELST | 8.10.15 | 9.30 p.m. | Rifle & Kit inspection this morning & the rest of the day has been spent in cleaning up kits. Total of 396 O.R. & 4 officers arrived this evening | |
| RENINGHELST | 9.10.15 | 9.30 p.m. | A & B companies had rifle inspection. Platoon drill & ceremonial. C & D Companies on stunt work from Trinchlos, C company having before one man wounded. | |

Army Form C. 2118.

# WAR DIARY
## or
## INTELLIGENCE SUMMARY.
(Erase heading not required.)

Instructions regarding War Diaries and Intelligence Summaries are contained in F.S. Regs., Part II and the Staff Manual respectively. Title pages will be prepared in manuscript.

| Place | Date | Hour | Summary of Events and Information | Remarks and references to Appendices |
|---|---|---|---|---|
| RENINGHELST | 10.10.15 | 9.30am | Church parade this morning at 10.15 am. | |
| RENINGHELST | 11.10.15 | 9.30pm | The Battalion moved this morning at 11.30 into huts which quite close to RENINGHELST. The new camp was found in a very dirty condition. News arrived this afternoon of the death on Oct 8th of Capt W. Howarth, who succumbed to wounds received on the 26 Sept. 1915. | |
| RENINGHELST | 12.10.15 | 9.30pm | Today musketry platoon and inner company arrangements, with a short route march this afternoon. Weather fine. | |
| RENINGHELST | 13.10.15 | 9.30pm | Companies carried out same programme as yesterday. Today CO, adjutant visited the trenches that we are shortly to take over. Bayonets not in very good condition. | |
| RENINGHELST | 14.10.15 | 9.30pm | Programme same as yesterday. Brigade route march in the afternoon via HERZEEN - WESTOUTRE - LAOLYTTE - RENINGHELST. Company Commanders to-day inspected their section of the line to be held. | |
| RESERVE DUGOUTS | 20.10.15 | 9.30pm | On the 17th went into the Battalion paraded at 11.15 am & marched one two miles to Caulf A, G.31 d 2.8 (Ref 28). Here a halt was made until 4 o'clock when the march up to the trenches was continued, via Dickebusch to the Café Belge, cross roads G.11.d.10 for each company + Head Quarters, supplied by the 11th Bn Royal Scots, was met at Café Belge movements. The relief of trenches 30. 31. 32 was completed at 11.45 pm. At 5 am the 16th kind enemy opened fire with high explosive & knocked in a dugout in 32 R. Retaliation was asked for and received from Belgian Battery. Situation quiet during rest of day. On the 17th went to bays in left of Trench 32 were recorded at 10 am an advance of R.E. Tunnelling Company Artillery fired all day in retaliation around | |

# WAR DIARY or INTELLIGENCE SUMMARY.

(Erase heading not required.)

Army Form C. 2118.

| Place | Date | Hour | Summary of Events and Information | Remarks and references to Appendices |
|---|---|---|---|---|
| RESERVE DUGOUTS | 20/10/15 | 9.30 p.m | On the 18th Huns situation remained quiet & weather remained fine. At 6.30 a.m Heavy Battery rang up & asked if we could confirm a report that enemy were advancing against Trench 39. Made necessary enquiries & found rumour false. Enemy have been shelling at some effort Trench 30. On the 19th most enemy aeroplanes were very active. Their artillery fire on while front behind 31 R but very little damage was done. At 5.30 an enemy shell of 32.S & 31.S vigorously for 15 minutes. Relaxation are aware of the entire garrison of Belgian observation post in 33.S & as no time taken then before reinforcements with them disappeared for one hour. Our men were wounded 2/R.E. Ploughman Pte R. 1330 Some inquiry were knocked in & four men wounded killed Pte Stewart in the Bluff. Today we have been relieved by the 3rd Rifle Brigade & have gone into the reserve dugouts on Canal Bank. Casualties O.R. 20 wounded. |  |
| RESERVE DUGOUTS | 21/10/15 | 9.30 p.m | A quiet day. Working parties being found for R.E. B Company in reserve R/12 K9 antlers who are holding Trench 39. Casualties O.R. 1 killed (……) |  |
| do | 22/10/15 | 9.30 p.m | Situation unchanged. Casualties O.R. 1 wounded. |  |
| do | 23/10/15 | 9.30 p.m | Weather rather fine. Situation unchanged. Casualties O.R. 2 wounded. |  |
| do | 24/10/15 | 9.30 p.m | Situation unchanged. Working parties are being found out of R.E. D Company every night for R.E. Casualties O.R. 2 wounded. |  |
| do | 25/10/15 | 9.30 p.m | Situation normal. |  |
| do | 26/10/15 | 9.30 p.m | Situation unchanged. Some artillery activity at 6 a.m. No damage reported. |  |
| WINCHELSEA M.P.D | 28/10/15 | 9.30 p.m | No more activity. Enemy night by 2nd Yorkshire Regt, relief being completed at 12.45 p.m. Coys were marched to independently. Hdrs & no. 2 to … |  |

Army Form C. 2118.

# WAR DIARY
## or
## INTELLIGENCE SUMMARY.
(Erase heading not required.)

Instructions regarding War Diaries and Intelligence Summaries are contained in F. S. Regs., Part II. and the Staff Manual respectively. Title pages will be prepared in manuscript.

| Place | Date | Hour | Summary of Events and Information | Remarks and references to Appendices |
|---|---|---|---|---|
| RENINGHELST CAMP D | 29.10.15 | 9.30pm | arriving at 3.30 am. Men were rested today, only an inspection of kit & rifles having taken place. It has rained heavily for the last 18 hours. Weather has cleared a little, but camp is in a very muddy condition. We have endeavoured to get thoroughly cleaned up. Assistance has been given to R.E. for construction of huts. Baths at RENINGHELST were allotted to this Battalion this afternoon from 1.30 to 3pm. 60 men proceeding every half hour. | |
| do | 30.10.15 | 9.30pm | We had the use of the baths again this morning from 9.30 till 12.30pm. | |
| do | 31.10.15 | 9.30pm | Church Parade this morning at 11.15 am at Y.M.C.A. hut at RENINGHELST. Weather has turned wet again. | |

A.P.H. Foreman Major

S.2.

8th E. Kent
Vol: 2

121/7761

17/ 24th Division
From 72nd Bde
18.10.15.

Nov. 15

CONFIDENTIAL.

WAR DIARY

OF

8th (SERVICE) BATN THE BUFFS

(Volume 3.)

From 1st November 1915.   To 30th November 1915.

Army Form C. 2118.

# WAR DIARY
## or
## INTELLIGENCE SUMMARY.
(Erase heading not required.)

| Place | Date | Hour | Summary of Events and Information | Remarks and references to Appendices |
|---|---|---|---|---|
| CAMP A NEAR DUDERDON | 1.11.15 | 9.30pm | The Battalion paraded at 11 o'clock this morning & marched to CAMP A, changing places with 12th Royal FUSILIERS. Orders received that we are to relieve 3rd R.BRIGADE tomorrow night. Heavy rain all day. JV. | |
| H.Q. DUGOUTS | 3.11.15 | 9.30pm | Battalion marched up yesterday evening from CAMP A to trenches 30, 31, 32 & relieved 3rd RIFLE BRIGADE. Roads up very difficult owing to recent heavy rains. Relief effected at 1am this morning. Quiet day. Trenches are in very bad condition - rain falling in many places & some dugouts have collapsed. Casualties 2 other ranks killed. JV. | |
| do | 4.11.15 | 9.30pm | Weather has much improved & work is being carried on as rapidly as possible in trenches. German aeroplane was shot down this morning by a British B plane in the vicinity on the left of 32. Some artillery activity this afternoon, but no casualties in this Battalion. Major General J.E. Capper made a tour of our trenches this afternoon. Casualties O.R. 2 killed 3 wounded. JV. | |
| do | 5.11.15 | 9.30pm | This has been a very quiet day except that at 11am six shells fell in B Company's line in trench 31S. Very little damage was done. Two guns by a Belgian Battery. Casualties O.R. 3 killed 1 wounded. JV. | |
| do | 6.11.15 | 9.30pm | Another very quiet day. Enemy being unusually quiet. Casualties O.R. 1 wounded. JV. | |
| do | 7.11.15 | 9.30pm | Orders have been received that we shall be relieved tomorrow night by the 3rd RIFLE BRIGADE. Enemy are still very quiet. Have practically no rifle or artillery fire between 12 noon & 3.30pm. JV. | |

# WAR DIARY
## or
## INTELLIGENCE SUMMARY.

*(Erase heading not required.)*

Army Form C. 2118.

| Place | Date | Hour | Summary of Events and Information | Remarks and references to Appendices |
|---|---|---|---|---|
| RENINGHELST CAMP A | 9.11.15 | 9.30 p.m | We were relieved last night by the 3rd RIFLE BRIGADE & the Battalion marched by Companies to CAMP A, where the arrangements made to meet the Battalion were well carried out. Today small fatigue parties have been found towards the building of dug outs in the Camp. Rifts to kit inspections have been held. Casualties on 8th Grunt. O.R. 1 wounded. JR. | |
| RENINGHELST CAMP A | 10.11.15 | 9.30 p.m | Today has been spent in camp, with short parades under company arrangements, for training of Bombers. JR. | |
| do | 11.11.15 | 9.30 p.m | Resting in Camp. The Battalion has been warned by the bulletin RENINGHELST this afternoon. JR. | |
| do | 12.11.15 | 9.30 p.m | Resting in Camp. Parades under company arrangements. JR. | |
| do | 13.11.15 | 9.30 p.m | Orders received that we are to relieve the 3rd RIFLE BRIGADE tomorrow night. JR. | |
| H.Q. dugouts | 15.11.15 | 9.30 p.m | We relieved the 3rd RIFLE BRIGADE last night, the arrangements were being delayed owing to enemy shelling the DICKE BUSCH - YPRES road. Today artillery on both sides has been very active, especially our heavy artillery & the smaller guns of the Belgian Batteries. No damage of any importance was done to our trenches. Weather has been very fine. Casualties O.R. 2 wounded JR. | |
| H.Q. DUG OUTS | 16.11.15 | 9.30 p.m | Artillery has again been active, but to a smaller extent owing mainly to consider ably more work than those of the enemy. Casualties O.R. 1 killed, 1 wounded. JR. | |
| H.Q. DUGOUTS | 17.11.15 | 9.30 p.m | This has been a fairly quiet day. Casualties O.R. 1 killed, 1 wounded. The new arrangements made recently by the 17 I.B. for the drawing of material, are a great improvement on previous methods. JR. | |

Army Form C. 2118.

# WAR DIARY
## or
## INTELLIGENCE SUMMARY.
(Erase heading not required.)

| Place | Date | Hour | Summary of Events and Information | Remarks and references to Appendices |
|---|---|---|---|---|
| HQ. DUGOUTS | 18.11.15 | 9.30 p.m | Another quiet day, except for some intermittent artillery fire from over our guns very little retaliation from the enemy. Casualties O.R. 1 killed 1 wounded. | |
| HQ. DUG-OUTS | 19.11.15 | 9.30 p.m | This afternoon two shells landed very close to H.Q. without doing any particular damage. Orders have been received that we shall be relieved on the 21st inst in trenches 30 & 31 by the 10 K.R.W.F. & in trench 22 by 1st at Gordon Highlanders. | |
| HQ. DUGOUTS | 20.11.15 | 9.30 p.m | The relieving units sent their reference taking to take over the trenches this morning. We have received orders that we are going into Army Reserve. There was some shelling this afternoon, but no retaliation was given by the Belgians. | |
| RENINGHELST CAMP G | 22.11.15 | 10 a.m. | Yesterday morning there was very considerable rifle fire between 7.45 & 8.15 am. But ourselves & the Germans were firing rapid fire, but as we had our men up on the fire step they were unable to see a single German. It was conclusive that the enemy were firing up in the air from the bottom of their trenches. They shelled our reserve line Kenny at |
| | | 11.30 a.m. | Kansas report good deal of damage, especially to the trench another Battery's dug outs. The reply that night was carried out in good order & without any firing from the enemy. | |
| EECKE | 23.11.15 | | The battalion paraded at 4.30 pm last night & marched to this village via BOESCHEPE - GODEWAERSVELDE. The roads were good, but for the last three miles very slippery owing to hard frost following |

Army Form C. 2118.

# WAR DIARY
## or
## INTELLIGENCE SUMMARY.

(Erase heading not required.)

Instructions regarding War Diaries and Intelligence Summaries are contained in F.S. Regs., Part II. and the Staff Manual respectively. Title pages will be prepared in manuscript.

| Place | Date | Hour | Summary of Events and Information | Remarks and references to Appendices |
|---|---|---|---|---|
| EECKE | 24.11.15 | 7.30 am | a shower of rain. The billets here for the men are quite good, but H.Q. suffered from lack of accommodation. The battalion parades this morning at 8.30 to continue the march to our rest area. | |
| ARNEKE | 24.11.15 | 9.30 pm | We arrived in this small town today at 1.30 p.m. having marched via ST. SYLVESTRE-CAPPEL – CASSEL. Paved roads nearly all the way. The men were troubled a good deal with sore feet & marched discipline was not all that it might have been. We move on again tomorrow morning. | |
| HOULLE | 25.11.15 | 9.30 pm | We arrived here this afternoon at 3 o'clock. The battalion paraded at 8.30 am marched via RUBROUCK – BROXEEL – CROME STRAETE – WATTEN – GANSPETTE – HELLEBROUCK. This has been a long march but the men responded very well indeed to an address by Major Trueman & the march discipline has been very good indeed. | |
| BAYENGHEM-LES-EPERLECQUES | 26.11.15 | 9.30 pm | The battalion moved this morning to the area LA COMMUNE – LE COMUNAL, where we have taken over our farm quarter billets. The men are spread about in a large number of barns, but the accommodation is good. For officers the accommodation is not good, but we hope to be able to improve this during the next few days. | |
| do. | 27.11.15 | 9.30 pm | In addition to the two villages mentioned above we have today taken over LA PANNE, where it is intended to move our Hd Qrs. Cos. Companies have had kit rifle inspections today. | |

Army Form C. 2118.

# WAR DIARY
## or
## INTELLIGENCE SUMMARY.
*(Erase heading not required.)*

Instructions regarding War Diaries and Intelligence Summaries are contained in F. S. Regs., Part II. and the Staff Manual respectively. Title pages will be prepared in manuscript.

| Place | Date | Hour | Summary of Events and Information | Remarks and references to Appendices |
|---|---|---|---|---|
| BAYENGHEM | 28.11.15 | 9 am | A Church of England service will be held this afternoon at 3 p.m. in an ex-tannery in BAYENGHEM. Head Quarters are moving this afternoon into LA PANNE. | |
| LA PANNE | 29.11.15 | 9.30 p.m. | Parades today have been under company arrangements & efforts are being made to make the men as comfortable as possible. | |
| do. | 30.11.15 | 9.30 p.m. | Today parades have been carried out according to a pre-arranged scheme of work. This programme has been made out on a progressive system & work carried out today has been of an elementary character. | |

A.P.H. Freeman ?/Lt
Comdg. 8th (SERVICE) Bn THE BUFFS

12/24.

Sir E. Grey
Vol: 3

December 1915.
151/7909

24th November

Confidential

War Diary

of

8th (Service) Batt. The Buffs.

From 1.12.15. To 31.12.15.

(Volume 4).

# WAR DIARY or INTELLIGENCE SUMMARY.

Army Form C. 2118.

(Erase heading not required.)

| Place | Date | Hour | Summary of Events and Information | Remarks and references to Appendices |
|---|---|---|---|---|
| LA PANNE | 1.12.15 | 9.30 pm | Parades today having been under company arrangements according to the Schedule of work. Baths for the men have been arranged & will be ready tomorrow. the 2nd inst. JV. | |
| do. do. | 2.12.15 | 9.30 pm | A short Battalion route march this morning. D Company have used the baths today. The accommodation admitting of 24 men per hour. JV. | |
| do. do. | 3.12.15 | 9.30 pm | To-day Training of specialists companies has been carried on. JV. | |
| do. do. | 4.12.15 | 9.30 pm | Training has been carried on. JV. | |
| do. do. | 5/6.12.15 | 9.30 pm | Church parade for C. of E. was held this morning at 10.30 am. Holy Communion at 10.60. R.C. Battended service at BAYENGHEM Church. JV. | |
| do. do. | 6.12.15 | 9.30 pm | Training of all men continues. The G.O.C. 2nd Division lectured to officers & N.C.O's of the Battalion this afternoon at 5 pm at H.Q. Billets JV. | |
| do. do. | 7.12.15 | 9.30 pm | A short Battalion route march this morning was followed by a parade of the whole Brigade in mass. JV. | |
| do. do. | 8.12.15 | 9.30 pm | Training has been carried on today. A party of 4 officers & 200 men worked for two hours this afternoon under the supervision of 103rd R.E. on the construction of a specimen German trench which will be used for practice purposes. JV. | |
| do. do. | 9.12.15 | 9.30 pm | Training is being continued. Particular attention has been paid to rapid & accurate fire. Four men were sent to WIZERNES for testing telescope & rifles. JV. | |
| do. do. | 10.12.15 | 9.30 pm | There has been an inspection of hutts by G.S.O. 2nd Division today. A draft of 40 O.R. arrived at 8 pm tonight evening. JV. | |
| do. do. | 11.12.15 | 9.30 pm | The Battalion paraded this morning at 9.45 a.m. for a short Brigade route march. The Brigade was inspected by G.O.C. 2nd ARMY. JV. | |

Army Form C. 2118.

# WAR DIARY
## or
## INTELLIGENCE SUMMARY.
*(Erase heading not required.)*

Instructions regarding War Diaries and Intelligence Summaries are contained in F.S. Regs., Part II. and the Staff Manual respectively. Title pages will be prepared in manuscript.

| Place | Date | Hour | Summary of Events and Information | Remarks and references to Appendices |
|---|---|---|---|---|
| EPERLECQUES | 12.12.15 | 9.30pm | Church parade was held this morning, arrangements being the same as on the 5th inst. JV. | |
| do do | 13.12.15 | 9.30pm | A party of 1 officer & 100 men continued the work on the German trench referred to on the 8th inst. Training has been continued. JV. | |
| do do | 14.12.15 | 9.30pm | There has been a demonstration of the efficiency of the late pattern helmet today. 500 N.C.O's & men in succession of 4 officers walked through a trench which had been filled with gas. No ill effects while were noticed. JV. | |
| do do | 15.12.15 | 9.30pm | Training continued today. A small party of 1 officer & 30 men were sent to EPERLECQUES for wood cutting. 1/4 of the Whole Battalion today. The usual German trench and places at our disposal today for training purposes each company carried out an attack. JV. | |
| do do | 16.12.15 | 9.30pm | A short Battalion route march this morning. At a meeting held on the Commandant Mess, attended by Company Commanders, the Quartermaster & C.O. & C.Q.M.S. arrangements were made for providing a good meal for all ranks in the Battalion on Christmas day. JV. | |
| do do | 17.12.15 | 9.30pm | Training has been continued today, according to schedule of work. JV. | |
| do do | 18.12.15 | 9.30pm | Training continued today. JV. | |

Army Form C. 2118.

# WAR DIARY
## or
## INTELLIGENCE SUMMARY.
(Erase heading not required.)

Instructions regarding War Diaries and Intelligence Summaries are contained in F.S. Regs., Part II. and the Staff Manual respectively. Title pages will be prepared in manuscript.

| Place | Date | Hour | Summary of Events and Information | Remarks and references to Appendices |
|---|---|---|---|---|
| LA PANNE | 19.12.15 | 9.30 p.m | Church parade was held this morning under the same arrangements as on the 12th Inst. News was received by telegram that a gas attack had been made on the 6th Division front. J.D. | |
| LA PANNE | 20.11.15 | 9.30 p.m | Training was continued today. A wreath of 24 O.R. arrived this afternoon. News was received of great activity of German artillery on British front N.E. of YPRES. The noise of heavy gunfire can be distinctly heard. J.D. | |
| LA PANNE | 21.12.15 | 9.30 p.m | Bad weather caused the postponement of a Brigade Route March, which was to have taken place today; training under cover has been carried on as possible. J.D. Training continued. | |
| LA PANNE | 22.12.15 | 9.30 p.m | Training continued. A lecture was given this afternoon of Mr DAVIES on the rest line. The Blue Taken over by the 2nd Battn J.D. | |
| LA PANNE | 23.12.15 | 7.30 p.m | Training continued. There will be a service for R.C. at midnight tonight. Special precautions are being taken against fire. J.D. A draft of 66 O.R. arrived today. J.D. | |
| LA PANNE | 24.12.15 | 9.30 p.m | Bad weather necessitated the C. of E. service on unavoidably [?] knowing Every arrangement had been made to give them a good time though the day [?] but a good Christmas dinner consisting of Roast meat, veg, Plum pudding & fruit. the fruit was bought locally J.D. | |
| LA PANNE | 25.12.15 | 9.30 p.m | | |

Army Form C. 2118.

# WAR DIARY
## or
## INTELLIGENCE SUMMARY.
*(Erase heading not required.)*

Instructions regarding War Diaries and Intelligence Summaries are contained in F. S. Regs., Part II. and the Staff Manual respectively. Title pages will be prepared in manuscript.

| Place | Date | Hour | Summary of Events and Information | Remarks and references to Appendices |
|---|---|---|---|---|
| LAPANNE | 26.12.15 | 9.30 am | Church parade was held this morning at 10.15 am. | |
| LAPANNE | 27.12.15 | 9.30 am | The Battalion was inspected while at training this afternoon by General Sir Douglas Haig. He expressed to the Junior that the men were smart in appearance & their drill movements. | |
| LAPANNE | 28.12.15 | 9.30 pm | Training continued. C & D Companies paraded at two pm for a church route march, the ammo being on parade for the first time since September 20. 1915. | |
| LAPANNE | 29.12.15 | 9.30 pm | Training continued. The 24th Divisional Cinema hall LWORDAYQUES was placed at the disposal of the Battalion this afternoon. A Coy of Engineers for an officer & 25 sentries for each man was furnished, & 470 men were provided with an afternoon's entertainment. | |
| LAPANNE | 30.12.15 | 9.30 pm | The Battalion this morning with the ammunition rest of the 73rd Brigade for inspection by Major General V.T.E. Capper C.B., G.O.C. 24 Division. Lt/Col B.O.S. Le Honour appeared. The inspection was very thorough. The General expressed himself as extremely pleased at the appearance & soldierly bearing of the men. | |
| LAPANNE | 31.12.15 | 9.30 pm | Training continued. Parties of men have been sent to 103 Battery R.F. today for further instruction in the working of Hurdles. Dagen & Gas Machine | |

A.R.H. Newman Lt.Col.
Comdg. 8th Bn. The Buffs

17th Brigade
24th Division.

8th BATTALION

"BUFFS" EAST KENT REGIMENT.

January 1916.

Dec 15

Dec '17

Confidential

War Diary

8" (Service) Bn. The Buffs.

From 1. I. 16 To 31. I. 16

Volume VI

**Army Form C. 2118.**

# WAR DIARY
## or
## INTELLIGENCE SUMMARY.
(Erase heading not required.)

Instructions regarding War Diaries and Intelligence Summaries are contained in F. S. Regs., Part II. and the Staff Manual respectively. Title pages will be prepared in manuscript.

| Place | Date | Hour | Summary of Events and Information | Remarks and references to Appendices |
|---|---|---|---|---|
| LA PANNE | 1.1.16 | 9.30 p.m. | A firing line attack on the specific German trenches at MINNECOVE was carried out this morning. The operation orders were carefully adhered to; the attack was quite successful. This evening a short night operation was carried out. The Battalion made an advance across country, wheeling on a compass bearing, to finish up finishing with the assault of a position marked by flags. AMM | |
| LA PANNE | 2.1.16 | 9.30 p.m. | Church of England service this morning at 10 a.m. Wesleyan & Non-Conformists at 10.30 a.m. Orders have been received that the Battalion will move into Reserve Divisional area by train on Thursday Jan. 6th 1915. This next two has been the greatest assistance in the training of specialists in particular to the whole battalion generally. AMM | |
| LA PANNE | 3.1.16 | 9.30 p.m. | This morning a short Brigade route march took place, all the other Transport accompanying the Battalion. The Brigade was inspected on the line of march by the G.O.C. 2d Division. AMM | Apx 193 |
| LA PANNE | 4.1.16 | 9.30 p.m. | Training has been continued. Apx 193 | |
| LA PANNE | 5.1.16 | 9.30 p.m. | In view of the move, the day has been spent in cleaning up the billets occupied during the rest. AMM | |
| POPERINGHE | 6.1.16 | 9.30 p.m. | The Battalion paraded at 2 a.m., marched to St. Omer. Arrived there at 6 p.m. & entrained. One train conveyed the whole battalion & all the 1st line Transport. We arrived at QUENTIN at 10.15 a.m., detrained & marched into POPERINGHE & occupied billets. AMM | |

# WAR DIARY
## or
## INTELLIGENCE SUMMARY.

(Erase heading not required.)

Army Form C. 2118.

| Place | Date | Hour | Summary of Events and Information | Remarks and references to Appendices |
|---|---|---|---|---|
| POPERINGHE | 7.1.16 | 9.30pm | Parades have been under company arrangements. AMW | |
| CAMP E. H19.6.4.b. SHEET 28. B SERIES | 8.1.16 | 9.30pm | The battalion paraded this morning & marched into this camp, which had been found in a very dirty condition. Turned food was lying about all over the camp. Haversack & other things that have been rolled are 9, 4.5 Howitzer shells with cartridge cases, 6 rifles, & about 500 bombs etc. AMW | |
| do | 9.1.16 | 9.30pm | Parades have been held for the purposes of cleaning & clearing the camp. AMW | |
| do | 10.1.16 | 9.30pm | Parades under company arrangements, particular attention having been paid to gas helmet drills. AMW | |
| do | 11.1.16 | 9.30pm | Parades under company arrangements. Weather windy & raining. AMW | |
| do | 12.1.16 | 9.30pm | Weather wet. Parades under Coy arrangements. AMW | |
| do | 13.1.16 | 9.30pm | Orders received that we are to relieve 3rd Bn R.B. tomorrow in left sector of the line held by 17th & 18th I.B. AMW | |
| RAMPARTS YPRES | 14.1.16 | 11.30pm | We have today relieved 3rd Bn R.B. A & D Companies are in the firing line & B & C companies in the Ramparts. AMW | |
| do | 15.1.16 | 9.30pm | A quiet day. Weather dry. Casualties O.R. 2 killed one wounded. AMW | |
| do | 16.1.16 | 9.30pm | Some artillery firing during the morning, but no material damage done. Casualties O.R. 1 AMW | |
| do | 17.1.16 | 9.30pm | Another quiet day. Casualties O.R. 1 wounded AMW | |

Army Form C. 2118.

# WAR DIARY
## or
## INTELLIGENCE SUMMARY.
(Erase heading not required.)

| Place | Date | Hour | Summary of Events and Information | Remarks and references to Appendices |
|---|---|---|---|---|
| BN.H.Q. in RAMPARTS YPRES | 18.1.16 | 11.30 p.m | Tonight B+C companies have relieved A+D Companies in the front line. The two latter companies returning to the Ramparts. Casualties O.R. 1 killed 1 wounded. | |
| do | 19.1.16 | 9.30 p.m | This morning enemy carried out a very heavy bombardment of the trenches held by B company. Casualties were slight but damage to trenches very considerable. Consumption O.R. 4 killed 6 wounded. | |
| do | 20.1.16 | 9.30 p.m | This has been a fairly quiet day; the enemy artillery being active against B company for a few minutes in the middle of the day. However tonight at 8.45 p.m. enemy fired four whizz bangs + six shells which did considerable damage. Killing while not wounding 15 + also killing 5 men + wounding 1/2 of the 3rd R.B. Casualties O.R. 2 killed wounded 15 | |
| do | 21.1.16 | 9.30 p.m | A quiet day on our front. Officers Capt & 2O/Gray attacked. | |
| do | 22.1.16 | 9.30 p.m | This morning enemy fired rifle grenades + also a trench mortar on to B Coy lines for two hours. Retaliation could not be obtained sufficiently quickly to silence enemy at once. D Coy relieved B Coy this evening. Casualties 2 Lt. A.G. Holland wounded O.R. 1 killed | |
| CAMP B | 24.1.16 | 9.30 p.m | We were relieved last night by the 8th Bn. The lines returned to this Camp, which was found to be in a fairly clean condition. Kit inspections have been held today. Casualties on 23rd O.R. 3 wounded | |

# WAR DIARY
## or
## INTELLIGENCE SUMMARY.
(Erase heading not required.)

Army Form C. 2118.

| Place | Date | Hour | Summary of Events and Information | Remarks and references to Appendices |
|---|---|---|---|---|
| CAMP B | 25.1.16 | 9.30 p | Parades have been held in 2 Company arrangements. Weather dull but fine. | AMM |
| do | 26.1.16 | 9.30 p | Today the 1st Bn. the Buffs marched to this camp, arriving here at 11 a.m. This is the first occasion on which this battalion has met another battalion of our own regiment, while on active service. The men were dismissed for half an hour. Major General T.E. Capper C.B. inspected the camp this morning. | AMM AMM |
| do | 27.1.16 | 9.30 p | Parades have been under company arrangements, C & D companies going over to visit the 1st/Bn. this afternoon. | AMM |
| do | 28.1.16 | 9.30 p | Parades under company arrangements. | AMM |
| do | 29.1.16 | 9.30 p | Orders have been received that we are to proceed tomorrow to Belgian Chateau Bivouac. Wind has changed to E.S.E. & the two letters "AMN" were received at 3.10 p.m. from 24th Division. | AMM |
| Bn H.Q. BELGIAN CHATEAU | 30.1.16 | 9.30 p | We have this evening relieved the 13th Middlesex Regt in the dugouts at BELGIAN CHATEAU. | AMM |
| do | 31.1.16 | 9.30 p | Very little work can be done here, as every available man is sent out at night on fatigue, working on the trenches. | AMM |

A.P. M Taulman

17th Brigade
24th Division.

8th BATTALION

"BUFFS"  EAST KENT REGIMENT.

*February* 1916.

Confidential

War Diary
of
8th (Service) Batn. The Buffs

From 1st February 1916. To 29th February 1916.

Volume 7

**Army Form C. 2118.**

# WAR DIARY
## or
## INTELLIGENCE SUMMARY.
(Erase heading not required.)

Instructions regarding War Diaries and Intelligence Summaries are contained in F. S. Regs., Part II. and the Staff Manual respectively. Title pages will be prepared in manuscript.

| Place | Date | Hour | Summary of Events and Information | Remarks and references to Appendices |
|---|---|---|---|---|
| BN.H.Q. BELGIAN CHATEAU | 1.2.15 | 9.30 p/m | A quiet day. There being no enemy artillery activity in this direction. Weather fine, but cold. | |
| do | 2.2.16 | 9.30 p/m | Another quiet day. Some artillery fire from batteries in this neighbourhood. Casualties 2 O.R. wounded. | |
| do | 3.2.16 | 9.30 p/m | Great aeroplane activity in spite of very strong wind. | A.Pt. Trueman M.L.t comdg 6 th Bn The Buffs |
| BN.H.Q. BELGIAN CHATEAU | 4.2.16 | 9.30 p/m | Some artillery activity during the morning. Weather cloudy. Orders received that we are to relieve 3rd Bn Rifle Brigade in the HOOGE SECTOR on Sunday 6 Feby. Casualties O.R. wounded 2 | |
| BN.H.Q. BELGIAN CHATEAU | 5.2.16 | 9.30 p/m | Trenches have been reconnoitred today by C.O, Adjutant, & Company Commanders. Casualties O.R. wounded 1 | |

Army Form C. 2118.

# WAR DIARY
## or
## INTELLIGENCE SUMMARY.
(Erase heading not required.)

| Place | Date | Hour | Summary of Events and Information | Remarks and references to Appendices |
|---|---|---|---|---|
| BN. H.Q. DUGOUTS | 6.2.16 | 11.30p.m. | We have tonight relieved the 3rd Bn. the Rifle Brigade. During the enemy shelled batteries in neighbourhood of BELGIAN CHATEAU, one shell bursting close to A Coy H.Q. & Captain J. HAMILTON was wounded. Casualties. O.R. wounded three. | |
| do. | 7.2.16 | 9.30p.m. | A fairly quiet day, but enemy have sent over a considerable number of whizz bangs. Casualties. O.R. killed 1 wounded 3. | |
| do | 8.2.16 | 9.30p.m. | More artillery fire today, mostly whizzbangs, but some 5.9" H.E. shells uncomfortably close to Bn H.Q. Casualties O.R. killed 2 wounded 2. | |
| do | 9.2.16 | 9.30p.m. | Artillery activity has continued all day. In there have been a large number of winds from the enemy. Casualties. O.R. wounded 1 | |
| do | 10.2.16 | 9.30p.m. | Less artillery fire during day, but there Red was heavily shelled at this evening. Casualties. 2/Lt. Wild wounded, O.R. killed 1 wounded 1. | |
| do | 11.2.16 | 9.30p.m. | Intense artillery fire on all our trenches all day. They are beginning to look considerably the worse for wear. Orders received that we are to be relieved by 3 Coys. the Rifle Brigade on 12 Feb. inst. | |

Army Form C. 2118.

# WAR DIARY
## or
## INTELLIGENCE SUMMARY.
*(Erase heading not required.)*

Instructions regarding War Diaries and Intelligence Summaries are contained in F. S. Regs., Part II. and the Staff Manual respectively. Title pages will be prepared in manuscript.

| Place | Date | Hour | Summary of Events and Information | Remarks and references to Appendices |
|---|---|---|---|---|
| BN.H.Q. DUG-OUTS AT BELGIAN CHATEAU. | 12.2.16 | 11.30pm | We were relieved tonight by 3rd Bn the Rifle Brigade. Very heavy artillery fire on our trenches all day. They were unfortunately handed over in a very bad state of repair. Casualties: O.R. killed 1 wounded 14 | |
| do | 13.2.16 | 9.8pm | A quiet day in the vicinity of the Chateau, but artillery active can be heard South of YPRES. | |
| do | 14.2.16 | 9.20pm | At 7pm. on the 14 inst. the Battalion moved up to ZILLEBEKE DUGOUTS in support of the 3rd Bn the Rifle Brigade, against whom the enemy attempted an advance. It was however dealt with by them. Our services were not required. Very prompt assistance from the artillery helped in stem a great deal. Orders received that we are to be relieved tomorrow by the 8th R.W.K. Casualties O.R. wounded 2. | |
| BN.H.Q. CAMP. C. | 16.2.16 | 11.20pm | We have been relieved tonight by the 8 Bn R.West Kent Regt. at BELGIAN CHATEAU, & have taken over CAMP. P. C. | |
| do | 17.2.16 | 9.30pm | The day has been spent in complete kit inspections by companies | |
| do | 18.2.16 | 9.3pm | Elementary Training, which did great platoon & company drill has been carried out so far as the ground, which is very muddy, allows | |

Army Form C. 2118.

# WAR DIARY
## or
## INTELLIGENCE SUMMARY.
(Erase heading not required.)

Instructions regarding War Diaries and Intelligence Summaries are contained in F. S. Regs, Part II. and the Staff Manual respectively. Title pages will be prepared in manuscript.

| Place | Date | Hour | Summary of Events and Information | Remarks and references to Appendices |
|---|---|---|---|---|
| CAMP C | 19.2.16 | 9.30pm | Weather very wet & windy. Training has taken the form of lectures in huts. | |
| do | 20.2.16 | 9.30pm | Church parade was held this morning at 10.30 am, the Brigade playing the Battalion to & from the service. | |
| do | 21.2.16 | 9.30pm | Training continued under schedule of work. | |
| do | 22.2.16 | 9.30pm | Training continued. This afternoon the Battalion attended a concert by the Princess Victoria's Concert Party, who gave a very good show which was much appreciated. | |
| do | 23.2.16 | 9.30pm | The audit from Res Camp to be moved from "C" £101 to VERBRANDENMOLEN have been recommended by Staff Serjeants N.C.O's of this Battalion under orders received from the G.R.T.D. | |
| do | 24.2.16 | 9.30pm | Major General J.E. Capper C.B. Commanding 24 Division gave a lecture to the officers & N.C.O's of this Battalion this afternoon on Discipline. | |
| do | 25.2.16 | 9.30pm | Weather has become very cold hence covers the ground. This has facilitated training, as the ground is frozen hard. | |
| do | 26.2.16 | 9.30pm | A lecture was given this afternoon by 2/Lt Greenwood, R.E. on Balloons. N.C.O.'s |

Army Form C. 2118.

# WAR DIARY
## or
## INTELLIGENCE SUMMARY.

(Erase heading not required.)

Instructions regarding War Diaries and Intelligence Summaries are contained in F. S. Regs., Part II. and the Staff Manual respectively. Title pages will be prepared in manuscript.

| Place | Date | Hour | Summary of Events and Information | Remarks and references to Appendices |
|---|---|---|---|---|
| CAMP. E. | 27.2.16 | 9.30a | Church parade was held this morning at 10 a.m. | |
| do | 28.2.16 | 9.30a | This morning at 10.30 the battalion practised the attack in some open ground near this camp. Weather has become warmer. | |
| do | 29.2.16 | 9.30a | Further attack practices took place this morning, by all companies. | |

A. C. Hamilton Major.
Commanding 8 Bn/p

17th Brigade
24th Division.

8th BATTALION

"BUFFS" EAST KENT REGIMENT.

*March* 1916.

Confidential

War Diary

8th (Service) Batt. The Buffs.

From 1st March 1916 to 31st March 1916.

Volume 6.

8 Buffs
Vol 6

# WAR DIARY or INTELLIGENCE SUMMARY

Army Form C. 2118.

| Place | Date | Hour | Summary of Events and Information | Remarks and references to Appendices |
|---|---|---|---|---|
| Camp C. G.11.c.5.5 Sheet 28 | 1.3.16 | 9.30pm | The battalion was practising the attack for two hours this morning. Weather wet, ground very heavy. | |
| | 2.3.16 | 7.30pm | Terrific artillery fire was heard this morning at 4.30 in a South easterly direction from here. At 9.15 a report was received from Bde H.Q. that the attack had been successful & that 200 prisoners & later this number was revised to 4 officers & 2200 men. The battalion is in a state of readiness & receives two hours notice of destination. | |
| do | 3.3.16 | 9.30pm | Training has been continued today. A & B companies practised the attack during the morning. | |
| do | 4.3.16 | 9.30pm | Training continued. C & D companies practising attack this morning. A & B companies doing musketry & close order drill. | |
| do | 5.3.16 | 9.30pm | Church parade this morning at 10 a.m. at YMCA hut at BUSSEBOOM. | |
| do | 6.3.16 | 9.30pm | Orders received that we are to relieve 4th YORKSHIRE Regiment on 8th inst. C.O., Adjutant, M.G.O., & Company Commanders had a view of the new line. The new line runs from I 30 b 2.1 to I 24 d 9.5 Sheet 28. | |

# WAR DIARY
## or
## INTELLIGENCE SUMMARY.

Army Form C. 2118.

| Place | Date | Hour | Summary of Events and Information | Remarks and references to Appendices |
|---|---|---|---|---|
| Contd. | 6.3.16 | | Trenches good but wet at bottom. Situated on high ground on which we overlook German lines. Our line runs from trench A4 to trench A8 both inclusive. Weather fine. | |
| Camp C | 7.3.16 | 9.30p | One officer per company went up today to reconnoitre the trenches with one man per coy. who will remain in the trenches to act as guides when battalion arrives. Machine guns relieved tonight. Snowing all night & day. | |
| BN HQ. I 24 a 2.1 to Rue de 8. | 8.3.16 | 11.20p | One officer per company, all O.C.'s & 2 men per company proceeded to trenches at 9am this morning. The object of sending the working parties having been all continuous thaw at least two men who knew their way all over the trenches. The relief took place this evening, the battalion being much hampered on the way up by R.E. transport. Relief was completed 9.50p.m. | |
| do. | 9.3.16 | 9.30p | Weather very fine but a lot of snow on the ground. A fight between two aeroplanes was witnessed this morning, the British machine falling to the ground in the neighbourhood of SHRAPNEL CORNER. A quiet day, 2 Lt Darling wounded in the head by a piece of shrapnel. | |

Army Form C. 2118.

# WAR DIARY
## or
## INTELLIGENCE SUMMARY.
(Erase heading not required.)

| Place | Date | Hour | Summary of Events and Information | Remarks and references to Appendices |
|---|---|---|---|---|
| BNHQ. I.24.a.2.1 | 10.3.16 | 9.30pm | Weather fine but quiet. Enemy shelled A Coy in trenches A4 & A5 with 20 whizzbangs without doing any damage. Casualties | |
| do | 11.3.16 | 9.30pm | A very quiet day. Much progress is being made in the work on the trenches. There is a great deal to do in the way of wiring, drainage, revetting trenches. Casualties. | |
| do | 12.3.16 | 9.30pm | Another very quiet day. This is apparently the quietest part of the YPRES SALIENT. Very heavy firing all the afternoon was heard at HOOGE. | |
| do | 13.3.16 | 9.30pm | A machine gun was enfilading A4 this morning from the south. Last night D company relieved A Company in trenches A4 + A5. B Coy, A Company relieving to BORDER DUGOUTS. | |
| do | 14.3.16 | 9.30pm | Enemy whizzbanged A4 + A5 this retaliation being difficult to get owing to the number of aeroplanes about. This evening A Coy relieved C Company in R1 & R2. C Company relieved B Company in trenches A5-6-7. & B Company relieved A Company in BORDER DUGOUTS. | |
| do | 15.3.16 | 9.30pm | A very quiet day. | |
| do | 11.3.16 | 9.30pm | Lt. Col. R.W. Ewens joined the Battalion today & taken over command | |

Army Form C. 2118.

# WAR DIARY
## or
## INTELLIGENCE SUMMARY.

(Erase heading not required.)

Instructions regarding War Diaries and Intelligence Summaries are contained in F.S. Regs., Part II. and the Staff Manual respectively. Title pages will be prepared in manuscript.

| Place | Date | Hour | Summary of Events and Information | Remarks and references to Appendices |
|---|---|---|---|---|
| BNHQ. T24c2.1 | 16.3.16 | 9.30pm | Orders received that on the night 18/19 inst. we are to increase our frontage, by taking in trenches A9. & A10. | |
| do | 17.3.16 | 9.30pm | A few whizzbangs on A4 this morning, no damage being done otherwise very quiet. | |
| do | 18.3.16 | 9.30pm | For the first time since we came this area, enemy activity has been considerable. He shelled BORDER DUGOUTS this afternoon inflicting some casualties to B Company. This evening D Company relieved C Company in A6 & B Company relieved C Company in A7 & A8 & also 1st R.F. in trenches A9. A10. C Company returned to BORDER DUGOUTS. | |
| do | 19.3.16 | 9.30pm | Enemy again shelled BORDER DUGOUTS inflicting some casualties on C Company. Orders received that we are to be relieved on night 21/22 inst, by 42nd Canadian Battalion. | |
| do | 20.3.16 | 9.30pm | Enemy very quiet all day. Our artillery caught a working party of the enemy this morning inflicting some 20 casualties. | |
| Camp A | 22.3.16 | 9.30pm | Enemy very quiet all yesterday. The 42nd Canadian B. did not arrive until late & the relief was not complete until 2.30 a.m. this morning. A train was provided at the Asylum Y/View. & brought | |
| G.11.c.5.5 Shect 28 | | | | |

# WAR DIARY
## INTELLIGENCE SUMMARY

Army Form C. 2118.

| Place | Date | Hour | Summary of Events and Information | Remarks and references to Appendices |
|---|---|---|---|---|
| FLETRE | 23.3.16 | 9.30 p.m. | the battalion back. We move tomorrow to 3rd Canadian Rest Area. | |
| | 23.3.16 | 9.30 p.m. | The Battalion paraded this morning at 11.45 a.m. preceded by the starting point at G.5.c.9.2. Sheet 28. The 17th Inf. Bde. marched as a complete unit, this Battalion leading the Brigade. We were followed on POPERINGHE – ABEELE – K.36.d. Sheet 27. GODESWAERSVELDE – FLETRE. We were halted for lunch at L.21.F.9.3 Sheet 27. The battalion marched well. We billets here are fairly but space is rather limited, more especially no upto do accommodation for officers. H.Q. is a farm at W.5.c.3.9. Sheet 27 | |
| do. | 24.3.16 | 9.30 p.m. | The day has been spent in hit inspections, short company parades. | |
| do. | 25.3.16 | 9.30 p.m. | Training has been carried on today according to a programme of work following letter was received today from 17 I.B. "To O.C. 8th R. W. Kent. The following letter dated 24.3.16 has been received from G.O.C. 24th Division by the B.G.C. 17th Inf. Bde. 'I have heard from General Fanshawe that he saw the 17th Brigade on the march yesterday & thought their turn out, and discipline & general soldier like appearance did them great credit, after the trying time they have had in the trenches. I also heard from senior officers who saw the 3rd Rifle Brigade & the 8 Buffs | |

# WAR DIARY
## or
## INTELLIGENCE SUMMARY.

Army Form C. 2118.

| Place | Date | Hour | Summary of Events and Information | Remarks and references to Appendices |
|---|---|---|---|---|
| | 25.3.16 | | that they thought they were looking & going very well. "Yful" are the Buffs" staff well worth while to glad to hear of this. | |
| FLETRE | 26.3.16 | 9.30 am | There was no Church Parade this morning, owing apparently to the universal distribution of the battalion training. | |
| do | 27.3.16 | " | Company has been continued today. | |
| do | 28.3.16 | " | Today the battalion has had theirs of the bathe at METEREN, where however there were so proper ware of clean underclothes. | |
| do | 29.3.16 | " | Orders have been received that we are to move up to BULFORD CAMP on 31st and relieve 7th British Columbia Regt. | |
| do | 30.3.16 | " | Training has been continued in accordance with programme of work. | |
| BULFORD CAMP T26 a 3.8 Sheet 28. | 31.3.16 | " | The Battalion paraded at 6.25am this morning & marched to this camp via METEREN – BAILLEUL. The men marched well, it being a very warm day. The camp is a good one & with ample accommodation. The Battalion were inspected this morning on arrival by GOC 24 Division. | |

Thomas H Alnel
C in cy B^n The Buffs

17th Brigade.
24th Division

8th BATTALION

"BUFFS"    EAST KENT REGIMENT.

*April* 1916.

XXIV

8 East Kent
Vol. 7

Confidential

War Diary

of

8' (Service) Battn. The Buffs

From 1st April 1916  To 30th April 1916

Volume 9

Army Form C. 2118.

# WAR DIARY
## or
## INTELLIGENCE SUMMARY.
(Erase heading not required.)

| Place | Date | Hour | Summary of Events and Information | Remarks and references to Appendices |
|---|---|---|---|---|
| BULFORD CAMP T26 a 3.8 Sheet 28 | 1.4.16 | 9.30/- | Short company parades today, including close order drill, musketry | |
| do | 2.4.16 | 9.30/- | Church parade was held this morning in a Y.M.C.A. marquee adjacent to the Camp. | |
| do | 3.4.16 | 9.30/- | Orders received today that we are to relieve 3rd Rifle Brigade on night 5/6 inst. in the front line. A Battalion was been started in this camp, this being the first occasion since we came on active service but August. | |
| do | 4.4.16 | 9.30/- | An attack practice for Lewis guns took place this morning. Other parades under company arrangements. | |
| BN.H.Q. ASH HOUSE U14 & U.S Sheet 28 | 6.4.16 | 9.30/- | We relieved the 3rd R.B. last night, relief being completed at 12.45 am this morning. Enemy shelled the roads & tracks in communication trench to the relief was held up in consequence. Today enemy has been fairly quiet but fired some 5.9's into Trench L 131 occupied by A. Coy. Casualties O.R. 1 killed 6 wounded. | |

# WAR DIARY
## or
## INTELLIGENCE SUMMARY.

(Erase heading not required.)

Army Form C. 2118.

Instructions regarding War Diaries and Intelligence Summaries are contained in F. S. Regs., Part II. and the Staff Manual respectively. Title pages will be prepared in manuscript.

| Place | Date | Hour | Summary of Events and Information | Remarks and references to Appendices |
|---|---|---|---|---|
| Bn.H.Q. ASH HSE | 7.4.16 | 9.30 pm | Everything has been considerably quieter than on 5th & 6th. Our artillery carried out a shoot on LA PETITE DOUVE farm this afternoon. Very considerable damage. Weather fine. | |
| do. | 8.4.16 | 9.30 pm | Enemy shelled Trench 131 with H.E. this morning causing little damage. Our Artillery carried out a shoot on AVENUE FARM this afternoon causing a fair amount of damage. A few W.&.3 shrapnel ranging Bn.H.Q about 9.30. An aeroplane flew along our front line from N. to S. dropping coloured lights. Casualties O.R. 3. | |
| do. | 9.4.16 | 9.30 pm | At 2.30 A.M & 3.30 A.M our machine guns fired on the enemy lines. There was no retaliation, in the afternoon the enemy fires on trench 131 we replied with rifle Grenades & completely silenced the enemy. Also 2 of our snipers crawled out about 150 yds from our trench & accounted for one of the enemy who was observing their artillery fire. Casualties O.R. 2. | |
| do. | 10.4.16 | 9.30 pm | Morning very quiet, in the afternoon the enemy again shelled trench 131 with M.G doing little damage, we replied with Grenades. | |
| do. | 11.4.16 | 9.30 pm | Very quiet during the day. We were relieved by the 2nd Batn R.B. the relief being completed at 10.p.m. W. the marched to GRAND MUNQUE FARM via HYDE PARK CORNER arriving there at 10.45 2/Lt BALDWIN was slightly wounded. | |
| Bn.H.Q. GRAND MUNQUE FARM | 12.4.16 | 9.30 pm | A.&.C Coy's were sent in a working party in the morning. The weather was very wet. | |
| do. | 13.4.16 | 9.30 pm | Found working parties both in the morning & evening. All leave was stopped. Weather fine. | |

# WAR DIARY or INTELLIGENCE SUMMARY

Army Form C. 2118.

| Place | Date | Hour | Summary of Events and Information | Remarks and references to Appendices |
|---|---|---|---|---|
| Bn. H.Q. GRANDE MUNQUE FARM | 14.4.16 | 9.30 pm | Found working parties bed in morning & evening. Weather very wet. | |
| do | 15.4.16 | 9.30 pm | Continued to find working parties for R.E. in morning & evening. Weather wet. One O.R. was D.I. very slightly in the evening. Casualties O.R. 1. | |
| do | 16.4.16 | 9.30 pm | Chief parade in the morning. Working parties both in morning & evening. The C.O. inspected the transport during the morning. | |
| do | 17.4.16 | 9.30 pm | Found a working party in the morning. | |
| Bn. H.Q. W.13.C.6.3 | 18.4.16 | 9.30 pm | The relief was not completed until 10 p.m. The enemy was quiet during the evening. | The relief in the evening we relieved the 3rd Batt. R.B. into trenches 130 & 131. |
| do | 19.4.16 | 9.30 pm | During the morning of 12 midday the enemy and some 5.9 shells into trenches 130 & 131. During the afternoon the enemy bombarded the trenches 128-131 doing very little damage on Bulstrode nr. MESSINES ROAD. At 7.15 the enemy replying. The enemy also shelled ASH HOUSE. MESSINES ROAD. At 7.15 the enemy fired a bombardment on HYDE PARK CORNER. At 7.15 the enemy artillery fired on trench 131. Trenches in 2 days. The remainder of the day was quiet. Our artillery carried on a shoot on the GAPPARD ROAD at 9 p.m. | Casualties Killed 2 O.R. Wounded 3 O.R. |
| do | 20.4.16 | 9.30 pm | The enemy was very very quiet all day. The weather still continues to be very bad. | Casualties Wounded 4 O.R. |
| do | 21.4.16 | 9.30 pm | In the morning the enemy shelled to try doing no damage. The ONLY IN MY ADVANCED ESTAMINET were also shelled. | Casualties Wounded 2 O.R. |
| do | 22.4.16 | 9.30 pm | The enemy came into reply. Very quiet all day. Weather very wet. Enfers trenches 128 & 129 at 5.0 p.m. | Casualties 1 O.R. wounded. |
| do | 23.4.16 | 9.30 pm | The enemy shelled trenches 128 & 129 in the morning, the remainder of the day was very quiet. In the evening we were relieved by the 3rd Batt. R.B. The relief was complete at 11.30 pm. Two new officers arrived 2/Lt MORRELL & Lt PRIEST. | Casualties 6 O.R. wounded. |

Army Form C. 2118.

# WAR DIARY
## or
## INTELLIGENCE SUMMARY.
(Erase heading not required.)

Instructions regarding War Diaries and Intelligence Summaries are contained in F. S. Regs., Part II and the Staff Manual respectively. Title pages will be prepared in manuscript.

| Place | Date | Hour | Summary of Events and Information | Remarks and references to Appendices |
|---|---|---|---|---|
| BUFORD CAMP | 24.11.15 | 9.25 pm | Two aeroplanes were flying this morning one of which landed quite near Bd. H.Q. All companies were out on working parties. | |
| do | 25.11.15 | 9.30 pm | Do again had a bath. Weather very fine. Parade water. Coy arranged that Coy supplied a working party of 5 men. O. football match was played in the evening. D of R.I. Bat M.C. Reveil D_3 Bat M.C. | |
| do | 26.11.15 | 9.30 pm | Weather very fine. Parade under Coy arrangement. Working parties were supplied morning & afternoon. Evening watch very fine. | |
| do | 27.11.15 | 9.30 pm | Parade in the morning for the C.O's inspection. Weather fine. A football match was played. Bay v Rest Bn. Reveil D_3 Rest M.C. | |
| do | 28.11.15 | 9.30 pm | The Lashing Gunners practised the attack in the morning. The B.G.C. came Weather very fine. Reveilled 3rd Bn R.B. starting at 8.30 pm. Reveil D_3 Rest | |
| do | 29.11.15 | 9.30 pm | Fine weather. Into clothing. A football match. Reveil D_3 Rest | |
| Bd.H.Q. W.15.6.13 | 30.11.15 | 9.30 pm | The relief was completed at 11 pm. At 1.30 am the enemy opened heavy fire and shelled the Hebuterne-Mailly road from 11 pm. At 1.30 am the enemy shelled RED LODGE during the afternoon, lasted until 3.10 pm. The rest of the day was very quiet. Weather fine. Casualties 5 O.R. wounded. | |

H. W. Swann H-Colonel
Comg 8th Bn R.B.

17th Brigade.
24th Division.

8th BATTALION

"BUFFS"  EAST KENT REGIMENT.

May. 1916.

XIV

8th Buffs
Vol 8

[stamp: ORDERLY ROOM, 8TH BN. THE BUFFS]

Confidential.

War Diary

of

8th Batn The Buffs.

Volume 10.

To 31st May 1916.

From 1st May 1916.

A.R.Owen
Lieut-Colonel
Comdg 8th Batn The Buffs

# WAR DIARY or INTELLIGENCE SUMMARY

Army Form C. 2118.

| Place | Date | Hour | Summary of Events and Information | Remarks and references to Appendices |
|---|---|---|---|---|
| B^n H.Q. | 1.5.16 | 9.30 p.m. | Very fine weather. Aeroplanes active on both sides all day. Enemy very quiet, only sending a few whizz bangs on the front line. Working party out to bury telephone cable to two posts in front line. | |
| " | 2.5.16 | 9.30 p.m. | Beautiful sunny day. Enemy quiet with his artillery. Aircraft very active. Enemy M.G's very busy after dark. Casualties killed 1 O.R. Wounded 1 O.R. | |
| " | 3.5.16 | " | Very hot & bright sunshine all day. Aircraft no active account. A few whizz bangs & H.E fired at front line during morning & again in the afternoon. Crest of Hill 63 was shelled intermittently. | |
| " | 4.5.16 | " | Still very hot. Few H.E shells on front line. Subsidiary line, & MESSINES ROAD, also few whizz bangs near Lunatic 1. A small "chape" organised consisting of artillery, + M.G.S, between 12 M.N. & 12.50 a.m. | |
| " | 5.5.16 | " | Very fine & bright day. Aircraft extremely active on both sides. One of our planes whilst spotting for heavy artillery attacked by enemy & brought down behind enemy lines in flames. | |
| " | 6.5.16 | " | Bright day. Few H.E shells on frontline. Relieved by 3^rd R.B. Relief completed 11 p.m. | |

Army Form C. 2118.

# WAR DIARY
## or
## INTELLIGENCE SUMMARY.
*(Erase heading not required.)*

Instructions regarding War Diaries and Intelligence Summaries are contained in F. S. Regs., Part II. and the Staff Manual respectively. Title pages will be prepared in manuscript.

| Place | Date | Hour | Summary of Events and Information | Remarks and references to Appendices |
|---|---|---|---|---|
| Grand Munque | 7.5.16 | 7.0 pm | Fine day. Church parade in farm yard at 11 am. The Hun small shells between this farm & Pissaro's. Some a few hundred yards N of farm. | |
| " | 8.5.16 | " | No aircraft up during day owing to wind. The Officers played 12th R. Scots at Rounders & beat them 2 to 1. | |
| " | 9.5.16 | " | Windy day & rain intermittently. Neuve Eglise baths open for the Batt: 60th yesterday & to-day. Working parties found for R.E. | |
| " | 10.5.16 | " | Windy & wet day. Very little activity. Working parties at night for R.E. | |
| " | 11.5.16 | 11.30 pm | Bright day but not hot. Our heavy guns fired at 3 pm on trenches opposite 131. Enemy put some Shrapnel South of Grande Munque at 5 pm. Usual working parties for R.E. | |
| Bn HQ U.13.b.6.3 Sheet 28 | | | We relieved the 2nd R.B. tonight in the same sector as before. Relief passed off quietly. | |

Army Form C. 2118.

# WAR DIARY
## or
## INTELLIGENCE SUMMARY.
(Erase heading not required.)

Instructions regarding War Diaries and Intelligence Summaries are contained in F. S. Regs., Part II. and the Staff Manual respectively. Title pages will be prepared in manuscript.

| Place | Date | Hour | Summary of Events and Information | Remarks and references to Appendices |
|---|---|---|---|---|
| BnHQ V13 c.6.3 Sheet 28 | 12.5.16 | 9 p.m | Weather fine. Very quiet day indeed. Casualties O.R. Killed 2. | |
| do | 13.5.16 | 9 p.m | Some shellange round the Hill 63 this afternoon. Not much done & very quiet on front line. | |
| do | 14.5.16 | 9 p.m | Enemy fired 6 H.E. to to left of our line early this morning. Machine guns are active this morning & evening. Weather hot. | |
| do | 15.5.16 | 9 p.m | Still raining today. Enemy very quiet. This is the quietest spell we have had in these trenches. | |
| do | 16.5.16 | 9 p.m | Heavy artillery fire by the enemy on our right this evening at 8 p.m. Enemy fired an extraordinarily large number of blind shells. | |
| Bulford | 17.5.16 | 11 p.m | We have been relieved tonight by the 3 R.B. & have come back into Divisional Reserve | |

# WAR DIARY
## or
## INTELLIGENCE SUMMARY.

(Erase heading not required.)

Army Form C. 2118.

Instructions regarding War Diaries and Intelligence Summaries are contained in F.S. Regs., Part II. and the Staff Manual respectively. Title pages will be prepared in manuscript.

| Place | Date | Hour | Summary of Events and Information | Remarks and references to Appendices |
|---|---|---|---|---|
| B.H.Q. BULFORD CAMP. | 18.5.16 | 9.30pm | Weather very fine all day. Great aeroplane activity. | |
| do. | 19.5.16 | 9.30pm | Glorious day. In the evening 36 officers were invited by Captain Summers to the Sergeants Mess. | |
| | 20.5.16 | 9.30pm | Very fine & very hot. A draft of 159 O.R. arrived today, the band playing them into camp from the Station. 2/Lt PEACOCK, 2/Lt RAINEY, 2/Lt FARMER | |
| | 21.5.16 | 2pm | Very fine. Church parade was held in the Y.M.C.A. tent. | |
| | 22.5.16 | 9.30pm | Weather still continues to be fine. Received a memo from BRIGADE informing us that influenza in period 1st to last of the week were only 8 days. COLONEL LUGAS was interviewed by the T.I.B. He was also needed. Still fine & hot to report 2 officers & 50 men of enemy troops during our visit. Very large convoys of enemy aeroplanes our very low. | |
| B.H.Q. | 23.5.16 | 9.30pm | Weather only fair with occasional storms were still continued of 2 on 3 each day. | |
| U.13. C.6.3. Sheet 6. | 25.5.16 | 2pm | Weather fair. In the evening it rained very hard. We relieved the 3rd RIFLE BRIGADE in the evening. A party of 1 Officer 1/Lt ELLIOTT & 12 men from the GRAND FLEET arrived during the afternoon. | |
| | 26.5.16 | 9.30pm | Weather fine. Very quiet all day. The men of the GRAND FLEET went up to the trenches. Casualties O.R. 2 WOUNDED | |
| | 27.5.16 | 9.30pm | Weather fine. During the afternoon the enemy hurled in a bay on the left of the line. Conspicuous conduct was displayed by No 5263 PTE BIGNALL. E. 1/Lt SHAFTO to 2nd LIEUT GRANT. Casualties O.R. 3 KILLED 1 WOUNDED | |

Army Form C. 2118.

# WAR DIARY
## or
## INTELLIGENCE SUMMARY.
(Erase heading not required.)

Instructions regarding War Diaries and Intelligence Summaries are contained in F. S. Regs., Part II. and the Staff Manual respectively. Title pages will be prepared in manuscript.

| Place | Date | Hour | Summary of Events and Information | Remarks and references to Appendices |
|---|---|---|---|---|
| BN H.Q. U13 c 6,3. | 28.5.16 | 9.30pm | Weather fine. Enemy m.g. fire all day. Machine guns were very active during the evening. | |
| do | 29.5.16 | 9.30pm | A draft of 7 officers L/Col. A.T.H. TRUEMAN + 131 O.R. arrived to-day. Enemy active. Weather fine. | |
| do | 30.5.16 | 9.30pm | The enemy shelled the left of our line from 12.30 - 2.30 p.m. doing a great deal of damage. One Lewis gun was put out of action, our retaliation was good. The following men were conspicuous for bravery. No 6799 Pte. DRAPER. Casualties NIL. | |
| do | 31.5.16 | 9.30pm | Very quiet all day. Plenty of machine gun fire during the evening. Weather fine. Casualties  Killed N.O.R. Wounded 5 O.R. | |

[signatures]

17th Brigade.
24th Division.

8th BATTALION

"BUFFS"  EAST KENT REGIMENT.

June 1916.

Confidential  XXIV

War Diary
of
8th Batt. The Buffs

Volume 11

From 1st June 1916.

To 30th June 1916.

A.S.Duncan.
Lieut-Colonel.
Comg. 8th Batt. The Buffs.

# WAR DIARY or INTELLIGENCE SUMMARY

Army Form C. 2118.

| Place | Date | Hour | Summary of Events and Information | Remarks and references to Appendices |
|---|---|---|---|---|
| Bn HQ O.13.c.6.3. | 1.6.16 | 9.30pm | Very quiet day. Aeroplanes very active. In the evening a coffin balloon hole tore from its moorings & was carried over the enemy lines by the wind. The occupants used parachutes & landed safely behind our lines. Casualties nil. | |
| do | 2.6.16 | 9.30pm | Weather fine. Enemy very quiet all day. We were relieved by 2nd R.B. during the evening. Casualties nil. | |
| GARDEN MINQUE FARM | 3.6.16 | 9.30pm | Relief was completed at 12.30 am. Weather fine. Battn paraded in the morning. During the afternoon the Bn Cmdr went to PETITE PORT St. the way to Beat through winning. Casualties nil. | |
| — | 4.6.16 | 9.30pm | Heavy bombardment on our left commencing 12.30 am. Weather wet. Among the Birthday List of honors were Lieut G Lindsay Military Cross. No 511 RSM Brooker I.G. & No 3265 Pte Peel Sr. D.C.M. No 1838 L/Cpl J. Buzzard & Pte No.5272 Pte C.S. Hall Military Medal. Weather continued wet. Very quiet along our front. Casualties nil. | |
| — | 5.6.16 | — | Weather fine. Artillery more active, especially north of ROMARIN – HYDE PARK CORNER ROAD. Towards evening aircraft very active. Our AA guns did some good shooting – Casualties nil. | |
| — | 6.6.16 | — | | |
| — | 7.6.16 | — | Weather fine – Artillery active on AU 63. Aircraft fairly busy. Casualties nil. | |

# WAR DIARY
## or
## INTELLIGENCE SUMMARY.
*(Erase heading not required.)*

Army Form C. 2118.

| Place | Date | Hour | Summary of Events and Information | Remarks and references to Appendices |
|---|---|---|---|---|
| GRANDE MUNQUE FM | 8.6.16 | 9.30 pm | Weather fine. Artillery active all day; during the afternoon a few shells fell on huts in the wood. Heavy rain in evening. Casualties OR wounded 2. | |
| | 9.6.16 | — | Weather still fine. Artillery quieter. Aircraft very active. at 4.30 pm very large enemy machine made three tours of hill 63 flying very low, though heavily shelled by our AA guns. Later, an machine appeared flying westward + though heavily shelled continued its course till out of sight. Casualties OR 1 wounded | |
| Bn HQ U.13.e.6.3. | 10.6.16 | — | Bn relieved the 3rd Rifle Brigade in right SubSector. Relief reported complete at 10.30 pm. Very quiet. Casualties nil | |
| | 11.6.16 | — | Very quiet all day except for a few Trench Mortars on Trench 131. Though did no harm but then is the first true that they have been used against our trenches here. Weather wet. CASUALTIES Nil Military Cross awarded 2/Lt SHAFTO inactive. Enemy very inactive. Goc Div came round | |
| | 12.6.16 | — | Weather still very wet. — Enemy quiet this morning. Casualties nil | |
| | 13.6.16 | — | Very wet indeed. — Enemy quiet on our front. — Very heavy bombardment to the north of us. Casualties. Nil | |
| | 14.6.16 | — | Weather still wet. Locality A shelled from 12 to 1 pm, one dugout being knocked in. Very good retaliation by our guns on ASH ROAD BARRIER | |

Army Form C. 2118.

# WAR DIARY
## or
## INTELLIGENCE SUMMARY.
*(Erase heading not required.)*

Instructions regarding War Diaries and Intelligence Summaries are contained in F. S. Regs., Part II. and the Staff Manual respectively. Title pages will be prepared in manuscript.

| Place | Date | Hour | Summary of Events and Information | Remarks and references to Appendices |
|---|---|---|---|---|
| — | 15 | 9.30 p.m | Very wet. Enemy still quiet. The following were mentioned in Gen. Sir D. Haig's despatch. Lt.Col. J.L.W. LUCAS. 3383 Pte CLANCEY J. 5196 Pte GARLINGE, W.J. | |
| — | 16 | 9.30 p.m | Weather cleared up - and N.E. The enemy sent up 2 small parachute balloons opposite ANTON'S FM presumably to test wind. CASUALTIES NIL. Brisk bombardment in neighbourhood of ARMENTIERES about 11. P.m. | |
| | 17 | 9.30 p.m | At 12.30 a.m - B Company on the left sent an S.O.S. for retaliation — Almost immediately afterwards "GAS" and the S.O.S came through from the 1st Bn Royal Fusiliers on our left. A brisk bombardment started on our front line + the top and South sides of hill 63. A barrage was put on the line CHATEAU LAHUTTE — LOCALITY I fought across our rear. The Gas itself was sent arrived in the wood 3 or 4 minutes after the warning and lasted half an hour. Its path was from ONTARIO FM — HILL 63 — Bde HQ (PETITE MUNQUE) and penetrated as far as KORTEPYP thus missing our front and subsidiary line. The Rarin Company and Bn HQ were in the area @ Communication with Company and Bn HQ and Bde Batte HQ owing to the shelling of line was cut between Bn HQ and Bde Batte HQ owing to the moving up of 6th Bde Batte HQ the wood. It was reestablished however by moving the wire Fore and the - Communication with Subsidiary line was maintained there a breaks by Lamp was received from the Right Coy + transmitted | |

# WAR DIARY or INTELLIGENCE SUMMARY

Army Form C. 2118.

| Place | Date | Hour | Summary of Events and Information | Remarks and references to Appendices |
|---|---|---|---|---|
| | 18th | 9.30 | to Bn HQ. Nowhere was the buried cable cut. Casualties OR 2 slightly gassed 2 shell shock. About 10 am the camp of 2/5 Anderson's party at PETIT PONT was shelled without damage. Fine. Slight shelling of Trench 128 about 5.30 pm. We were relieved by 3rd Bn the Rifle Brigade - relief being complete at 11.25 pm. Party of 4 Officers and 207 OR engaged on tramline cable into new Bn HQ this afternoon. False gas alarm about midnight for which the party stood to in the SUBSIDIARY LINE. Bn work which has been carried on during the tour. Casualties OR 1 wounded from rose cap of Anti aircraft Shell. Bn moved to BULFORD CAMP. Casualties nil. | |
| BULFORD CAMP | 19th | | Wet nearly all day. Rehearsal for raid at 10.15 pm. Companies fans out. Sergeants Mess started. Casualties nil. | |
| | 20th | | Nothing of importance. Casualties nil. | |
| | 21st | | Orders received for our relief by the 2nd Australian Bde. Casualties nil. | |
| | 22nd | | Left Bulford Camp 1.45 pm - & marched via BAILLEUL to ST JANS CAPELLE Billeted in farms - Bn very close together. Raining. Strength 27 X 5. Party left at PETIT PONT FM | |

Army Form C. 2118.

# WAR DIARY
## or
## INTELLIGENCE SUMMARY.
*(Erase heading not required.)*

Instructions regarding War Diaries and Intelligence Summaries are contained in F. S. Regs., Part II. and the Staff Manual respectively. Title pages will be prepared in manuscript.

| Place | Date | Hour | Summary of Events and Information | Remarks and references to Appendices |
|---|---|---|---|---|
| ST JANS CAPELLE | 23rd | | Heavy storm at start in the afternoon - Bn went for Route march in morning for about 2 hours. Rehearsal of Raiding Party | |
| | 24th | | Bn rested - no parades except Swedish Drill. under a CSM from Army Gymnastic Staff working on new System. weather showery | |
| | 25th | | Church parade at 11.15 am at Bn HQ | |
| | 26th | | Companies did route marches. Military Medal awarded to 3377 Cpl. C. BATCHELOR for his conduct on the night of the late gas attack. | |
| | 27th | | Raiding party at PETIT PONT did a final Rehearsal. weather wet | |
| | 28th | | A detachment of the Bn under 2/Lt ANDERSON and 2/Lt TEMPLE carried out a raid on GERMAN TRENCHES at ASH ROAD BARRIER Sheet 28 U 15 A. The two parties moved out so as to be in position outside our wire when an intense bombardment started on the points to be attacked. under Cover of this the parties Crept forward, while the guns lifted at 50 yards at a time to their barrage line. The raid | |

# WAR DIARY or INTELLIGENCE SUMMARY

Army Form C. 2118.

| Place | Date | Hour | Summary of Events and Information | Remarks and references to Appendices |
|---|---|---|---|---|
| | | | Unfortunately, also at once as a surprise light the right party rather 2/Lt ANDERSON succeeded in entering the enemies front line trench and bombing 2 dugouts where they killed 5 Germans. 3 Rifles went bombing back as far as pegs. They i.e. the enemy was holding the trench in considerable force and after some stout fighting the raiding party withdrew successfully being nearly all wounded. The left party met with less success as they found the enemys wire in front of them uncut. On hearing the signal for withdrawal from the right Lt TEMPLE withdrew his party also, having no dead man who was subsequently brought in. Telephone communication with both parties was attempted at the outset and the cables to two Signallers being wounded. The enterprise was carried out according to plan but by shrapnel being given by means of a live tube, being cut by shrapnel. The artillery support was in command of the covering party, Capt GULLICK. A total of 3 officers + Lt. HALL was in command. | 12.1 AM |
| | | | C. D. GULLICK commanded the parapet casualties officer 100 Other ranks went over the parapet. Capt GULLICK returned the nil OR killed 4 wounded 20. to the night and came away company by the 5th Avalanche |  |

# WAR DIARY or INTELLIGENCE SUMMARY

Army Form C. 2118.

| Place | Date | Hour | Summary of Events and Information | Remarks and references to Appendices |
|---|---|---|---|---|
| ST JANS CAPELLE | 29th | 9.30p | next morning at 7 am. Raiding party returned from PETIT PONT in lorries, arriving about 5 pm. Weather fine. Orders received that we are to move to LOCRE to billets before taking over the line. The Raiding party received the Congratulations of Corps & Div. Commanders. | |
| LOCRE | 30th | 9.30p | CO, Company Commanders Signal officer & MGO went to inspect new trenches Sheet 28. N.36.a. HQ at COOKERS TM N 35 C49. Battalion marched to billets at LOCRE starting at 1.30 pm. & were inspected en route by G.O.C. 24th Div. Billets very scattered. | |

Andreas Lt Colonel
Comdg 8th Bn. Queens

REPORT ON RAID CARRIED OUT BY A PARTY
OF 8TH BUFFS ON 2ND AUSTRALIAN BRIGADE
FRONT ON NIGHT OF 28TH/29TH JUNE.

********************

1. The programme was carried out in accordance with the time table arranged up to 20 minutes after Zero, i.e. 11.50 p.m., at which hour the raiders were to enter the enemy's trenches. Subsequent events were as follows:-

2. The Right Party on approaching the point of entry were seen by two of the enemy in the sap. These were fired on but apparently succeeded in giving the alarm. The wire was found cut and the Commander and leading men of the party entered the enemy's trench. They were then immediately heavily bombed, the enemy being evidently in readiness for them. In these circumstances the commander decided it was useless to attempt to proceed and gave the signal for withdrawal, and the party retired to our trenches.

The Left Party found the wire not cut. As they approached it they were fired on by Machine Guns and suffered some casualties. They continued their advance and began cutting wire and placing their mats in position, in the face of renewed machine gun fire. They then heard the siren of the Right Party Commander ordering a retirement, whereon they withdrew to our trenches.

3. The Right Party captured three German rifles.

4. The telephonic communication with the parties was not very successful. Touch was entirely lost with the Left Party, (the signallers were probably wounded very early), and the Right Party were in touch only as far as the HALF WAY HOUSE. No report was therefore received of the moment of entering the enemy's trench.

5. <u>Casualties.</u>  The casualties amongst the raiders amounted to 3 killed, 2 missing, 14 wounded. Casualties in the trenches were slight.

6. The artillery co-operation was satisfactory.

7. The enemy's retaliation was not heavy. The first shell was noticed 7 minutes after our bombardment commenced. Most of the fire was over our front line trenches, and did little damage.

   No damage to our gas cylinders has been reported.

   A red flare was sent up from the enemy's trenches 42 minutes after our bombardment had begun, i.e. after our raiders had retired.

   A red and green rocket was seen north of Trench 129 at 12.51 a.m.  All was quiet by about 1.20 a.m.

8. The wind being too gentle, it was decided at 12.40 a.m. that gas could not be used. This was notified to all concerned. About 1.45 orders were given to dismount pipes and sandbag up the cylinders again.

*Ashton-Morgan*

Major, G.S.

29/6/16.                                           24th Division.

## Report on Raid carried out by 8th Batn The Buffs.
### 28th/29th June. 1916.

1. **Start.** The Raid started on time and all times as laid down in scheme were kept. The Right Party entered the Enemy's trench at 11-53.pm, the Left Party reported entry impracticable, at 12-1.am.

2. **Right Party.**

    (a). Right Party got out of our trench at 11-21.pm and and moved off at 11-31.pm. At 11-35.pm two Signallers were wounded rendering the laying of the ladder wire impossible. So only a single wire was laid. At 11-41.pm. the Party reached HALF WAY HOUSE and reported. After this the wire was broken. About 11-48.pm after crossing one barbed wire entanglement the party entered the enemy's forward trench which was made in the form of a Horse shoe joining enemy's fire trench at each end. This forward trench was held by a post of three men who ran down it to their fire trench as Party approached.

    Two of them left their rifles behind; these were captured and sent back.

    Leaving one Bombing Squad to hold this trench, the Party went on - crossed another wire entanglement and entered the enemy's fire trench, at U15 a 4.7.

    The Party was received by salvoes of bombs, but our bombers were able to drive enemy back about 10 yards.

    The leading Bayonet man shone a light in a dugout and was shot through the chest and died from the wound.

    This dugout however and one other were successfully bombed - five Germans were killed, another rifle was captured in this trench making three in all.

    The enemy's rifles were loaded but bayonets were not fixed. MACC or MAX was written on the door of one of the dugouts.

Sheet 2.

Considering no further point would be obtained owing to the strength of the enemy in the trench Lieut. Anderson withdrew his party leaving one dead and bringing back three wounded (ours) out of the enemy's trench.

The party then came back meeting a barrage on the way. All wounded were brought back.

Left Party. (b). Left Party moved out in front of our wire and started to move forward to time, 11-31 pm arriving at half way at 11-43 where TOMBRIDGE was reported (this message was not received.).

This party moved forward at 11-46 pm. and reached a single strand of (barbed concertina) wire. This was crossed at 11-48. The enemy opened with Machine Gun fire from the left. The party proceeded and came across another obstacle consisting of several strands of the same wire.

As soon as the party started to cut this the Machine Gun opened fire again.

One wirecutter was wounded.

This obstacle was crossed and another was met; this was partially crossed - the machine gun playing the whole time and Very Lights going up. Hearing the syren of the other party (the signal for withdrawal) Lieut. Temple withdrew his party.

At this time it was 12-1 am.

During the journey back the enemy opened rifle fire as well as Machine Gun Fire.

NOTES.

1. Miscellaneous. Enemy's Machine Guns traversed our parapets about 11-15. pm very much more heavily than he has ever done before.

On the Right the enemy were found to be holding their front line trench strongly and were on the alert.

Sheet. 3.

The enemy's trench _which was about 7' deep_ was not traversed which increased the difficulty of the raiding party.

2. **Artillery Support.** The timing of the Artillery Fire was excellent.

The Trench Mortars did not produce the volume of fire anticipated.

3. **Very Lights.** During our Advance no Very Lights were put up on our immediate front, but were sent up from each flank.

During the withdrawal Very Lights were sent up in quick succession on our immediate front.

4. **Wire.** The wire was well scouted, but no gaps were found.

On the right wire cutters were hardly necessary as the wire entanglements were very poor.

On the left the reverse was the case. The Mats were excellent.

5. **Tape.** Luminous tape was very useful and made the withdrawal simple. Without it several of the party would have been considerably delayed in getting back.

6. **Signals.** The ladder system of cable was used and this entailed a minimum of 4 men to work it. It is thought that 4 single wires would have caused less confusion.

The pull system - i.e. the same as is used on L.P.s might be better, but this would work up to 150 yards.

7. **Casualties.** Our Casualties were:-

    4. Killed.

    20 Wounded.

The total number of men to cross our parapet was 3 Officers and 100 other ranks.

8. **Conclusions.** The raid did not come as a surprise to the enemy.

The 2 men seen in the advance trench undoubtedly gave the warning to the German troops in the front line.

This emphasises the necessity for men on listening posts to remain on their posts no matter how heavy the bombardment.

Sheet. 4.

All details had been carefully thought out and were carried out to the last letter.

The alertness of the enemy and his preparedness for resistance solely accounted for the fact that the raiding parties were not able to achieve their primary object, the capturing of a Prisoner.

Strength of party.
Right Party 1 officer 37 O.R. 2 Lt. L. Anderson
Left Party 1 officer 29 O.R. 2 Lt. W.H. Temple
Covering party 1 officer 18 O.R. Lt. E.F. Hall.
In addition 6 Prisoner runners
& 7 Signallers.

L.W. Lucas, Lieut-Colonel,
Cmdg 8th Batn The Buffs.

Field.
30th June. 1916.

17th Inf.Bde.
24th Div.

**WAR DIARY**

8th BATTN. THE BUFFS (EAST KENT REGIMENT).

J U L Y

1 9 1 6

Army Form C. 2118.

1 E Kent Regt July 24 Vol 1 b

# WAR DIARY
## or
## INTELLIGENCE SUMMARY.
(Erase heading not required.)

| Place | Date | Hour | Summary of Events and Information | Remarks and references to Appendices |
|---|---|---|---|---|
| B'n HQ COOKERS FM Sheet 28 N35.C.49 | 1st July | 9:00 | Relieved 1st Bn. N. Staffordshire Regt in trenches D5. D6. N36A. A + C Coys in line. B Coy in Support at R.E. FARM. D Company in Reserve in GHQ 2nd Line. Relief reported at 12.20 am. Front trenches very much knocked about and untidy. The whole area has been heavily shelled in the last two months and all works very much knocked about. Casualties Nil. | |
| | 2nd | | A quiet day with the exception of some shelling to the south of us. Casualties OR wounded 1. General repairs to parapet + dugouts and large working party on wire entries both day + night. Weather very fine. | |
| | 3rd | | Still fine and very quiet all day – two Sentries shot while looking over parapet at by a Sniper, the Officer probably a stray. 17 NCC1 was counted and a third man – 2 of the men being killed and himself OR killed 2 wounded. CASUALTIES Officers — wounded | (3²) |
| | 4th | | Officers wounded 1. OR killed 3 wounded 2 | (4ᵃ) |
| | 5th | | Artillery cut wire all afternoon in front of D6 French this provoked some retaliation which was effectively stopped by our counter retaliation + wire cutting proceeded. From 11.30 pm to 12.15 Am a continued artillery shoot took place. The enemy replied with trench Mortar, Minenwerfer + Skoepfel barraging the line of the loop running back from R.E. FARM. Casualties Officer wounded 1 killed 2 | |

# WAR DIARY
## or
## INTELLIGENCE SUMMARY.
*(Erase heading not required.)*

Army Form C. 2118.

| Place | Date | Hour | Summary of Events and Information | Remarks and references to Appendices |
|---|---|---|---|---|
| Bn HQ COOKERS FM | 6th | | A quiet day. Some trench mortar bombs dropped behind D5. Officers wounded 1 (Capt. Gullick slightly) OR wounded 17 Chiefly owing to the enemy's retaliation to our shoot. | |
| | 7th | | Bn was relieved by 3rd Bn the Rifle Brigade and moved to Brigade Reserve in AIRCRAFT FM (Sheet 28 N 32.B 2.2.) Relief reported complete at 12.15 AM. OR wounded 1 | |
| AIRCRAFT FM. | 8th | — | Bn rested. Working party of 2 Officers + 50 men in KINGSWAY Casualties nil. | |
| | 9th | — | A fine day — large working parties by day and night on new CT KINGSWAY. AIRCRAFT FM was shelled this afternoon with shrapnel + 5.9 HE. The first few shells caused casualties but the Bn took up positions in the adjacent trenches whilst the shelling was harmless. CASUALTIES nil. | |
| | 10th | — | Working parties continue on KINGSWAY. Bn HQ in ARCHIE FM shelled this afternoon between 5.30 + 6.30 p.m. two direct hits being obtained on the farm. without casualties however. The peasant decided to evacuate + Bn HQ moved to dugouts behind the know. Casualties 1 OR killed, 4 wounded in previous day's shelling. | |

Army Form C. 2118.

# WAR DIARY
or
## INTELLIGENCE SUMMARY.

(Erase heading not required.)

Instructions regarding War Diaries and Intelligence Summaries are contained in F.S. Regs., Part II. and the Staff Manual respectively. Title pages will be prepared in manuscript.

| Place | Date | Hour | Summary of Events and Information | Remarks and references to Appendices |
|---|---|---|---|---|
| AIRCRAFT FARM | 11 | | Bn "stood to" in trenches of KEMMEL DEFENCES from 12.30 to 2.30 am. An morning to avoid possible retaliation for shoot and raid carried out on our front by 3rd Bn the Rifle Brigade. No shells came near us. | Military Cross awarded to 2/Lt L ANDERSON 2/Lt. W.H. TEMPLE |
| Do. | 12. | | Some working parties on KINGSWAY. New Code for telephone messages introduced to this Brigade by 2nd Army. Nothing of importance to report. | Military Medals to Pte S/Sgt WILLIS Pte. MARSH |
| Do. | 13. | | Working parties as usual. Weather cold. Casualties 1 O.R. wounded. | PTE. IMBER |
| Do. | 14 | | One shell behind AIRCRAFT Fm in afternoon. Casualties 2 OR wounded on working party. | |
| Bn HQ | 15. | | Relieved 3rd Bn the Rifle Bn in D5, D6 + BULL RING. Relief complete at 11.30 p.m. B + D Coys in line. A at RE Farm, C at Dayrial Corner in reserve. Casualties nil | |
| | 16th | — | Military Medal awarded to 8116 Pte J. PHILIPS. At about 1 am At about 1 am the enemy attempted to raid the BULL RING. The first indication was a rather short fired at the LEWIS GUN in the "CASTLE" - which it was apparently their intention to seize. Two smoke bombs were then | |

# WAR DIARY or INTELLIGENCE SUMMARY

| Place | Date | Hour | Summary of Events and Information | Remarks and references to Appendices |
|---|---|---|---|---|
| COOKERS FARM | 18th | — | thrown out the enemy attempted to advance. Our Lewis gun then burst over our wire to which the enemy replied with about 20 Mt. They then rifle bomb flared a bomb Rifle & Lewis gun fire which caused some casualties though no hits were discovered. 2/Lt R.T. HESLOP & No. 7738 Corporal Cooper (both did excellent work. Casualties. 1 officer wounded (2/Lt HESLOP.) OR 2 killed 9 wounded | |
| | 19th | — | A quiet day - Some trench mortars on our right and on the next Bn but no damage done. Casualties. OR killed 1 wounded 1. Orders for relief by 5th Bn the BORDER REGT. Coy Commanders and specialist Officers arrived about 4pm. Relief complete by 4.45 am. Bn moved to DONCASTER HUTS at LOCRE. Casualties OR wounded | |
| LOCRE | 20th | — | Bn rested. Orders received 10.15 pm trench out training programme then cancelled. Bn to be ready to move at short notice. Move orders early in morning to proceed to R.22. Sheet 27. Casualties 1 OR killed | |

Army Form C. 2118.

WAR DIARY
or
INTELLIGENCE SUMMARY.
*(Erase heading not required.)*

| Place | Date | Hour | Summary of Events and Information | Remarks and references to Appendices |
|---|---|---|---|---|
| SHEET 27 X | 21 | | Area changed to X 22 and neighbourhood. Bn inspected by GOC 24th Divn at LOCRE at 11.30 pm and moved off to new area. marched through BAILLEUL. arrived 3 pm. Billets close together and ample room. Training area Anzefras west of METEREN. | |
| BELCROIX FARM | 22nd | | Demonstration of signaling between infantry & aircraft at 5 pm at X.I.D.A. Orders received to leave BAILLEUL by train on Sunday. | |
| | 23rd | | Day spent in packing. Discussion & lecture by Major King RE on Consolidation of Trenches at 3 pm attended by nearly all officers. | |
| | 24th | | Bn. left BAILLEUL Station at 7.28 am for LONGPRÉ (2 miles E. of AMIENS) & proceeded by train via HAZEBROUCK, CHOCQUES, ST POL & AMIENS to LONGPRÉ station which was reached at 3.30 pm. No orders for billets to hand on arrival, so the Battalion marched to a field on the edge of the town & halted for tea. Orders received that our billeting area is LE MESGE 15 miles from LONGPRÉ back along the railway; | |
| BREUILLY | | | Bn paraded at 8 pm again and marched through AMIENS where Drums a great reception was accorded us by the inhabitants: the Band | |

# WAR DIARY
## or
## INTELLIGENCE SUMMARY.
(Erase heading not required.)

Army Form C. 2118.

| Place | Date | Hour | Summary of Events and Information | Remarks and references to Appendices |
|---|---|---|---|---|
| LE MESGE | 25th | | Drums The Bn especially armed enormous enthusiasm, so that at one time the Company following (B Coy) was completely cut off from it by 7 or 8 rows of civilians. Several of the men were seized and kissed by the female portion of the inhabitants, and badges + numerals were freely removed. The Bn halted for the night in a field near BREVILLY and bivouacked. | |
| | 26 | | Marched off at 6 am and arrived at our area LE MESGES at 9.30 am. Billets are numerous but large numbers of them are in empty houses of which not ½ the village seems to be occupied. | |
| | 27. | | Training in progress. Parades 8.15 am to 12.45 pm. Close + extended order drill. | |
| | | | Programme of training similar to yesterday. G.O.C. 24 Div came round billets + training areas this morning. Major A.G. Hamilton left for the base, on a tour of 2 months duty in instructing reinforcements. | |
| | 28 | | B Coys practised attack in morning. Concert at 6 pm in the garden of the Chateau. Ph. de St Hilaire. Capt. M. ASPREY The BUFFS attached to the Bn with 2 STOKES GUNS and 17/2 TM Battery. | |

A.D.S.S./Forms/C.2118.

Army Form C. 2118.

# WAR DIARY
## or
## INTELLIGENCE SUMMARY.
(Erase heading not required.)

| Place | Date | Hour | Summary of Events and Information | Remarks and references to Appendices. |
|---|---|---|---|---|
| | 29 | | Battalion attack practice on ground NE of SORIES where some dummy trenches have been constructed. Practice commenced at 10 am ended 1 pm. Coys returned between 3 & 4 pm. | |
| | 30 | | Battalion attack practise in morning. Orders received that we are to move tomorrow. Transport to be loaded ready to start by 8 pm. Rendezvous for Brigade transport at BREILLY | |
| | 31. | | Battalion started at 7.30 am to reach station at PICQUIGNY at 12 Noon. 12th arrived to time and found 3rd Bn the Rifle Brigade on the platform. Sherwood Foresters arrived within ½ hr of us. We waited all afternoon in the station approaches and street, and eventually shared train with Sherwood Foresters and moved off at 6.5 pm. Detrained at MERICOURT at 8.30 pm about, and marched via MORLANCOURT to huts in the BOIS DES TAILLES which was reached about 11 pm. All the brigade is in this wood, and accommodation is small. Weather very hot. Water very short. | Sheet 62 D R 17 B |

Andrews Lt Col
Cmdg 8th Bn The Suffolk.

17th Brigade.
24th Division.

8th BATTALION

"BUFFS" EAST KENT REGIMENT.

*August* 1916.

Vol 11

War Diary

8th (Service) Battalion The Buffs.

For the month of

August 1916

Sept 8th 1916.

Volume 12.

Army Form C. 2118.

# WAR DIARY
## or
## INTELLIGENCE SUMMARY.
*(Erase heading not required.)*

Instructions regarding War Diaries and Intelligence Summaries are contained in F.S. Regs., Part II. and the Staff Manual respectively. Title pages will be prepared in manuscript.

| Place | Date | Hour | Summary of Events and Information | Remarks and references to Appendices |
|---|---|---|---|---|
| BN HQ FRANCE Sheet 62D E.18.D | Aug 1st | 9.30 p.m. | The Bn marched in brigade from BOIS des TAILLES to the SANDPIT. S.E. of MEAULTE (France sheet 62D E.18.D) The Brigade was inspected en route by GOC 24 Div. There are a few tents out for officers, orderly room etc., the rest of the Bn being billeted bivouaced. | |
| | 2nd | | Very hot. A brigade signalling scheme was practised with a contact patrol aeroplane from No 9 squadron RFC. at 5pm this afternoon. Only one message was acknowledged from the aeroplane, sent by 12th Royal Fusiliers. Military Cross awarded to Lieut. E.T. HALL for gallantry during the raid at PLOEGSTEERT on 28 June, and on patrol on July 4th. Companies ordered to wear a distinguishing star. A Coy Red. B. green. C red. D. Yellow; below the shoulder on the sleeve. | |
| | 3rd | 11 pm | Day spent in kit inspections etc. Signalling scheme practised again. Sunday transport drivers drawn from all units in the Bde of our own yesterday. The ROYAL FUSILIERS played at rituel. Very heavy bombardment commenced at 10 pm on our corps & French front, and still continuing. | |

# WAR DIARY
## or
## INTELLIGENCE SUMMARY.
(Erase heading not required.)

Army Form C. 2118.

| Place | Date | Hour | Summary of Events and Information | Remarks and references to Appendices |
|---|---|---|---|---|
| THE SANDPITS | 4. | 9.30 p.m. | Training continued in morning. The Bn attended a demonstration of bayonet fighting at 10 a.m. At 5 p.m. G.O.C. 24 Divn lectured the Bn. + two companies of the 8th Queens on the attack + consolidation of trenches. Weather very much colder. An enemy aeroplane came into view over the ridge this evening. This is the first we have seen in this area. | |
| | 5th | | Training by companies – weather dull + cold. | |
| | 6th | – | Brigade Church parade at 10.30 am N.E of camp. Orders received that the Brigade is to take over the line between GUILLEMONT & DELVILLE WOOD. The Brigade to be in depth, the 12th Royal Fusiliers being in the line + then 6n in support in BERNAFAY WD. with the 12th Ry. Fusiliers; the 3rd Rifle Brigade in Gr between CARNOY + MONTAUBAN. A signaling practice with an aeroplane was held at 5 p.m. which was completely unsuccessful. | |
| | 7th | | The Adjutant + 4 Coy. Commanders went at 4 am to reconnoitre our new position in BERNAFAY WOOD. Bn. practised the attack | |

# WAR DIARY
## INTELLIGENCE SUMMARY

Army Form C. 2118.

| Place | Date | Hour | Summary of Events and Information | Remarks and references to Appendices |
|---|---|---|---|---|
| THE SANDPITS | 7th | | Bn. moving to the farm & M.E. of the Camp. | |
| Cr.Hqr. Shel 62c A9 6.2.7. | 8th | | B'n boarded at 11 a.m. in fighting kit and moved via CARNOY to the "CRATERS" where guides met us & pointed out positions we occupied in case of shelling. None the less we had to halt till nightfall before proceeding to BERNAFAY WOOD to relieve Australians. Before we went forward to the Bde. we were informed that the Brigade on our left had not moved up or arrived until about 8 pm. When we settled down for the night in trenches — for any few of the trigate. So everyone settled down for the night in trenches — any thing that might turn out shells were as— | |
| | 9th | | The C.O. & Officers went to Bde. HQrs. at 8 AM. & were told that the Brigade was to attack ARROW HEAD COPSE would take responsibility for operations in front of 169 Bde. South of ARROW HEAD COPSE & that the 169 Bde. HQrs. at 8.12 am. returned informed that owing to 163 Bde. & 169 Bde. Hqrs. to 8pm. previous rowing & true again. Cancelled. On returning to HQ 1st R.F. went & registered our request at WATERLOT FARM & at 6.30pm at Minefor. marched up to Bde. Reserve in place of 1st Buffs. 2 Lieut. Stuart on the CARNOY—MONTAUBAN ROAD at Shel 62c A 8.C.6.0 control. Suffered carrying party trying to relieve 1st R. Fus. in expeditionary which has casualties H.Q. moved to We have in Hanf at A. 6.5.1.8. & 1 O.R. accidently wounded. & to rate Bde. H.Q. Casualties 1.O.R. accidently the dust. H.Q. moved Camp Officers went up the line. Day Sgent. cleaning rounds on salvage yard. 4 to 6.30 pm. Is scarely 4 gun split billing bombing shell. At 10.30pm the shelled by own heavy artillery from the 1st R.F. before the war billeted by a piper rolling sage. Severe casualties among | |
| T.24.G central | 10th | | This was returned out slipped staff accept about 4 am. & returned 1st Division at hot such after 6 hours but plenty of 15 cay Relieving party of Rifle Brigade exhausted a rush trench in part of our left. | |
| | 11th | | Battalion down waking party of 15 & 4 R. 4th W. wot working done. NEW TRENCH and Bn HQ | |

# WAR DIARY
## or
## INTELLIGENCE SUMMARY.

Army Form C. 2118.

| Place | Date | Hour | Summary of Events and Information | Remarks and references to Appendices |
|---|---|---|---|---|
| | 11th | | II & A Coys improving their own trenches. 2° Lt J.S.H. SHAFTO killed by sniper about 12-15 am whilst reconnoitring bombing posts. Casualties 3 O.R. wounded (1 accidental) Weather still fine. | 2° Lt J.S. Shafto |
| | 12th | | C.T. improving trenches & men forward from Guillemont carried on while resting bombing posts. Killed by sniper at Machine Gun house at 5.15 pm. Heavy shelling on our right rear area from Littered Mainpas. Working party from 7 D.R.L. going out to send up his S.O.S. signal of a rocket bursting into 4 red lights, that a barrage who sent up his S.O.S. behind WATERLOT also a TRONES WOOD † BARNAFAY WOOD on the front line & his barrage heavy shrapnel upon the whole area during the greater part of the night. He kept up this barrage heavy shrapnel upon the whole area during Capt ASHREY (Comdg B/½ Tm. Battery was killed by a splinter about 2 am. Casualties about 17 an working party of 3 Rifle Bde + 2 of 1° Royal Fus. 2 wounded men who had been lying out about 3 days were brought in by B Coy. They belonged to Essex Regt. 1/2 8th Lanes Fusiliers. During an attempt to get at a third wounded man Pte JORDAN + STEVENSON B Coy were themselves wounded by M G fire from GUILLEMONT. | |
| | 13th | | Some shelling on front line + WATERLOT FARM. Otherwise a quiet morning. A great many officers from different regiments were supporting artillery in C. Coy came round VK trenches. We were relieved in the afternoon by the 18 Royal Fusiliers relief being completed at 9.45 pm later. Man was at owing to the fact that it was impossible to relieve the Lewis Guns in the two new forward trenches before dusk. Capt DAWSON was slightly wounded by a splinter while coming down to Relieve B° where as in reserve occupying the position we left on August 11th. | |

#353 Wt. W3544/1454 700,000 5/15 D. D. & L. A.D.S.S./Forms/C. 2118.

# WAR DIARY
## INTELLIGENCE SUMMARY
*(Erase heading not required.)*

Army Form C. 2118.

| Place | Date | Hour | Summary of Events and Information | Remarks and references to Appendices |
|---|---|---|---|---|
| | 14ᵗʰ | | The Bn. found a working party of 50 men to complete new C.T. through N. of TRONES WOOD: also large carrying parties to make dumps of reserve S.A.A. etc. in the forward area. | |
| | 15ᵗʰ | | Working & importance to repair. This all day: situation generally quiet, further carrying parties were supplied for the forward area | |
| Bn. Hq. Nr. Platoon CARNOY | 16ᵗʰ | | Working & importance to repair. 2/Lt. G.L. Brees took over command of Battalion Stokes mortar section. The afternoon was spent in packing up. C.O. explained proposed Operation Orders to its attack on N.C.A. M.U.R.E. and the Z.Z. Trench. | |
| Bn. H.Q. Sheet 57, 1/W. S 29, d 2.5 | 17ᵗʰ | | The Battn. with Bath. Royal Fusiliers in the line at WATERLOT FARM, took early hours of the morning. Commanding Own the town given on the guide arriving at Brick Kiln. A NEW TRENCH which now on the west of Bde. on to Brigade. Two sections. B Coy to HATTON and BOSKY Trenches to form a Reserve C.O., ment to Brigade. He Brigade moved out with us own. Zero time on B. 15 am tomorrow. During the night both moved to their assembly positions. | |
| | | | A. By. } Forms Bn. H.Q.<br>B. " }<br>C. " In BOSKY Trench.<br>D. " In HATTON Trench. | 2 Platoons in HATTON Trench & 2 Plats. in BOSKY Trench. |

| Place | Date | Hour | Summary of Events and Information | Remarks and references to Appendices |
|---|---|---|---|---|
| BN HQ Sect SP.S.W Sqn. R2L | 19th | | Operation Orders received about 5am. Held a Conference of Officers at 9am. The plan of attack is:- Two Platoons of A Coy under 2/Lt J. GRANT to rush MACHINE GUN HOUSE and connect it into a strong point to await the advance of the Rifle Brigade. The 9th Batt. Rosslin to find and from their old posts to fill in the gap between M.G. House and the left flank of the Batt. R.B. A 3rd Platoon of A Coy to be at the disposal of 2/Lt GRANT in support. C Coy with two platoons of B Coy in close support to attack the Z.Z. trench from about B19 D74 to T19 A17 and to form a strong point at the further junction. The Rosslin and the Z.Z. trench will be taken by the 6th Batt SOMERSET. LIGHT INFANTRY. The remaining B Coy to be at the disposal of CPT GULLICK. Battalion Reserve to consist of the remaining Platoon of A Coy, D Coy, and one Coy of Royal Fusiliers in TROYES TRENCH. Reorganisation opened at 11am into the New dugouts in KULLEN TRENCH. At 2.45pm the attack commenced. The mopping party (C Coy) on its Platoons Blew under CPT KERICK moved out of their trenches and keeping close under the barrage successfully reached their objectives with |  |

# WAR DIARY or INTELLIGENCE SUMMARY

Army Form C. 2118.

| Place | Date | Hour | Summary of Events and Information | Remarks and references to Appendices |
|---|---|---|---|---|

no/ten Casualties. 2/LT PEACOCK was killed about halfway across. On reaching the trench they found the enemy completely surprised — On nearing the wire and the parapet, not a German was noticed at all and went across to our trench. An Officer and a Rabbi were turned out and put up a fight but they were quickly knocked out. Lt Pt. LINDSEY was badly wounded in the head & arm for a time. The 3 a time there were Captured and at once turned against the enemy. Reinforcements were asked for. CAPT HODGSON at once brought up his company to reinforce and this by repairing was kept on tenaciously. Known to remainder of his Coy arrived to [reinforce] him and in command of [the men just] on CAPT HODISON had discussing wounded a CAPT PENNY at once arrived on kind the Coy in. DUSKY TRENCH and the CO men and the platoon of D. Co also about the German TRENCH Consolidation was advanced when a party of Lanky fund. Cont. to a our left England arms though has they were considerably hung there and [German] heavy tremendous Sho CRITERIA

L f. L q t cef. 1 on per hours lost, Matron's War force has received

# WAR DIARY or INTELLIGENCE SUMMARY

Army Form C. 2118.

| Place | Date | Hour | Summary of Events and Information | Remarks and references to Appendices |
|---|---|---|---|---|

And the Trench was strongly held. The right Bombing party, under Cpl Barrington, was attacked by 15 of the enemy with Bombs from their flanks but they succeeded by keeping in diving their in and forcing up with Lt GRANT and the R.B. 20 Bombers worked down to about the back of M.G. HOUSE. The Lt. Bombing Capt, then proceeded to work up the Trench towards the point where C Coy's right flank should have rested. They met with considerable resistance, especially about the Machine Gun near the Trench Junction at Tig A7. The Machine Gun they captured as well as 2 Prisoners. A few civilians were caused by a Sniper lying on a Stretcher near M.G. HOUSE but he was quickly dealt with by one of the Bombing Squad. A third Bombing Squad blocked and held the enemy head running down HIGH HOLBORN towards GUILLEMONT

# WAR DIARY or INTELLIGENCE SUMMARY

Army Form C. 2118.

The position at M.G. HOUSE was greatly consolidated and the C.T. forward to the Z.Z. Trench cleared and deepened into a good trench. The old C.T. had to our left hand (South) Coys was found very much choked with dead from previous attacks and the work on this part was very slow and difficult. By this time the R.D. Regt. had taken their front objective and the STATION which they converted into a strong point. Their Lg Flank was well in touch and 2/Lt GRANT at B.G. HOUSE. The C.O. now called up the remaining two platoons of the 1st R.F. and at his request awoke 1st Cy of D. Coy 1st R.F. was moved up into TRONES' TRENCH to take his place. Afterwards this half Coy was brought up and ordered to garrison the C.T. from M.G. HOUSE to the front line and to form advanced flank Consolidation was on all night. A second C.T. was dug from BOSKY TRENCH to the Centre of the Captured Position. This work was carried out by a Coy of the Brigade Reserve the 12th Batt. ROYAL FUSILIERS. An armoured Cable was carried along machine gun C.T. to the front line and telephonic communication established which linked with R. Coy. Three Vickers and four Lewis Guns were placed in the front line, one Vickers and one Lewis Gun in M.G. HOUSE and C.T.

# WAR DIARY
## or
## INTELLIGENCE SUMMARY.

*(Erase heading not required.)*

Army Form C. 2118.

| Place | Date | Hour | Summary of Events and Information | Remarks and references to Appendices |
|---|---|---|---|---|
| | | | Only Indian Officers including Bn. HQ and the M.O. were taken into action and by this time all C. Coy's Officers were casualties and the Officers on the line were, CAPT. HODGSON, 2/LT HONNOR, UNDERHILL and MORRELL of B. Coy and 2/LT BOWKES & D. Coy 2/LT GREIG had been wounded coming across, the first Bowers of Officer. 2/LT TAYLOR, MARIKTON, VARGE and GRIFFIN now arrived. 2/LT GRIFFIN relieved 2/LT BOWKES on the line as the latter had been wounded in the Leg. The M.O. CAPT. RANKIN had been wounded in the face and part of the Dressing Station blown in, he continued on his honours, job another hour until relieved by CAPT. BRISCO 73rd Field of Ambulance. Altogether we captured about 120 Prisoners (including 2 Officers) 3 Machine Guns 2 of which were subsequently destroyed by Shell fire and many valuable and interesting trophies, Automatic Pistols, Rifles, Field Glasses, and Shrapnel and Fuse Bows helmets. All the Equipment was brought in and very great large quantities of Rations were found in the trench. Casualties. All the Officers of C. Coy became Casualties during the assault. | |

# WAR DIARY
## or
## INTELLIGENCE SUMMARY.
(Erase heading not required.)

C.S.M. Dankeldon and 5 Sgts N.C.O's of A Coy were killed. 1 C.L.M. & other Coy Sergeant Majors were wounded. Casualties in 16.

Officers.

| Killed | Wounded | Missing |
|---|---|---|
| 1 | 6 | — |

Other Ranks

| Killed | Wounded | Missing |
|---|---|---|
| 38 | 297 | 16 |

Communication was kept up with the most remarkable completeness by means of Runners. No case has yet come to light in which any message failed to reach its objective. The Signalling Sergeant (Sergt. Y. Shaw) did excellent work, laying the wires from the old Battalion Headquarters and informing BN. HQ of the progress made. He also succeeded under heavy fire in getting the message "PTE. OK" acknowledged by the Contact Control Aeroplane. The Advance Signalling Wires to men were cut.

# WAR DIARY or INTELLIGENCE SUMMARY

Army Form C. 2118.

| Place | Date | Hour | Summary of Events and Information | Remarks and references to Appendices |
|---|---|---|---|---|
| | | | to return. The Aeroplane flew low but by the excellent keeping in touch this by engine but we have not heard whether they were seen. All units in the attack sent in excellent messages and Battalion & Brigade Headquarters were kept informed of the attack throughout. | |
| Ltn. | 19th | | About 4.30 am Brigade extra was received that no assault would take place to-day. The morning was quiet. CAPT. HODGSON and 2/LT. HONNOR both of whom were wounded yesterday, were relieved and went down to the Field Ambulance. CAPT. PEARCE took charge of the Front Line. Work was continued on the new line of the Two New C.T.s, the position now held by what is left of B.Co. & D.Coy on the ZZ Trench and 2 Platoons of the 1st R.F. and 3 Platoons of A Coy on M.G. HOUSE and C.T. The 17TH MACHINE GUN. Coy have 3 Vickers Guns in the line, viz. 1 M.G. HOUSE and 2 thereabouts near our BN. HQ. There are also 2 captured German Guns in action. 2/LT. T.W. UNDERHILL was killed about 11 pm by shells fire. There are plenty of rations and water in the line but few rifles & few as are short. | |

# WAR DIARY or INTELLIGENCE SUMMARY

Army Form C. 2118.

Were all however no chart of Agmetters. The C.O. sent for 2nd P.O. Casualties OR. Killed 3. D.O.W. 1. Wounded 10. Missing 2.

The Enemy have been shewing our position & we have been getting a considerable amount of shelling especially about M.G. HOUSE. One shell hit the Signal Station wounding 2/Lt. HUBBARD and 2/Lt. McCOE operator. Runners & some others entangled for some time as the instrument room fared. There has been so the only disheartening. The men are very disappointed at no being relieved but the operation deceived them up. About noon the C.O. deemed to withdraw the bulk of the Infantry and hold the line with LEWIS and MACHINE GUNS. This was carried out in the evening and early part of the night our boys going back to ROSKY HEAD the R.F. to HATTEN wood. The L.G.O. (2/Lt ALLEN) is in command of the line aid 2/Lt TAYLOR and an Officer of the Machine Gun Coy. There are also two Bombing Posts and a Listening Post in the ZZ Trench and the R.F. are finding a Bombing and a Lewis gun in MACHINE GUN C.T. 2/Lt MONKELL reported to Battalion on relieving the ZZ Trench Southwards and found it unoccupied. Garrison retained this by the R.B. and the 72nd Inf. R.B. will carry on the attack at H. Bo tomorrow the after noon

# WAR DIARY
## or
## INTELLIGENCE SUMMARY.
(Erase heading not required.)

Army Form C. 2118.

| Place | Date | Hour | Summary of Events and Information | Remarks and references to Appendices |
|---|---|---|---|---|
| | 21st | | We are to be relieved on the night of the 22nd and 23rd though this is not most likely. Men are expected every hour, in order to get a definite time and the men have settled down and in ordinary trench life. Casualties Officers killed 1, wounded 1. O.R. wounded 14. | |
| | | | In preparation for their attack the R.B. sent a Lewis Gun and Team forward and by a Bombing Squad, an to establish themselves in the trench continuation of ZZ Trench which they did without opposition. The ZZ Trench and the remainder of Hughes Trench has been named DUFF'S TRENCH. Arms & Waggons and Stand had amounds only, have been yesterday before Relief. Orders are on Lacy body immensely cleared. At 4.30pm the R.B. attacked. Lieut HAMER & 2/Lt TAYLOR proceeding from old BN HQ were able to spot the advance from positions to positions and report. BN HQ. At about 5pm the sky listening in on the telephone we heard O.C. 2nd R.B. report that large numbers of Germans are coming out into the open between GREENSTREET and BROMPTON RD. Whereupon the C.O. offered to turn upon Machine Gun fire for on RKR1 Hunt. There was done by firing a few Guns put on this morning. | |

# WAR DIARY
## or
## INTELLIGENCE SUMMARY.
(Erase heading not required.)

Army Form C. 2118.

| Place | Date | Hour | Summary of Events and Information | Remarks and references to Appendices |
|---|---|---|---|---|
| | | | and the eye in S.P. in Trig. A17. Ten minutes later a verbal message came though that the R.B. had reached their objective & Trig. 1 was along side the N.E. corner of GUILLEMONT. About 6.30pm O.C. 3rd R.B. asked for complete be carried to the Station 2/Lt RAINEY and 40 men of B. Coy carried their down the place, though a certain amount of Shrapnel & the German turn barrage when they got through which only 2 Casualties. This party was probably taken by the Enemy as the commencement of another attack for he at once put a strong barrage on Buff's trench and the Priory. High Holborn & Dept.1 etc for the 10 part of an hour. The R.B. were withdrawn during the night and we have been in dearth taken over the 2/Lt held by them this morning. Two platoons have been sent to Buff's trench to strengthen the Garrison in the trenches in night line to remedy their objective and our Dept. 4 coy's opposite the Contentmaker trench is being moved in to this. Casualties OR 1 Killed 2 wounded | |
| | 22nd | | A great morning a number of men of an in (DSK) hand gun let by a few under 2/Lt  Felsen. The C.O. & O.y Commanding of the 7th Batt. KOYLI. | |

# WAR DIARY
## or
## INTELLIGENCE SUMMARY

*(Erase heading not required.)*

Army Form C. 2118

Instructions regarding War Diaries and Intelligence Summaries are contained in F.S. Regs., Part II. and the Staff Manual respectively. Title Pages will be prepared in manuscript.

| Place | Date | Hour | Summary of Events and Information | Remarks and references to Appendices |
|---|---|---|---|---|
| | | | Came up to arrange relief this morning. They are very strong and eventually decided to leave two Coys behind and to take over position with A & B. Coys (One Company to one 2 Platoons). Relief started at about 6.30 pm and when not completed and 11.35 pm the Front Line being very thin. On relief the Coys were conveyed to HAPPY VALLEY by Motor Lorries from CARNOY. The following orders were received by the C.O. on the 19th August. "The following wire from G.O.C. 2nd Div Regina AAA. Corps Commander has asked me to convey to troops his extreme appreciation of gallant conduct of troops and refer to gallant of Regina AAA. We have our teeth into GUILLEMONT and must grip like Bull-dogs to what we have AAA. Message ends. "Following from XXth Corps AAA following from Army Commander as at Msgs SECOND ARMY Regina AAA. Many congratulations on your success. ENDS. "Congratulations from B.G.C. Hope casualties are not heavy." Casualties O.R. killed 3. wounded 6 | |

1875. Wt. W593/826 1,000,000 4/15 J.B.C. & A. A.D.S.S./Forms/C. 2118.

# WAR DIARY or INTELLIGENCE SUMMARY

Army Form C. 2118

| Place | Date | Hour | Summary of Events and Information | Remarks and references to Appendices |
|---|---|---|---|---|
| HAPPY VALLEY | 23 | | Bn rested and received congratulations. Casualties 6 OR. | # drafts 1/20 fm Base hurry, 1 SGTS 1 Major A.G. HAMILTON |
| N. BRAY | 24 | | Battg further went down to the Somme. Rejoined fm Base | |
| SHEET 57D E15 | 25 | | Bn marched in Brigade via MORLANCOURT and DERNANCOURT to this camp which is the worst we have ever seen. There appears to be nothing beyond 11 tents and the earth. | BURE SUR ANCRE |
| — | 26 | | Drawing clothing and commenced training again | |
| — | 27 | | GOC 24 Div addressed the Bn at 10. a.m and congratulated them on their success | |

# WAR DIARY or INTELLIGENCE SUMMARY

Army Form C. 2118

| Place | Date | Hour | Summary of Events and Information | Remarks and references to Appendices |
|---|---|---|---|---|
| E.15 | 28th | | Training continued during intervals of showers | |
| Sheet 57 D | 29th | | Training during morning. Exceptionally heavy rainstorm during the afternoon. The camp was swamped. | |
| | 30th | | Parties reconnoitred the route to MONTAUBAN during the afternoon. Rained hard practically all day. At 7.0 p.m. Battalion paraded & moved to Bayonet Reserve Bivouac camp at F.8.d, arriving about 10 p.m. A very dirty camp. The rain stopped about this time. | |
| F.8.d. | 31st | | Battalion cleaned itself & the camp in beautiful sunshine. After receiving preliminary orders to be prepared to move at half an hour notice, we were ordered at 7.30 p.m. to move up to POMMIERS REDOUBT to support the 72nd Bde. On arrival there we were ordered to occupy/then after a very trying march the by roads choked with traffic, we were ordered to occupy MONTAUBAN ALLEY with Bn HQ near the function of this trench with CATERPILLAR TRENCH. | |

A.W. Andrews Lieut Colonel
Cmdg 8th Bn Rl Rifles

17th Brigade.
34th Division.

8th BATTALION

"BUFFS" EAST KENT REGIMENT.

*September 1916.*

17/24

24/24

Vol 12

Confidential

War Diary

of

8th Battalion The Buffs.

For Month of September 1916

Volume 13

**Army Form C. 2118**

# WAR DIARY or INTELLIGENCE SUMMARY

(Erase heading not required.)

| Place | Date | Hour | Summary of Events and Information | Remarks and references to Appendices |
|---|---|---|---|---|
| BN. HQ MONTAUBAN ALLEY 57.C.S.W S.26.D.3.5 | 1st Sept | | After a very uncomfortable night we set about cleaning the trench and cleaning dugouts. All morning we awaited orders & about noon operation orders arrived to the effect that the enemy had occupied TEA TRENCH & ORCHARD TRENCH and that the 3rd Bn. the Rifle Brigade would retake them that afternoon: zero time 6.30. We watched the short from MONTAUBAN ALLEY nothing coming back to about 8 pm news that the Rifle Brigade had retaken the first & further ORCHARD TRENCH. We supplied 220 men to carry rations & water for the Rifle Brigade & the N.R.F. & the two Bns. in the line. D Company are now at the disposal of the 72nd Brigade. Casualties 1 O.R. wounded. | The following reinforcement officers joined: Lt R.T. Davidson 2/Lt A13 NICOLS  F. Russell, T.V. Hitchcock R.C. Phillips A13. Blood-Smyth, A1 Sherwel, H.R. Sterrett |
| CARLTON TR. S.16.B.6.3 | 2nd | | D Company moved off to support the 72nd Brigade in DELVILLE WOOD. During the morning the CO went to meet the GOC at Bde HQ. There he was told that we are to relieve the remainder this afternoon and attack the 72 | |

# WAR DIARY or INTELLIGENCE SUMMARY

Army Form C. 2118

| Place | Date | Hour | Summary of Events and Information | Remarks and references to Appendices |
|---|---|---|---|---|
| | 2nd | | Strong point at the junction of TEA TRENCH + WOOD LANE along S.11.A.1½.3. We relieved the tenants in WORCESTER, McDOUGAL TRENCH and PONT ST: relief being over about 9 p.m. We are sharing Bn HQ with the Royal Sussex Regiment who are in Brigade support. | |
| | 3rd | | Morning spent in preparation for the attack. Great difficulty was met with in synchronizing watches as this had to be done with the battalion on our left the CAMERONS. Eventually we got the time from the gunners and it reached companies only a few minutes before zero time 12. Noon. The attack was made by B Coy, supported by C Company — the B Coy Bombers attacked on the right by bombing up WORCESTER TR. within 1 minute of starting all the officers and the C.S.M. of B Coy on barrage became casualties, and the company itself was stopped by machine gun fire from which they suffered heavily. News of the failure of the attack reached | The following officers [were] hit or wounded |

| Place | Date | Hour | Summary of Events and Information | Remarks and references to Appendices |
|---|---|---|---|---|
| CARLTON TR. | 3rd | | Bn HQ about 12.30 pm & the CO at once ordered Major HAMILTON who was in command of the front line, to make every effort to organise a fresh attack. This was arranged for, at 4 pm with the support of similar artillery programme. Lt Col STEWART, Cmdg the group & the 14th Dur. Art. who were covering us, were luckily in CARLTON TRENCH at the time. The front line & PONT ST were shelled intermittently the whole afternoon. at 4 pm the second attack took place but was at once stopped by M.G. fire from the strong point. The bombers succeeded in working up the trench towards the strong point but all the infantry supporting them became casualties. Two more officers were hit. Also the CSM of C Company. It seemed probable that the strong point is held only by M.G.s, a | |

# WAR DIARY
## or
## INTELLIGENCE SUMMARY

*(Erase heading not required.)*

Army Form C. 2118

| Place | Date | Hour | Summary of Events and Information | Remarks and references to Appendices |
|---|---|---|---|---|
| CARLTON TRENCH | | 3:10 a | snipers & bombers. The enemy was quiet on our front though the enemy counter attacked the First Division on our left. | |
| F.B.D | | 4:45 | We were relieved in the front line about 1 am by the 1st Bn the Royal Fusiliers and the three Companies withdrawn to SAVOY TRENCH. Most of the Companies spent in resting. Relief when came in about 11 am and about 5 pm the relieving Battalion the 5th Kings Liverpool Regt arrived. On relief the Bns went in the Reserve Brigade Camp at F.8.d. sheet 62.d. All were in by 9 pm. Casualties in the three Coys. 1 Officer killed (2/Lt T. FIRMINGER) and 6 wounded 2/Lts D. GRANT, C.B. HAMILTON, J.C. TWYMAN C Company & 2/Lt H.V. EYRE, C.H RAINEY & E.H. VARGE B Company. O.R. killed (Wansley) | |

1875  Wt. W 593/826 1,000,000 4/15 J.B.C. & A. A.D.S.S./Forms/C.2118.

| Place | Date | Hour | Summary of Events and Information | Remarks and references to Appendices |
|---|---|---|---|---|
| F.8.D | 4 | | Meanwhile D Company had gone up to support the Great Surrey in DELVILLE WOOD. They were apparently placed in DEVILS TRENCH and suffered very heavily from shell fire. About 4 p.m. yesterday Pte Crick, one of D Company's stretcher bearers, made his way to our HQ in CARLTON TRENCH, a journey of over a mile (laterally) along the trenches, and informed us that all the officers had been killed & not of the Company wiped out. Though we believed him to be exaggerating, we found on our arrival myself that 2/Lt MORREL who had been sent up | |

# WAR DIARY
## or
## INTELLIGENCE SUMMARY

Army Form C. 2118

(Erase heading not required.)

| Place | Date | Hour | Summary of Events and Information | Remarks and references to Appendices |
|---|---|---|---|---|
| | 4th | | from the transport lines to take charge of the Company was ordered after to an over a few stragglers. Another killed. Capt D. G. PEARCE, 2/Lt B. G. BOWLES +/Lt B. B. BLACKWOOD O.R. no figures yet available. Communications throughout the two attacks were very bad, as the distance to the front line was very great (nearly a mile) and an time for preparation was limited. Runners were used forward of Bn HQ. - but the ng Brigade wire held the whole time. Bn HQ was well behind the barrage line | |

| Place | Date | Hour | Summary of Events and Information | Remarks and references to Appendices |
|---|---|---|---|---|
| AREA "A" E.14 57 D.S.E. | 5th | | Bn. handed this morning from Bois Reserve Camp by TRICOURT starting at 1.30 p.m. and arriving 3.45 p.m. This Camp is quite comfortable being composed of 9 new canvas huts which give plenty of accommodation for our reduced numbers. A few more stragglers of D. Company came in. Orders are in for a move to the rest area near ABBEVILLE tomorrow to proceed by road starting at 7. a.m.; also all cyclists in a Brigade Party starting at 10. a.m. | |
| YAUCOURT | 6th | | Up very early as everything had to be packed by 7 a.m. During the morning 2/Lt OVERY visited the Bns of the 72nd Brigade and collected 5 more stragglers of D Coy still to come down from trenches. Of a team from team paraded at 12. noon and marched to EDGEHILL station near DERNANCOURT where we entrained; the team | |

| Place | Date | Hour | Summary of Events and Information | Remarks and references to Appendices |
|---|---|---|---|---|
| | | | Left just after 3 p.m. after the usual Brad [Brigade] journey - 40 miles in 7 hours we detrained at LONGPRE at marched by devious routes to YAUCOURT which we reached at 1 a.m. Billeting parties were not able to arrive in time so the adjutant walked on ahead and accomplished the extraordinary feat of billeting the whole battalion in 3/4 of an hour commencing at midnight. | |
| YAUCOURT | 7th | | Spent the day resting and cleaning up. The billets are very good. HQ being in an half empty chateau. There is room for three times our strength in the village, which is conveniently compact. Weather very fine. | |
| | 8th | | Training commenced | |

# WAR DIARY
## or
## INTELLIGENCE SUMMARY

Army Form C. 2118.

| Place | Date | Hour | Summary of Events and Information | Remarks and references to Appendices |
|---|---|---|---|---|
| YAUCOURT | 9th | - | Nothing of importance to report | |
| | 10th | - | Church parade in morning | |
| | 11th | - | 3 Officers + 150 OR went to the AULT Rest Camp for 48 hrs. Lt DAVIDSON was OC party | |
| | 12th | - | Training continued with | |
| | 13th | - | Training cancelled as Small drafts of men north wounded on Aug 18th | |
| | 14th | - | Draft of 117 OR joined | |
| | 15th | - | Nothing of importance to report - weather continues fine but colder | |
| | 16th | - | Brigade ordered to be prepared to move at certain at short notice on transfer from 4th Army | |
| | 17. | | Church parades in morning - 8 officers joined | |

# WAR DIARY
## or
## INTELLIGENCE SUMMARY

Army Form C. 2118.

| Place | Date | Hour | Summary of Events and Information | Remarks and references to Appendices |
|---|---|---|---|---|
| | | | 2/LTS J.H. DINSMORE, C. HALL, F.D. WILKINSON, C.S.V. ALLEN C.M. KNIGHT, S.A. HARVEY, H.D. COCHRAN, F.B. KIRKMAN Received notification that we should probably entrain at PONT - REMY about midnight 18/19th | |
| | 18th | — | Weather soaking wet. Very little training. Caused a army to rain + packing. | |
| | 19th | | Left YAUCOURT at 2 am + entrained at PONT REMY about 4 am. Detrained unexpectedly at PERNES-CAMBLAIN + marched to FLORENGHEM. For the first time on record we detrained at the station nearest our destination, but "we are still on the edge of the map." Billeting was difficult as advance parties only arrived 10 minutes ahead of the Bn. Also all Barns are full of new wheat and the accommodation about one fifth of that advertised. | |

Army Form C. 2118.

# WAR DIARY
## or
## INTELLIGENCE SUMMARY
(Erase heading not required.)

Instructions regarding War Diaries and Intelligence Summaries are contained in F.S. Regs., Part II. and the Staff Manual respectively. Title Pages will be prepared in manuscript.

| Place | Date | Hour | Summary of Events and Information | Remarks and references to Appendices |
|---|---|---|---|---|
| | 20th | | CO took over temporary command of 17th Infantry Brigade. Nr. in under command of Capt. J. VAUGHAN. Parades 9am to 12.30 pm much interrupted by showers. | |
| | 21st | | Parades 9 to 12.30 pm. CO + Coy Commanders went to reconoitre the new line which is just South of SOUCHEZ with HQ in ZOUAVE VALLEY. They went by bus to CARENCY. 2/Lt. CHICK joined {Military Medals} /SGT. LORAM / Pts FLIGHT, STEVENSON + JARMAN. | |
| | 22nd | | 7 Other officers went to look over line. | |
| | 23rd | | Bn paraded at 8.15 am and marched into Billets at HAILLICOURT— billets commodious but not very comfortable. Major. R.S. Studd joined + took temporary command. Lt HALL MC joined + took over C Company; also 2/Lts H.P.R. ROBERTSON. C.S. NEWCOMB C.H.F. NESBITT R.L.F. FORSTER C.M. SANKEY | |
| | 24th | | Paraded at 7.45 am in marched in Reserve Brigade area at GOUY-SERVINS we relieved the 2nd South African Bn. | |

# WAR DIARY
## or
## INTELLIGENCE SUMMARY

Army Form C. 2118.

(Erase heading not required.)

| Place | Date | Hour | Summary of Events and Information | Remarks and references to Appendices |
|---|---|---|---|---|
| | 25th | | The whole Bn is billeted in the Citadisn + at built up. The weather for the last two days has been perfect. | |
| | | | We relieved the 6th Bn. KINGS OWN SCOTTISH BORDERS in 74th Street, The CHORD + P79.5 (S 21 A+B. Sheet 36c) Bn HQ is in ZOUAVE VALLEY. A Coy on right B+C in remainder of front line. D is in support in BROADSTREET + SNARGATE STREET. Trenches are foul in most places though the first rains of autumn are beginning to fall on the unrevetted sides. There is plenty of work to do. This area is extremely quiet, more so than any we have known. Casualties nil. Relief was complete about 4 pm. | |
| | 26. | | Very quiet. Work in progress consists of clearing the duckboards and making drains; and revetting and sandbagging the worst places. Casualties nil. | |
| | 27th | | Very quiet & fine. The following known have been | |

**Army Form C. 2118.**

# WAR DIARY
## or
## INTELLIGENCE SUMMARY
*(Erase heading not required.)*

Instructions regarding War Diaries and Intelligence Summaries are contained in F.S. Regs., Part II. and the Staff Manual respectively. Title Pages will be prepared in manuscript.

| Place | Date | Hour | Summary of Events and Information | Remarks and references to Appendices |
|---|---|---|---|---|
| | 28th | | announced by wire. DSO. Lt. Col. to L.W. LUCAS. MCs. Capt C.D. GULLICK. Capt. N. McRANKIN R.A.M.C. + 2/Lt D. GRANT. DCMs — (CSM. J. CARPENTER (B Coy) SGT. BUTLER (A Coy) + Pte SHUARD (C Coy). Casualties nil. Weather rather colder + damp. Casualties nil. | |
| | 29th | | Weather wet + misty. About 5.30 p.m the enemy sent several heavy T.M bombs (pineapples can fathers) onto B Coys trenches about OLD BOOTS STREET. — One man was buried but not severely hurt. Some slight retaliation fm howitzers + Stokes mortars was obtained. | |
| | 30th | | Fence + still quiet. Military medals awarded to 3429 L/C F. TINMOUTH; 10932 Pte J.W. BAKER; 3111 Pte R.S. HART. Winter time begins at 1 am tomorrow. Casualties. 1 OR wounded. | |

[signatures]
Lt Col Kent Stead
Comdg 8 Batt De Buffs

17th Brigade.
24th Division

8th BATTALION

"BUFFS"    EAST KENT REGIMENT

*October* 1916.

24/ vol 13

Confidential

War Diary

of

8th Service Battalion The Buffs

October 1916

Volume 14

13.

Army Form C. 2118.

# WAR DIARY
## or
## INTELLIGENCE SUMMARY

*(Erase heading not required.)*

| Place | Date | Hour | Summary of Events and Information | Remarks and references to Appendices |
|---|---|---|---|---|
| Bn. HQ | 1st | | Very quiet. A memorial service for LOOS was held by the 72nd Brigade | |
| ZOUAVE VALLEY | | | at LES QUATRE VENTS. Representatives from the Bn. were invited and a party of 2 officers + 50 O.R. attended | |
| | 2nd | | Wet all day. The Battalion was relieved by the 8th Bn the QUEEN'S OWN. Relief being complete at about 4 pm. On relief we moved in to our Bn. billets at GOUY-SERVINS | |
| GOUY SERVINS | 3rd | | Men bathed. Little else being done. 2/LTS. A. C.F. GOOD + H.R. NUDDS joined. | |
| | 4th | | A quiet day. Nothing of importance to report. Weather generally wet | |
| | 5th | | Finer: nothing to report. | |
| | 6th | | Wet still autumnal: nothing to report | |
| | 7th | | Training programme started on: hours 6.30 am to 7am + 8.30 am to 12.30 pm. | |

# WAR DIARY
## or
## INTELLIGENCE SUMMARY

Army Form C. 2118.

| Place | Date | Hour | Summary of Events and Information | Remarks and references to Appendices |
|---|---|---|---|---|
| GOUY SERVINS | 8th | | Church parade at 11 am in Divisional Theatre. | |
| | 9th | | Nothing to report | |
| "DALY'S" | 10th | | Relieved 2nd Bn Leinsters in Brigade Reserve - during the afternoon. | |
| X7 C.I.D. | 11th | | Nothing to report. Working parties of 225 men per day - all under RE. | |
| | 12th | | Working parties as yesterday. | |
| — | 13th | | C Company went up to ZOUAVE VALLEY to be in close support to the 3rd Rifle Brigade. | |
| — | 14th | | D Coy met Royal Fusiliers arrived in CARENCY. They are under our command to replace C. Coy which is at disposal of Oc 3rd R.B. | |
| — | 15th | | Nothing to report | |
| | 16th | | Nothing of importance. One casualty on a working party | |
| | 17th | | Relieved 3rd Bn the Rifle Brigade in Right Subsection CARENCY. Relief complete about 4.15 pm. Very wet. | |

**Army Form C. 2118.**

**WAR DIARY**
or
**INTELLIGENCE SUMMARY**
*(Erase heading not required.)*

Instructions regarding War Diaries and Intelligence Summaries are contained in F.S. Regs., Part II. and the Staff Manual respectively. Title Pages will be prepared in manuscript.

| Place | Date | Hour | Summary of Events and Information | Remarks and references to Appendices |
|---|---|---|---|---|
| | 18th | | A few TM's and Rifle Grenades on A Coy's area in morning about 8.30 am. The following officers left to be transferred to 6th B". 2nd Lieuts. F.B. KIRKMAN. H.B. BLOOD-SMYTH. J.H. DINSMORE. H.R. STERRETT. C.H.F. NESBIT. B. FARMER. R.L.T. FORSTER. G.F. GOOD. H.D. COCHRANE. S.A. HARVEY. | |
| | 19th 20th | | Very quiet + very wet - 60 lb. T.M. fired 4 rounds into an emplacement reported that enemy might be about to throw a camouflet near Kennedy Crater. | Camouflet near Kennedy Crater |
| | 20th | | 2/Lt. A.B. NICOLLS while patrolling near IRISH CRATER discovered Bosch working party about 9.1 am. A Lewis Gun drum was fired at them and 20 rounds from B Bombers but no result could be observed as party was slightly over the ridge. During the day the 1st R.F. captured them and also (-I. Stokes from + 60lb. T.M. was arranged - a patrol standing by to pick up the implements. They however found enough wire impenetrable. | |
| | 22nd | | 6" Howitzer fired during morning on new enemy Sap at Irish | |

Army Form C. 2118.

# WAR DIARY
## or
## INTELLIGENCE SUMMARY

(Erase heading not required.)

Instructions regarding War Diaries and Intelligence Summaries are contained in F. S. Regs., Part II. and the Staff Manual respectively. Title Pages will be prepared in manuscript.

| Place | Date | Hour | Summary of Events and Information | Remarks and references to Appendices |
|---|---|---|---|---|
| Crater | 22(d) | — | B but of the first 23 rounds were duds. 2nd Lt. E.T. YOUNG joined from 4th Entrenching Battalion. | |
| | 23rd | — | A quiet day — 2 or 3 minnies during the afternoon. At 10 pm 2 Camouflets were blown just opposite our left. 2/Lt. HALL again heard noise of working especially something that sounded like a crane clanking. This has been reported the 176th Tunnelling Co. R.E. | |
| | 24th | | Canadian officers came to look over the line; In the afternoon there were a few minnies in B Coy's area, for which we saw very prompt retaliation. One minnie unfortunately obtained a direct hit on a Stokes gun emplacement completely knocking out the gun & wounding men on | |

Army Form C. 2118.

# WAR DIARY
## or
## INTELLIGENCE SUMMARY

*(Erase heading not required.)*

| Place | Date | Hour | Summary of Events and Information | Remarks and references to Appendices |
|---|---|---|---|---|
| GOUY SERVINS | 25. | | We were relieved by the 4th Canadian Bn: relief being complete at 1.55 p.m. We then moved to GOUY-SERVINS to our old billets. Casualties one OR wounded. | |
| NOEUX LES MINES | 26th | | Bn: started at 8.15 am & marched through HERSIN into Huts at- NOEUX-LES-MINES. The officers are billeted in the VILLAGE | |
| MAZIN GARBE | 27th | | Moved to MAZINGARBE during the morning where we relieved 2 coys 12th SUFFOLKS, & 2 coys 2/1st MIDDLESEX in Div Reserve. Encamp is of huts, fitted with electric lights and to the most part with beds. The officers are billeted in the town. Very wet. | |
| MAZINGARBE | 28th | | Day spent in clearing up & refitting the men. | |
| do. | 29th | | Church Parade cancelled owing to continuous rain. | |
| do. | 30th | | Officers & NCOs have today reconnoitred the trenches up to section 14 bis, recently taken over by the 17 IB. Found to be very taken front line system of trenches | |

# WAR DIARY
## or
## INTELLIGENCE SUMMARY

Army Form C. 2118.

| Place | Date | Hour | Summary of Events and Information | Remarks and references to Appendices |
|---|---|---|---|---|
| MAZINGARBE | 21.10.16 | 9.30 p | Trenches muddy & in poor condition. Orders received today that we are to relieve 3rd R.B. in Rifle Bde in right subsection of the 74th in section on Nov 2nd 1916. Weather a little better. His Majesty the King has been graciously pleased to award the Military Medal for bravery in the field to the Undermentioned:– A/Sjt Lauder Sj. 84. 11.10.16 P.566 Pte B Kennan 2440 Pte J Allard 5763 Pte S. Pargh 5780 Pte L Page 1373 Sjt G Franklin 5768 A/Cpl A Stevens 4709 Sj S Slack 10760 A/Cpl C Inguine The D.C.M. has been awarded 4202 A/Cpl Hambleton V. | |

M. Sneed. Lieut Colonel
Commanding 8" Battn. The Buffs.

17th Brigade.
24th Division

8th BATTALION

"BUFFS"   EAST KENT REGIMENT

November 1916.

Secret & Confidential

War Diary

of

8th (Service) Battalion The Buffs.

Volume 15

Jakhalabad, November

Army Form C. 2118.

# WAR DIARY
## or
## INTELLIGENCE SUMMARY

*(Erase heading not required.)*

Instructions regarding War Diaries and Intelligence Summaries are contained in F. S. Regs., Part II. and the Staff Manual respectively. Title Pages will be prepared in manuscript.

| Place | Date | Hour | Summary of Events and Information | Remarks and references to Appendices |
|---|---|---|---|---|
| MAZINGARBE | 1.11.16 | | A very wet day. Little outdoor training possible. We were visited today by Lieutenant-Colonel H.W. Green, Commanding the 10th Bn. The Buffs; his adjutant Captain W. Berrill & other officers of the First Battalion who are at present at Bethune. | |
| Bn. H.Q. LOOS G.36.a.5.4. | 2.11.16 | | We relieved the 3rd Bn. The Rifle Brigade today, relief being complete at 1.30 p.m. We are holding a very long line & have a lot of work to be done. Weather very wet. | |
| do. | 3.11.16 | | Quiet day. | |
| do | 4.11.16 | | Enemy active with heavy trench mortars this afternoon. Our artillery gave heavy retaliation & effectually silenced the Huns. | |
| do | 5.11.16 | | Wet weather continues & trenches are beginning to fall in. These trenches were not revetted during the summer months, & in consequence are in a very bad state. | |

# WAR DIARY
## or
## INTELLIGENCE SUMMARY

Army Form C. 2118.

| Place | Date | Hour | Summary of Events and Information | Remarks and references to Appendices |
|---|---|---|---|---|
| South of LOOS. | 6/11/16 | | Very quiet day. | |
| do | 7/11/16 | | There was a combined artillery & trench mortar shoot. Enemy trenches on our right. A heavy trench mortar fell short & killed 3 men in our support line. Enemy retaliation very slight. Raining all day. | |
| do | 8/11/16 | | Trenches are falling in very fast. The support line is blocked at present & the front line was cleared during the night by stopping other work & putting every available man on to the work. | |
| do | 9/11/16 | | Enemy heavy trench mortars very active this morning. The first fine day since we came in. | |

**Army Form C. 2118.**

# WAR DIARY
*or*
# INTELLIGENCE SUMMARY
*(Erase heading not required.)*

Instructions regarding War Diaries and Intelligence Summaries are contained in F. S. Regs, Part II. and the Staff Manual respectively. Title Pages will be prepared in manuscript.

| Place | Date | Hour | Summary of Events and Information | Remarks and references to Appendices |
|---|---|---|---|---|
| QUALITY STREET | 10/11/16 | | Battn relieved by 3rd Bn The Rifle Brigade & went into Village Line & Gun Trench. HQ at Quality Street. Battn was in Bde. Reserve. | |
| | 11/11 | | Nothing to report | |
| | 12/11 | | The war continues as usual | |
| | 13/11 | | Officers Rugby team started practice | |
| | 14/11 | | Wet & cold. Relief orders received | |
| | 15/11 | | Normal | |
| | 16/11 | | Relieved 3rd Bn The Rifle Brigade in the 14Bde Rgtl Sub Section. Disposition 3 Companies, Rgt Coy C Centre Coy B Left Coy D. | |

14 Bde Section

# WAR DIARY
## or
## INTELLIGENCE SUMMARY

Army Form C. 2118.

(Erase heading not required.)

| Place | Date | Hour | Summary of Events and Information | Remarks and references to Appendices |
|---|---|---|---|---|
| 1stBn Section | 17/11 | | Quiet day. L.G.O. (2Lt F.C. ALLEN) went away to a course | |
| | 18/11 | | Enemy rather active with pineapples & R.G's. | |
| | 19/11 | | Normal | |
| | 20/11 | | 2Lt C.L. CARTER wounded by R.G. & pineapple in the shoulder during the evening. | |
| | 21/11 | | Capt T. Vaughan went down sick after serving continuously with the B" since its arrival in France. During only the Transport Officer 2Lt C.H.C. HEARPATH will be continuous ??. 2Lt A.L TAYLOR assumed the duties of assistant. | |
| Mazingarbe | 22/11 | | Batt" relieved by 3rd B" The Rifle Brigade in the afternoon & returned to MAZINGARBE | |

# WAR DIARY
## or
## INTELLIGENCE SUMMARY

Army Form C. 2118.

| Place | Date | Hour | Summary of Events and Information | Remarks and references to Appendices |
|---|---|---|---|---|
| Happegarbe | 23/11 | | Battn rested - rested required to find working parties. Lecture by gas sergeant from Div² in the afternoon | |
| | 24/11 | | Letting of box respirators. No casualties. In the afternoon the Batt⁴ played the 1ˢᵗ Batt⁴ The Buffs at Rugby & lost by one try to nil. | |
| | | | Nothing to report. | |
| | 25/11 | | | |
| | 26/11 | | Batt⁴ put in quarantine on account of a case of scarlet fever & Baths were stopped - but not working parties. | |
| | 27/11 | | Cold & wet. Relief orders came in. A very miserable day | |

# WAR DIARY
## or
## INTELLIGENCE SUMMARY

Army Form C. 2118.

| Place | Date | Hour | Summary of Events and Information | Remarks and references to Appendices |
|---|---|---|---|---|
| 14 Bde Section | 28/11 | | Relieved 2nd 13th R.B. in 14 Bde Right Sub-section by Companies B Right Coy A Centre Coy D Left Company C of support. Relief very late. | |
| | 29/11 | | Normal | |
| | 30/11 | | Enemy minenwerfer was heard to be active but soon silenced. | |

18/12/16

F.M. Wiener Major
Commanding 8th Battalion The Buffs

17th Brigade.
24th Division

8th BATTALION

"BUFFS" EAST KENT REGIMENT.

December 1916.

Secret and Confidential

War Diary
of
8th Battalion The Buffs.

For the Month of
December 1916.

Volume. 16.

Army Form C. 2118.

# WAR DIARY
## or
## INTELLIGENCE SUMMARY
(Erase heading not required.)

| Place | Date | Hour | Summary of Events and Information | Remarks and references to Appendices |
|---|---|---|---|---|
| | 1/2/16 | | Major Sinda (Commanding) went to bed with Trench fever | |
| | 2/2/16 | | Major Sinda Recovers | |
| | 3/2/16 | | Nothing | |
| | 4/2/16 | | In the morning about 10 a.m. a man of "D" Company walking along our front line found a hun sitting on the Duckboards smoking a pipe. The hun went to the left. | |

Army Form C. 2118.

# WAR DIARY
## or
## INTELLIGENCE SUMMARY

(Erase heading not required.)

| Place | Date | Hour | Summary of Events and Information | Remarks and references to Appendices |
|---|---|---|---|---|
| 14th Bn Section | 4/12 | | of our left post. 2 men kept concealed as the BOCHE got round up & fled. Our men failed to catch him before he reached the R.F.s. who claimed him. We however got his rifle & equipment. Batt^n was relieved by the 3rd Bn the Rifle Brigade & went into Bde Reserve. A,B,& D coys in Village Lane, C coy in Fan trench. | |
| Quality St. | 5/12 | | Nothing to report | |
| | 6/12 | | Normal | |
| | 7/12 | | Still Normal. Christmas Concert party began work. | |
| | 8/12 | | A few 5.9's fell unpleasantly near Quality Street Col | |

Army Form C. 2118.

# WAR DIARY
## or
## INTELLIGENCE SUMMARY

*(Erase heading not required.)*

Instructions regarding War Diaries and Intelligence Summaries are contained in F.S. Regs., Part II. and the Staff Manual respectively. Title Pages will be prepared in manuscript.

| Place | Date | Hour | Summary of Events and Information | Remarks and references to Appendices |
|---|---|---|---|---|
| PICCADILLY STREET. | 9/12 | | did no damage | |
| | 10/12 | | Nothing to report. | |
| 14 B is Right Sub-Section. | | | Batt'n relieved the 3rd Rifle Brigade in the right subsection. 14 B is Section in the morning. Only 14 Officers including the M.O. went up, the remainder being on courses etc. The 40th Div's Artillery has gone and are not covered by our own artillery. | |
| | 11/12 | | Attempts to get retaliation for meanies during the evening failed. Our front line was badly knocked about. | |
| | 12/12 | | A test S.O.S. about 11.30pm was a failure. He could not get through to our left and centre & the battery did not fire till about 12.30. Much correspondence about this. | |

2449 Wt. W14957/Mgo 750,000 1/16 J.B.C. & A. Forms/C.2118/12.

# WAR DIARY or INTELLIGENCE SUMMARY

Army Form C. 2118.

| Place | Date | Hour | Summary of Events and Information | Remarks and references to Appendices |
|---|---|---|---|---|
| 14B15 SECTION. | 13/12 | | Still worrying about the artillery support. This is being improved. Orders for 2Lt Walker 2Lt M Allen 2Lt Cheek & 2Lt Knight to join the M.G.C. Heavy Branch. Gentlemen are sent but the others will be returning us to 14 officers. | |
| | 14/12 | | Nothing to report | |
| | 15/12 | | "The leaves will start today." About three rounds actually came over. Very poor. | |
| Mazingarbe | 16/12 | | Relieved by 3rd Bn The Rifle Brigade in the afternoon & returned to Mazingarbe, after a very satisfactory tour, without casualties. Arrangements for the Christmas festivities are commencing. | |

# WAR DIARY or INTELLIGENCE SUMMARY

Army Form C. 2118.

| Place | Date | Hour | Summary of Events and Information | Remarks and references to Appendices |
|---|---|---|---|---|
| Hazigarbe. | 17/12 | | Nothing to report. | |
| | 18/12 | | Active preparations for Christmas celebrations. | |
| | 19/12 | | The same again today. Col. Lucas returned. | |
| | 20/12 | | Christmas festivities. In the morning sports were held. The 12th Sherwood Foresters band played for 1 p.m. Men's dinners were served in the BREWERY during which the Div'n band performed. In the afternoon the Buffs played the 1st B'n The Buffs at Rugger with the assistance of both bands. The 1st Buffs won by 1 try to nil. At 5.30 p.m. the Buffs Concert Party gave a concert arranged by Lt Lankey in the Brewery. The Foresters | |

Army Form C. 2118.

# WAR DIARY
## or
## INTELLIGENCE SUMMARY
(Erase heading not required.)

| Place | Date | Hour | Summary of Events and Information | Remarks and references to Appendices |
|---|---|---|---|---|
| Mazingarbe | 20/1/12 | | Band played during the internal. Afterwards all officers dined together with many guests from Brigade, 1st Battn etc. Weather was cold & frosty & the day was distinctly successful. | |
| | 21/12 | | Nothing particular | |
| 14 Bris Section | 22/12 | | Battn relieved the 3rd RB in the morning. C coy on the right, A coy centre D coy left with B coy in support. About 11 p.m. we "choked" a German wiring party with great success. The enemy immediately banged with T.M's & appeared to expect a raid. Casualties 2 OR killed 1 OR wounded. | |

Army Form C. 2118.

# WAR DIARY
## or
## INTELLIGENCE SUMMARY
*(Erase heading not required.)*

Instructions regarding War Diaries and Intelligence Summaries are contained in F. S. Regs., Part II. and the Staff Manual respectively. Title Pages will be prepared in manuscript.

| Place | Date | Hour | Summary of Events and Information | Remarks and references to Appendices |
|---|---|---|---|---|
| 14 B is Section | 23/12 | | Enemy minnied us all day & doing considerable damage. The front line hardly exists & the C.T's are bad. Our artillery retaliation was very poor & the 2" T.M.s (2) were destroyed. The Stokes fired mostly the time. Messages from the Left are rather disturbing. The next brigade reports reinforcements coming up, & the enemy certainly seems rather aggressive. Casualties Nil. | |
| | 24/12 | | Enemy quiet & seems nervous. He is very much on the alert. In the evening a short sharp bombardment by 18 pdrs caused him hopeful up very lights, open with M.G. & generally to show wind right up. We are working hard on our damaged trenches. | |

# WAR DIARY or INTELLIGENCE SUMMARY

Army Form C. 2118.

| Place | Date | Hour | Summary of Events and Information | Remarks and references to Appendices |
|---|---|---|---|---|
| 14 B 13. | 24/12 | | 2/Lieut Warden voluntarily reported to have gone to England sick & struck off strength. | |
| | 25/12 | | Christmas Day. This being the season of goodwill to all men, a nice little programme of artillery strafe has been worked out. During the day the enemy was quiet but in the evening soon after 10 p.m. he started with Oysters, Tomatoes & Pineapples for a short time on the Centre & Left Companies. Later he retaliated & kept going until a shower of 4.5's quietened him. | |
| | 26/12 | | Wet & miserable but quiet. Relief orders in. | |

2449 Wt. W14957/M90 750,000 1/16 J.B.C. & A. Forms/C.2118/12.

Army Form C. 2118.

# WAR DIARY
## or
## INTELLIGENCE SUMMARY

(Erase heading not required.)

Instructions regarding War Diaries and Intelligence Summaries are contained in F. S. Regs., Part II. and the Staff Manual respectively. Title Pages will be prepared in manuscript.

| Place | Date | Hour | Summary of Events and Information | Remarks and references to Appendices |
|---|---|---|---|---|
| 14 Bis Right Sub Section | 27/12 | | Nothing to report. | |
| | 28/12 | | Relieved by 3rd Bn R.B. in the morning. After relief the Bn moved into support A B & C, being in Village Line & D in fun trench. Bn H.Q. has moved from QUALITY STREET to NORTHERN Advanced Bde. H.Q. in NORTHERN UP. This H.Q. consists of a system of deep dugouts & a splinterproof mess. | |
| Village Line | 29/12 | | hut. The rain is soaking through & dripping into the dugouts. | |
| | 30/12 | | Dry. but the dugouts still drip. | |

# WAR DIARY
## or
## INTELLIGENCE SUMMARY

Army Form C. 2118.

| Place | Date | Hour | Summary of Events and Information | Remarks and references to Appendices |
|---|---|---|---|---|
| Village line | 31/12/12 | | Battalion of 93rd went into trenches today. 2nd Lt Pelley reported for duty. A draft of 100 odd has also turned up. N. D. Rice Lieut Captain for Major Commanding 8" Bn Ke Suffk | |

Secret and Confidential

War Diary
of
8' Battalion The Buffs.

Vol 16

Volume 9.

Month of January 1917

# WAR DIARY or INTELLIGENCE SUMMARY

Army Form C. 2118.

| Place | Date | Hour | Summary of Events and Information | Remarks and references to Appendices |
|---|---|---|---|---|
| Village Lipp | 1/1/17 | | The new year was welcomed in by the Boche with Gas & Lachrimatory Shells all along village lines. A rumour is spreading that whisky can no longer be got out here. 2/Lt Edwards joined. | |
| | 2/1/17 | | The rumour mentioned is true - we are now expected to go on with the war drinking lemonade. Whisky cannot be got anywhere. | |
| | 3/1/17 | | Received the 3rd R.B. in the afternoon. Slight relief with one Lewis gun. We are now holding the line with 2 companies. Bus on the right, D on the left. | |

Army Form C. 2118.

# WAR DIARY
## or
## INTELLIGENCE SUMMARY

*(Erase heading not required.)*

| Place | Date | Hour | Summary of Events and Information | Remarks and references to Appendices |
|---|---|---|---|---|
| 14 Bis Right Sub Sector | 4/1/17 | | A quiet day. Towards night the enemy became rather active with their T.M.s. This activity continued throughout the night. | |
| | 5/1/17 | | At about 4.30 a.m a large enemy raiding party entered our trenches at the junction of the two companies. The raiders avoided our sentry groups & got into our support line, bombing dugouts & capturing prisoners. We killed & recovered the bodies of six of the enemy & can account for three others. Our casualties were 3 killed 3 wounded & 42 missing. This disaster seems to be almost entirely due to the fact that | |

# WAR DIARY
## or
## INTELLIGENCE SUMMARY

*(Erase heading not required.)*

Army Form C. 2118.

the higher authorities order us to send over N.C.O's to all corners of the earth. The result is that we have to leave inexperienced N.C.O's in charge of important posts, & these failed to show the leadership that is so necessary in case of emergency. Particularly fine work was done by 2Lt Darling, Cpl Morley (B Coy) & Pte Littlefield. (D Coy) 2Lt Darling organised & led bombing squads with great success. Cpl Morley with three men held the bombing post at Seaforth Crater although completely surrounded & cut off. Only three enemy got into the post & these were

| Place | Date | Hour | Summary of Events and Information | Remarks and references to Appendices |
|---|---|---|---|---|
| | 6th | | killed. Pte Schofield was company runner to white company messages killed thus enemy of received one of our men. All was quiet soon after 6.15pm. The rest of the day was quiet. A quiet day. | |
| | 7th | | In the evening the Boche shelled round Bn. H.Q. with 4.M.5. One casualty, wounded. | |

# WAR DIARY or INTELLIGENCE SUMMARY

Army Form C. 2118.

| Place | Date | Hour | Summary of Events and Information | Remarks and references to Appendices |
|---|---|---|---|---|
| LOOS | 7th | | We were relieved by the 8th Batt. The R.B.s the relief being complete at 12 noon. We then moved into our rest billets at MAZINGARBE. | |
| MAZINGARBE his Reserve | 8th | | ½ of the Battalion employed in fatigues. The remainder were inspected and all deficiencies in kit equipment etc. noted for replacement. | |
| | 9th | | Training programme commenced, chiefly with company arrangements. Carried out provisional rdress rehea. | |
| | 10th | | Battn of Infantrcere to repair. Working parties supplied to harden up Maida Road Trenches. | |
| | 11th | | Usual programme/work carried out. Kit inspection | |
| | 12th | | Clothing parade. Fine. Nothing to Report | |
| | 13th | | Battn of Infantrcere trained. Football matches between Coys during the afternoon. | |

Army Form C. 2118.

# WAR DIARY
## or
## INTELLIGENCE SUMMARY.
(Erase heading not required.)

| Place | Date | Hour | Summary of Events and Information | Remarks and references to Appendices |
|---|---|---|---|---|
| MAZINGARBE | 14th | | Rifle Inspection. Usual parades. Nothing of importance occurred. | |
| | 15th | | Draft of 5 O. Ranks arrived. Companies rested all afternoon. Lewis Guns teams set up to 6 hours ready to which had to be completed by 8am | |
| | 16th | | Relieved the 3rd Battle Rifle Brigade in the Right Sub Section. Relief was completed by 11pm. Disposition of Companies was A Regale, C left Coy, B + D Companies in support in the Cellars. | |
| | 17th | | Bosche roller was active. Heavy shelling of the cellars causing several casualties. Walking post on enemy trenches. | |
| | 18th | | Quiet. Enemy attitude quieter. Little of importance to record. | |

# WAR DIARY
## or
## INTELLIGENCE SUMMARY.

Army Form C. 2118.

| Place | Date | Hour | Summary of Events and Information | Remarks and references to Appendices |
|---|---|---|---|---|
| LOOS | 19th | | Quiet day today, parties busy all night until Trenches after heavy artillery bombardment. Trenches filled in in many places also had to be withdrawn. | |
| | 20th | | Schacht hamel. Trenches fully [illegible] badly own to slight thaw. Both parties sent right for the Reserve Coy employed catching and [illegible] a few. | |
| | 21st | | taken [illegible] Supporting. Carried on successfully every quiet except for occasional minnies, still havoc nearly fell in our own. | |
| | 22nd | | Slight and[?] activity. Several Enemy planes seen flying over our lines. Very patchy today alright all [illegible] was as it is very weak in places especially in vicinity of further Rws. | |

# WAR DIARY or INTELLIGENCE SUMMARY

Army Form C. 2118.

| Place | Date | Hour | Summary of Events and Information | Remarks and references to Appendices |
|---|---|---|---|---|
| Village Huts | 23 | | Moved into Brigade Reserve at Village Huts taking over from the 12/Royal Fusiliers. Battalion Headquarters are at Old Pele Ordnance H'Qrs. Accommodation not good. Relief completed by 11.30pm. | |
| | 24 | | Fine but extremely cold enough to freeze hands. Snow continues. Ground is a frozen condition. Bathe parties formed. No parties to go to work in the village are staff. Raiding party still under training. | |
| | 25 | | Preparations for raid now completed. Coronary App'r Col. down to the Bombers to inspect new special party. Signallers head to have to fix up telephone arrangements for raiding party. | |
| | 26 | | Raiding party of 4 officers and 120 O.Ranks made a raid on German Trenches between Spantail Crater & Bootle Alley. Zero time was 6.30am. Gas put on at western slag's lab. Still damage was perfect. See 12" R.S. trailer on the scene hard down kept. Casualties: Officers killed 1 OR killed 14 O.Ranks wounded. Prisoners taken were 19. No body of 2/R.S. Phillips could not be recovered – majority of prisoners were of same group. | |

# WAR DIARY
## or
## INTELLIGENCE SUMMARY.
*(Erase heading not required.)*

Army Form C. 2118.

| Place | Date | Hour | Summary of Events and Information | Remarks and references to Appendices |
|---|---|---|---|---|
| Village Inn | 26" | | Several dugouts were blown in with whole chaps. Snow. Casualties two heavy. Received information was hoped rest of the enemy wire & Ken dugouts should not be fired out. Raid party which started 9.30am. while snowstorm raged a security measure was with cut by hostile artillery. | |
| | 27" | | 10th of inparana hospital. Weather fine cold. Congratulatory messages from Capt Div & Brigade commanders and also neighbouring Battalions in the newspapers received. | |
| | 28" | | Marked absence of snipers to the contemplated general not being cancelled. Supply train has not arrived till very late. Bren Rohans has to be conveyed accordingly by Anchally 1 BSC. 270 of the ration were expended for thanks. | |
| | 29" | | Major Shedd Capt North Lunt Rea and 2/Lt Stunqull went down to the trenches Hagnanh to hand down with the rest of the raiding party. The men were much elated. Ran very high spirited. Weather still intensely cold but quite fine. | |

Army Form C. 2118.

# WAR DIARY
## or
## INTELLIGENCE SUMMARY.
(Erase heading not required.)

| Place | Date | Hour | Summary of Events and Information | Remarks and references to Appendices |
|---|---|---|---|---|
| Loos. | 30th | | We were relieved by the 2nd M du Rifle Brigade previous to the Braeline Trenches. Relief was noted not to commence before 1pm. Slight snow was falling. It was very cold. | |
| | 31st | | Weather still extremely cold. Dark quiet day except for a few applies which killed 1 of C Coy men. Trenches unproven greatly on account of working parties constantly absent. A Km (?) Support line almost completed, duckboarded and revetted. | |

F W Stone Lieut Colonel
Commanding 8 Battalion The Buffs

17/6
(17

17.

Secret and Confidential

War Diary

of

8th Battalion The Buffs.

March & February 1917

Volume 18.

# WAR DIARY
## or
## INTELLIGENCE SUMMARY.

Army Form C. 2118.

| Place | Date | Hour | Summary of Events and Information | Remarks and references to Appendices |
|---|---|---|---|---|
| LOOS | 1st Sept | | Enemy very active with his heavy Trench mortars doing much damage to our trenches. Our heavy artillery carried out a short bombardment on the enemy support line doing much damage. | |
| | 2nd Sept | | Very quiet day. COs weather still continues. No trench mortar fire however. | |
| | 3rd | | Enemy suldedan CTs with heavy machines very good shooting. It was very aeroplane with two heavy TMs in the afternoon killing three men in C Coy. | |
| | 4th | | Sniper & rifle activity on both sides. Nothing of importance to report | |
| | 5th | | Trenches was dull. Trench mortar activity especially on redoubt line with heavy TMs and in the neighbourhood of the Cellars. Effected takeover in pairs. | |
| NAZINGARBE | | | Relieved by the 3rd Bn. the Rifle Brigade. Relief to be carried out during afternoon. Weather extremely fine. Relief completed by 5.30 p.m. | |

# WAR DIARY
## or
## INTELLIGENCE SUMMARY

| Place | Date | Hour | Summary of Events and Information | Remarks and references to Appendices |
|---|---|---|---|---|
| Mazingarbe | 6th | | Been extremely fine. There was nothing happening during the late evening. | |
| | 7th | | Very fine day. Busy with arrangements for Andrew Sfeast & jury upstands etc. The usual programme of work was drawn up. Battl'n of parade from 8.30 to 1 for each day. The afternoons were mostly spent games and sports. | |
| | 8th | | Hay + Dix was busily engaged in training another Raiding Party of about 125 NCOs + men for a Counterattack Raid in the event Truckle Phillips was wanted to spend training found by the Regimental Band. | |
| Mazingarbe | 9th | | Healy, Cadman, [?] fought during this period to experience a retaliation attack. Special attendance was given to Bayonet fighting during this period. | |
| | 10th | | Usual parade took place. 2 Lieuts S.J. Collison Harley & 2 Lt W.S. Donelan a S.S. Phillips with 6th & 3rd Battalion joined. About 35 Officers & [?] w.l.th Battalion. | |
| | 11th | | 2nd RD Reported from Allonque from the Traing Bn most of the men of course had a little experience, otherwise they will with up to standards. | |
| | 12th | | Preparations made to move off the following day to Noeux-les-Mines for a | |

Army Form C. 2118.

# WAR DIARY
## or
## INTELLIGENCE SUMMARY.

(Erase heading not required.)

Instructions regarding War Diaries and Intelligence Summaries are contained in F. S. Regs., Part II. and the Staff Manual respectively. Title pages will be prepared in manuscript.

| Place | Date | Hour | Summary of Events and Information | Remarks and references to Appendices |
|---|---|---|---|---|
| Mazingarbe | 12th | | Period of Rest. O Crews had been arranged to hor night between to the [illeg.] Battalion billeting over the half the [illeg.] to be attended | |
| Noeux les Mines | 13th | | Battalion moved by Platoons at 5 minute interval to noeux les mines. 1st platoon relieved of a gun arrived by 8th Battalion Somerset Regiment. Relief completed by 1 p.m. Transport moved independently. The distance is only about 2½ kilometres good billets were obtained in the town. Battalion was in Corps Reserve. | |
| | 14th | | Training programme as approved by G.O.C. Division was commenced. The companies were billeted a with close to the main Road. The training ground was just in rear of the hutments. The afternoons were spent in spade chiefly the work of the monastery of a strenuous nature I.2.O.C. in Sankey & 2/Lt Barley were arrived with trey from in recognise of their valour [illeg.] acknowledges the their Raid made by us at [illeg.] The weather continued fine facilitating the carrying out of the Trainy programme where was much adhered to. Beyond ordinary town [illeg.] [illeg.] were unimportant features of the programme in the [illeg.] of a few operations | |
| | 15th | | | |

2353  Wt. W2544/1454  700,000  5/15  D. D. & L.    A.D.S.S./Forms/C. 2118.

| Place | Date | Hour | Summary of Events and Information | Remarks and references to Appendices |
|---|---|---|---|---|
| Moeux les Mines | 16th | | Work carried out three a week. Boxing was inaugurated and last night the sport was indulged in by all who wished to take part. | |
| | 17th | | Reveille was ordered to be an hour later there was some rain but work was carried on as usual. In the afternoon hay Sports attack(?) took place between No officers Tom Swallows in equitation. Incidentally they were at two amusing exhibitions. 2nd R(?) Infantry(?) from the 3rd Buffs. Captain the Huxley from army RSC. Renaming. | |
| | 18th | | Sunday full fine. Services for all denominations. Catholics attend at the local Church the CofEs Presbyterians held parade services at 10.45 & 11.30 respectively, the InCA. The Rev Gray Jones temporarily attached to the Battalion officiated at the. at the CofE service. Holy Communion was celebrated at the InCA at 7.30 a.m. to any who might wish to attend. The remainder of the day was free. | |

# WAR DIARY or INTELLIGENCE SUMMARY

Army Form C. 2118.

| Place | Date | Hour | Summary of Events and Information | Remarks and references to Appendices |
|---|---|---|---|---|
| Meaux les Mines | 19th | | Training Programme continued. The Training of Specialists carried out by the Specialist Officers concerned. A class of specialists obtained weekly the rotation of our hill. Several cases occurred where it was necessary to isolate about 6 men. | |
| | 20th | | A site was selected for a Rifle Range at L.19.d.1.9 from Eastwards a fatigue party of 10 men per day were supplied to for the work. The Range & the Signal Officer found up telephone communication which he from point the stop mills. | |
| | 21st | | The hours between relief were placed at the disposal of the Battalion on certain days & the groupes of the whole Battalion was systematically carried out. The Command Officer held the Adjt Repr at 12 noon daily. The cases now not heinous. During this period the establishment of N.C.O's was checked and vacancies filled by men or substantive rank as the occasion required. | |

# WAR DIARY
## or
## INTELLIGENCE SUMMARY.

*(Erase heading not required.)*

Army Form C. 2118.

| Place | Date | Hour | Summary of Events and Information | Remarks and references to Appendices |
|---|---|---|---|---|
| Acheux Les Mines | 21st | | A draft of about 39 O.Ranks joined the Battalion from the 24th "DS" Train Battalion which was situated at ALLOUAGNE. This draft was the last the Train Bn ceased to exist from this date. The Battalion now at full strength. Casualties this Battalion since returned viz. — about 10 S.B. O.R. | |
| | 22nd | | The Train as usual carried out during the morning. Football match 1st Bn Royal Fusiliers v 8" Buffs took place at 24th Div School. Kick off was at 2.30 p.m. Our opponents were in fine form and although our side rallied were slightly outplayed, they being apparently in better preparation. We lost 3 – nil. | |
| | 23rd | | Still occasional rain. Rifle range completed. Competitions were now set to be fixed. The 3rd B/Gde Rifle Brigade arranged today tournament with Lewis & Hotchkiss guns to all ranks of 111 R.I.B. We sent a few representatives who fairly creditable performance. The Rifle Bde also engaged the 1st R.F. several contests. | |
| | 24th | | Gun Day parades carried out as usual. A friend Cameron arranged for the enemy. Musketry was a long period rifle | |

# WAR DIARY or INTELLIGENCE SUMMARY

Army Form C. 2118.

| Place | Date | Hour | Summary of Events and Information | Remarks and references to Appendices |
|---|---|---|---|---|
| Porte Said (contd.) | 24th | | horse was crowded: many being unable to effect an entrance until after the first three or four days. Classes were arranged by Battalion then forwarding to figures 1st offering particular time for the PLAN FAIR CYPHER. Unequally offering superquipy of came afterwards totals. | |
| | 25th | | Sunday. Church parades for all denominations. Very fine day. | |
| | | | Seven seemed cases of Kemplow were taken to Hospital. Staff Sergt Cartwright, No. 5 Pluto attached to Coy E Party to F1006 Church parade from Rifle Range. | |
| | 26th | | Rifle Range was used to full advantage during our last few days as no others had just been received that 28th instant would probably be the last day of training. | |
| | 27th | | As a previous days from 8 a.m. to 12.30 p.m. the various Companies carried out training according to the programme issued to all Caserne. Special lecture to N.C.O.'s of same Battalion was given by Col. Ord... afternoon of same was left to progress. The D route played from Isa a Shaftali races also felt Ruhital eve rg for the paste 2 days. | |
| | 28th | | Blg. the Roy Stuarts fini. The Battale paraded as shown on Parade to take part in an Air plane scheme which had been planned by the Brigade. | |

# WAR DIARY
## INTELLIGENCE SUMMARY

| Place | Date | Hour | Summary of Events and Information | Remarks and references to Appendices |
|---|---|---|---|---|
| Acheux les Hues | 28 | | It was an all day scheme and divisors were taken. Battn HQrs was tracked at E.19.d.4.4. messages were sent and received illustrating the system of Co. signals. Wireless Aircraft & Infantry have now been felt. All methods of communication was practiced between Brigade HQ applied upto a line crossing was kept all messages in each case being transmitted correctly. Battalion returned about 5.30 pm. The weather during the whole period of training was extremely fine & facilitates the carrying out of work to its advantage. The period was altogether fully carefully arranged. When opportunity of an infantry Battalion was carried out. The Companies having been told off refitted, received their new provisions & all Companies will be fitted & equipped, all deficiencies being made good as far as possible. | |

F.W.Lumsden RMA Col
Commanding 8 Bahama Bn Suffs

Vol 18

Secret and Confidential

War Diary

of

8th Battalion The Buffs.

Volume 19. Sixteenth of March 1917.

# WAR DIARY
## or
## INTELLIGENCE SUMMARY.
(Erase heading not required.)

Army Form C. 2118.

| Place | Date | Hour | Summary of Events and Information | Remarks and references to Appendices |
|---|---|---|---|---|
| Neux les Mines | 1/3/17 | | The Preparations for departure were made and a party of 12 Officers went by lorries (one to meet the Western Party) on August 1 Regt Left section which was held by the 10th Battalion Canadian Inf. Regt. The 1st Infantry Brigade took over all the Centre Canadian Brigade Angres section on the front M.32.a.2.6. to M.20.6.3.6. The 2nd Bn Brigade being on the Right CALONNE section and the 3rd Inf. Brigade on the Left SOUCHEZ section. Still rested all day. | |
| Cité du Sorci 10 | 2/3/17 | | Battalion paraded at 9 am and moved off by Platoons at 5 minutes interval via BRAEQUEMONT to door 10 Rq.a. (Sheet 36 c.) This is a small village about 24 Kilomet. away for Neux les mines and the hour 6.57 mm. Aux nouilles Rd. Battalion arrived in about 11.30 a.m. The billets were rather scattered and accommodation was not good. The night even spent but treated fine but dull. | |
| | 3/3/17 | | Battalion proceeded to Regt Left section August 1 Section in relief of 10th Canadian Inf. Battalion. Platoons were off as soon as entered at 9 am in order of Coys A.B.C.D. Platoon next us at entrance of | |

| Place | Date | Hour | Summary of Events and Information | Remarks and references to Appendices |
|---|---|---|---|---|
| Right Sub Section | 3/3/17 | | Cones d'Aix Tunnel. The disposition of Companies was as follows A Coy Equivalents by Ray Left Montsou Coy. C Coy Close Support D Coy in Reserve with Sponney Relays as far as (?) by 11pm. Battalion HQ. to extend to Sand Mill Tunnel. Six Lewis guns in position in sub Coms Stan. There are numerous OPs in very elevated unenclosed Shrapnel Battalion HQ. Artillery activity by 9pm. 15mm in Steamer near Athies and the Porch sent up Green & Red Rockets. Very bright day. Enemy Lines quiet. Slight Aeroplane activity. Rather tranquil. If at night a rather Hypos railway from Annes Roads Brigade HQ used up from house to house to Bully Grenay. | |
| | 4/3/17 | | | |
| | 5/3/17 | | Early morning fine, sunset very cold. Dismounts for all. Companies left at 11 + marched cross at Same Enfilade number short a stab of parades is arranged for the details work is carried on. Our Supervisor of Spans reported instructions like an Left tutors in accordance with the advance Scheme the orders of Bt. Division. Our Signalling Officer was evacuated sick. He is expected to return in a few days as he is not very ill really. | |

Army Form C. 2118.

# WAR DIARY
## or
## INTELLIGENCE SUMMARY.
(Erase heading not required.)

| Place | Date | Hour | Summary of Events and Information | Remarks and references to Appendices |
|---|---|---|---|---|
| Right Sub Sector | 6.3.17 | — | The weather continued fine. Our Heavy Artillery carried out a shoot on the enemy's back areas. The Boche did not retaliate. There was great aerial activity on both sides, at one time 15 Boche planes, not twelve of ours, and in the fight which ensued two Boche were seen to crash, and one of ours. | |
| | 7.3.17 | | Weather still fine. Enemy attitude very quiet. Considerable aerial activity again, especially on the part of the enemy. | |
| | 8.3.17 | | Weather mild. Our Snipers were active. Enemy seems to be getting some more Artillery into this Sector. Battalion were relieved by the 3rd R.B.S. | |
| BULLY - GRENAY | 9.3.17 | | The relief did not take place until late in the day, so that we did not get back to Bully-Grenay until 5 P.M. The Orderly Room which had stayed at SAINS-EN-GOHELLE with the training Platoons, as an experiment, rejoined the Battalion again. The experiment was not a success. We find we cannot get on without our Orderly Room. | |

Army Form C. 2118.

# WAR DIARY
## or
## INTELLIGENCE SUMMARY.
(Erase heading not required.)

| Place | Date | Hour | Summary of Events and Information | Remarks and references to Appendices |
|---|---|---|---|---|
| BOUY -GRENAY | 10th | — | The weather was fine. Most of the men were employed by day on working parties, and two officers and 60 men had to go up the line every night wiring the support line. The Companies were paid out, and accordingly were able to enjoy themselves in the evening. | |
| " | 11th | — | Weather misty, slight rain in the evening. The Cinema seems a great attraction and is crowded nightly. A "dud" aeroplane shell fell in the village this morning and killed a child and wounded two children and a soldier. | |
| " | 12th | — | Great enemy artillery activity last night, and we were just preparing to "Stand to". The firing continued from about 2.45 AM to 3.45 AM and then subsided. More working parties added to the list, so that every possible man is taken now. | |
| " | 13th | — | Enemy shelled our back areas behind PETIT SAINS but did not do any damage. Rain started falling at about | |

Army Form C. 2118.

# WAR DIARY
## or
## INTELLIGENCE SUMMARY.
*(Erase heading not required.)*

Instructions regarding War Diaries and Intelligence Summaries are contained in F. S. Regs., Part II. and the Staff Manual respectively. Title pages will be prepared in manuscript.

| Place | Date | Hour | Summary of Events and Information | Remarks and references to Appendices |
|---|---|---|---|---|
| BULLY GRENAY (cold) | 13/3/17 | 12.30 P.M. | and continued till well into the afternoon. | |
| " | 14 | — | Nothing of interest happened. Weather still wet, which makes things bad for working parties who get caught in the rain as we expect to go back into the line again to-morrow. | |
| R‍t Sub sector | 15 | — | We relieved the R.B's in the Right Sub-Sector. The enemy probably "spotted" us coming up for he started shelling the C.T.'s just as the Sergt Major and the Orderly Room Sergt started up. No casualties occurred. The Boche is noticeable more active now than during our last tour and there has been a lot of counter-battery work. The day has been clear and a good deal of aerial activity. | |
| " | 16 | — | Weather fine. A new "minnie" has made its appearance but we have not been able to locate it yet. Our Patrols were out most of last night but found nothing — | |

Army Form C. 2118.

# WAR DIARY
or
# INTELLIGENCE SUMMARY.
(Erase heading not required.)

| Place | Date | Hour | Summary of Events and Information | Remarks and references to Appendices |
|---|---|---|---|---|
| P¹ Sub Sector | 17 | — | The "Minnie" has been quite active on the Right Company front, but shut up when our Howitzers replied. The trenches in places are almost impassable owing to the depth and stickiness of the mud. The Trench Artillery has been busy but no casualties so far. | |
| " | 18 | — | Our Right Company have suffered severely from the attentions of the Minnie. We have discovered two Boche periscopes & houses behind their lines. We propose to get the Artillery to destroy them to MORROW | |
| " | 19 | — | Three Boche ties active will be hanging than yesterday, hull aerial aeronly by no aeroplane apparently engaged taking photographs. Casualties nil | |
| " | 20 | | was a commi. Enemy has all morning of unknown o Afen | |

Army Form C. 2118.

# WAR DIARY
## or
## INTELLIGENCE SUMMARY.
*(Erase heading not required.)*

Instructions regarding War Diaries and Intelligence Summaries are contained in F. S. Regs., Part II. and the Staff Manual respectively. Title pages will be prepared in manuscript.

| Place | Date | Hour | Summary of Events and Information | Remarks and references to Appendices |
|---|---|---|---|---|
| Pt Sub-Sector | 21st 37 | — | Relieved by 3rd Bn Rifle Brigade. Record relief. The whole operation only taking 4 hours. Weather splendid. We moved to Divisional Reserve at FOSSE 10 in billets | |
| FOSSE 10 | 22nd | — | Most of the day spent cleaning and recuperating after a strenuous 18 days. A large working Party consisting of one whole Company nightly (?) has to be found, wiring support lines on account of rumour that Huns were coming over in force here — | |
| FOSSE 10 | 23rd | | Very cold with snow storms. Frost from Brigade Armourer. Noblette road packed with traffic all night. Heavy large guns seen here. | |
| — | 24th | | Thaw set in. Mud plentiful. Drums paraded at N.O. and played retreat. | |
| — | 25th | | Usual training carried out. Football match in afternoon against A.S.C. We lost 8 - 5. A Company continue her special training for minor enterprise. | |

| Place | Date | Hour | Summary of Events and Information | Remarks and references to Appendices |
|---|---|---|---|---|
| Janval 10 | 26th | — | The G.O.C 24th Division motored over to address the Special Party previous to their enterprise. He also interviewed about 20 candidates for temporary Commissions about 4 pm. The Trench Platoon of 2 Officers and 62 other Ranks proceeded to ALLOUAGNE the party parading under 2/Lt A LE MAY at 1pm. The Platoon was late in returning from Aley will the expiration of the 4 Battalion instructors in Bullets, Bombing, Physical Drill & Bayonet Fighting, Bombing, Lewis Gun Firing during the manning Seniors within. | |
| | 27th | | Battalion relieved the 3rd & 8th Sea Rifle Bde in the Right Sector Re- first Platoon arriving at entrance of CORONS D'AIX at Maroc. The Grenadiers Council all without casualties being completed by 3 pm. Final Preparations for the wire enterprise were being made. (D) Special Party of Arty came up to Coy Headquarters at 2am trench in preparation by 3.30 pm. Captain Stoney took up his position in advanced line this evening. The party moved across no man's land opposite the Ry [?] at 3.10 am under a perfect barrage. Dawn was just breaking soon to be his light. | |

# WAR DIARY
## INTELLIGENCE SUMMARY
*(Erase heading not required.)*

Army Form C. 2118.

| Place | Date | Hour | Summary of Events and Information | Remarks and references to Appendices |
|---|---|---|---|---|
| Right Subsector | 27 | | The two parties carried together to a certain amount of confusion occurred in consequence of everyone the enemy parties. A delayed gas alarm in the left party provided some any danger to CT. Intense enemy wire encroachers during the whole raid. The Bosche retaliation was extremely futile. Our party remained in the German front line about 15 minutes. Our losses raid to our line. An isolated enemy OP was 1 killed 2 wounded. | |
| Right Subsector | 28th | | Standing still by the Bosche. Still not much of a day. Aerial battle between 1 and 6 British Company. One fast Hun was totally rammed by hostile machines. One was forced alight quickly, the other told Shepherd. | |
| | 29th | | Saw many Provincial activity on both sides. Bosche planes flying very low on our line were taking off by an our machines. A barrage fire from AA guns. In other respects the day was quiet. | |

Army Form C. 2118.

# WAR DIARY
## or
## INTELLIGENCE SUMMARY.
*(Erase heading not required.)*

Instructions regarding War Diaries and Intelligence Summaries are contained in F. S. Regs., Part II. and the Staff Manual respectively. Title pages will be prepared in manuscript.

| Place | Date | Hour | Summary of Events and Information | Remarks and references to Appendices |
|---|---|---|---|---|
| Right Section | 30th | | Still cold. Vimy Ridge was heavily shelled by the enemy who put a great many shells ranging along our support line beyond and wanted to take out a large portion of the line. This was held by the Royal Sussex Battalion on our right, its round on a piece on our left to the 1st Royal Fusiliers Company. Commanders were sent to reconnoitre the new line. | |
| | 31st | | Some snow during the early morning again in the evening. The enemy guns were active. It is thought that from the new battery positions. our front support lines received attention from whizz bangs, heavily were damaged & falling in in many places. | |

F.W. Stewart. Lieutenant
Commanding 1st Battn The Buffs

8th BATTN. E. KENT REGIMENT

17th INFANTRY BRIGADE

24th DIVISION

APRIL 1917

Army Form C. 2118.

# WAR DIARY
## or
## INTELLIGENCE SUMMARY.
(Erase heading not required).

| Place | Date | Hour | Summary of Events and Information | Remarks and references to Appendices |
|---|---|---|---|---|
| [Bois?] April 1917 | | | more rain. All available men have to be employed clearing up the trenches where they have fallen in. In spite of the weather the Huns did a considerable amount of flying, chiefly over our gun positions. | |
| Right Sub Sector | April 2nd | | Battalion relieved by 3rd Battalion the Rifle Brigade. Relief was by night and was not complete until about 11.30 P.M. The Battalion returned to BULLY-GRENAY and were in support. | |
| " | 3rd | | The usual number of working parties were found, which took absolutely every available man from the Battalion, once every 24 hours. The Boche has been searching for our artillery with some very heavy calibred guns and several shells have fallen in BULLY GRENAY. The Boschè still continues to shell the village, and one artilleryman was wounded in the street. The weather was fine and many Hun aeroplanes tried to fly over BULLY GRENAY. The Regimental | |
| | 4th | | Concert Party – The B. Infellows, gave a concert in the evening which was well attended in spite of the fact that shells fell very near the Hall all the time. | |

| Place | Date | Hour | Summary of Events and Information | Remarks and references to Appendices |
|---|---|---|---|---|
| BULLY -GRENAY | April 5th | — | The Bosche shelled the village so heavily during the night that it was thought advisable to find cellars for all the men. Matts were however brought to a heap about tea-time when the enemy obtained a direct hit on the billet & occupied by 2nd Lieut W.t. Donelan, killing him instantaneously. Permission was obtained from the Brigade to break up the Battalion as follows:- One Company went up the line to MECHANICS TRENCH, one Company to LES BREBIS, one Company to PETIT-SAINS, and one Company remained with Headquarters and slept in the cellars of BULLY GRENAY. Whilst the detail for this was being gotten out, the Hun threw a large number of gas shells into the village and badly gassed one of our Sergts, and a HQ Runner and some many others felt the ill-effects of the gas for several days. | |
| | | 6P | Shelling of BULLY-GRENAY and the surrounding villages still continues. Weather fine and warm. The 6th Division "Fancies" gave a Concert | |

Army Form C. 2118.

# WAR DIARY
## or
## INTELLIGENCE SUMMARY
*(Erase heading not required.)*

Instructions regarding War Diaries and Intelligence Summaries are contained in F. S. Regs., Part II. and the Staff Manual respectively. Title Pages will be prepared in manuscript.

| Place | Date | Hour | Summary of Events and Information | Remarks and references to Appendices |
|---|---|---|---|---|
| BULLY GRENAY | 6th | — | In BULLY-GRENAY in the afternoon during which the village was again shelled. | |
| | 7th | — | More artillery bombardments during which several soldiers were wounded. The Divisional Band gave a very good performance in the afternoon. Weather fine & warm. Very little work done owing to relief. Much aerial activity. We relieved the 3rd Battalion The Rifle Brigade by night. All the way up the ground was pitted with gas shell craters and the air was pungent. Whilst the relief was in progress the Huns threw some very large shells into BULLY-GRENAY and round about the ration dump wounding a Sergeant and three Officers servants. The Relief was complete about 1.30 AM | |
| ANGRES [?] Right sub Sector | | | | |

# WAR DIARY or INTELLIGENCE SUMMARY

Army Form C. 2118.

| Place | Date | Hour | Summary of Events and Information | Remarks and references to Appendices |
|---|---|---|---|---|
| BIVVAC CAMP ANGRES II Right Sub section | 8th April | — | Day beautifully fine and observation excellent. Our Artillery bombardment, especially in the direction of VIMY RIDGE, increased enormously and continued all day. The Huns shunned our front line and PYRENNEES considerably. | |
| | 9th | | At 5·30 A.M. the Artillery bombardment of VIMY RIDGE reached its climax, at which moment the Canadians attacked. We watched the barrage creep forward and knew that the Canadians must be gaining their objectives. Several troskes in the trenches opposite us, obviously taken by surprise at the suddenness of the blow at VIMY stood up in the trenches opposite us - the better to see the show - and three of them were promptly knocked out by our Sniping Officer. | |

# WAR DIARY
## or
## INTELLIGENCE SUMMARY

*(Erase heading not required.)*

Army Form C. 2118.

| Place | Date | Hour | Summary of Events and Information | Remarks and references to Appendices |
|---|---|---|---|---|
| ANGRES | 10th April | — | 12th Rfy al Fusiliers joined 3rd Brigade, and we extended our line to the right towards the ARRAS-ROAD in relief of the 9th Royal Sussex Regiment, and the 1st Royal Fusiliers, on our left, took over a portion of our line as far as "VASSEAUX" TRENCH. The Hun was too preoccupied to bother us much. | |
| " | 11th | | A great deal of aerial activity. The Bosche seems to be blowing up a great many places behind ANGRES | |
| " | 12th | | The LEINSTERS and ROYAL SUSSEX attacked the BOIS EN HACHE on our right, last night. The Hun had obviously been expecting us to attack to-day as he has been shelling us pretty heavily most of the day. | |

# WAR DIARY
## or
## INTELLIGENCE SUMMARY

Army Form C. 2118.

(Erase heading not required.)

| Place | Date | Hour | Summary of Events and Information | Remarks and references to Appendices |
|---|---|---|---|---|
| ANDRES | 13th April | | Orders came through for the Battalion to be relieved to-day but later on these were cancelled. The Boches shelling has become very desultory, and the shells seem to come from a long way off. It is quite the quietest day we have had for a long time. The weather is very fine but very cold at night. The Hun fired very lights intermittently all day and night. There is not a sound to be heard. No shelling. No sniping. | |
| | 14th | | The first thing of interest that happened was to an Orderly rushed in to Headquarters in the middle of lunch to fetch the Adjutant to the Observation Post. Hundreds of Germans were seen moving in the Bois HIRONDELLE. The artillery Officer at Headquarters got the guns on to them very quickly and scattered them. | |

# WARDIARY
or
## INTELLIGENCE SUMMARY
(Erase heading not required.)

Army Form C. 2118.

| Place | Date | Hour | Summary of Events and Information | Remarks and references to Appendices |
|---|---|---|---|---|
| ANGRES II | 14 | 3 PM | Enemy suspected to have left their trenches. Message from Brigade to that effect received about 2.30 PM. We left our trenches about 4 PM and by 6 PM had gained the line of ANCHOR TRENCH, unopposed, our left resting on ALCOHOL TRENCH, and our right in ARSON TRENCH. Touch was established with the Marine Light Infantry on our left and the Royal Fusiliers on our right. Patrols were pushed forward from this point and the CITÉ de ROLLENCOURT was reached by dusk. Our line was advanced to this point and we were in position by 10 PM. | |
| | 15/4/17 | | | |
| | 16/4/17 | | The 3rd R.B.'s passed through us about midday and we followed in support and billeted for the night in LIÉVIN. Relieved the R.B.'s in the evening on the line:- CRIMSON - CROOK - CRAZY - CHÂTEAUX. | |

# WAR DIARY
## or
## INTELLIGENCE SUMMARY

*(Erase heading not required.)*

Army Form C. 2118.

| Place | Date | Hour | Summary of Events and Information | Remarks and references to Appendices |
|---|---|---|---|---|
| | 17/4/17 | | Orders to advance against Enemy positions between N.13 Central and ALARM Trench at 9.10 AM. Attack started at the appointed hour after a feeble Artillery preparation. Enemy at once opened heavy M.G and rifle fire from strong points in his line, 2 M.G's on HILL 65 proving most offensive. He also shelled our advancing troops heavily, more particularly in the neighbourhood of FOSSE 9. The Brigades on our left and right flank were reported "hung up" by 10.30 A.M, the former in COLLEGE Trench at N.13.a.50.95. and the latter at the BOIS DE. RIAUMONT, and were it was obvious that we could not push forward without serious casualties and without losing touch on both flanks, a halt was called and our troops were ordered to hold the positions where they stood, and not to advance further | |

**Army Form C. 2118.**

# WAR DIARY
## or
## INTELLIGENCE SUMMARY

*(Erase heading not required.)*

Instructions regarding War Diaries and Intelligence Summaries are contained in F. S. Regs., Part II. and the Staff Manual respectively. Title Pages will be prepared in manuscript.

| Place | Date | Hour | Summary of Events and Information | Remarks and references to Appendices |
|---|---|---|---|---|
| | 17/4/17 | | The situation remained unchanged, till dusk when we were holding the line M.18.d.70.30 – M.18.d.60.50 along Railway line to M.18.a.75.00. Thence to M.24.c.90.80. The troops were ordered to consolidate this line as far as possible during the night. Our total casualties during the days fighting were roughly, one officer and 30 O.R's put out of action. | |
| | 18/4/17 | | Enemy shelled our positions fairly heavily during the day. We were relieved by the 1st R.F. during the night and proceeded to ROLLENCOURT. | |
| | 19/4/17 | | Relieved by North Staffordshire Regiment, 24th Division being relieved by the 46th Division. Our men are very tired but in high spirits. Proceeded on relief to LES BREBIS where we spent the night. | |

# WAR DIARY
## or
## INTELLIGENCE SUMMARY

Army Form C. 2118.

| Place | Date | Hour | Summary of Events and Information | Remarks and references to Appendices |
|---|---|---|---|---|
| LES BREBIS | 20/4/17 | — | We moved again to-day, still further back. This time to HESDIGNEUIL. This sudden marching is causing a great deal of sore feet in the Battalion, as the men have done very little marching for the last few months. | |
| HESDIGNEUIL | 21/4/17 | — | Moved again to-day to BOURECQ. In spite of sore feet the men are already much better, and marched in to BOURECQ as a Battalion, with the drums at their head in fine style. | |
| BOURECQ | 22/4/17 | — | All the day spent in refitting as far as possible and in cleaning up generally. This is the first real opportunity that officers have had of getting hold of the men and finding just how things stand. Casualty lists are completed and checked and deficiencies counted up. | |

Army Form C. 2118.

# WAR DIARY
## or
## INTELLIGENCE SUMMARY
*(Erase heading not required.)*

Instructions regarding War Diaries and Intelligence Summaries are contained in F. S. Regs., Part II. and the Staff Manual respectively. Title Pages will be prepared in manuscript.

| Place | Date | Hour | Summary of Events and Information | Remarks and references to Appendices |
|---|---|---|---|---|
| BOURECQ | 23/4/17 | — | All the Companies paraded in the morning and were inspected by the CO. Considering the difficulties, the men looked very clean and smart. The weather for the last ten days has been excellent. | |
| BOURECQ | 24/4/17 | | We are on the move more again, further back still, this time to ERNY St JULIEN. It is a quiet country village, with good training grounds and playing fields | |
| ERNY ST JULIEN | 25/4/17 | | Training started seriously. The surrounding districts are all full of Portuguese who take a great interest in the doings of the British "Tommy". Football is played every evening. The French civilians cannot yet understand the Englishman's love for games. | |

Army Form C. 2118.

# WAR DIARY
*or*
# INTELLIGENCE SUMMARY
*(Erase heading not required.)*

Instructions regarding War Diaries and Intelligence Summaries are contained in F. S. Regs., Part II. and the Staff Manual respectively. Title Pages will be prepared in manuscript.

| Place | Date | Hour | Summary of Events and Information | Remarks and references to Appendices |
|---|---|---|---|---|
| ECNYST ST JULIEN | 26/4/17 | — | We had just settled down to a good safe period of training, but we are on the move again. This time back to BOURECQ. We are on our way to be in Support to the 199th Brigade in case they are attacked. We are only to spend one night in BOURECQ. The people of BOURECQ seem delighted to see us. | |
| BOURECQ | 27/4/17 | — | We moved again to-day to ANNEZIN on our way up to LA-BOURSE. The march was very trying as it does on *pavé* roads the whole way. | |
| ANNEZIN | 28/4/17 | — | We moved to-day to LA BOURSE via BEURY and SAILLY LA-BOURSE, and have obtained excellent billets here | |

2449 Wt. W14957/M90 750,000 1/16 J.B.C. & A. Forms/C.2118/12.

Army Form C. 2118.

# WAR DIARY
or
## INTELLIGENCE SUMMARY
(Erase heading not required.)

| Place | Date | Hour | Summary of Events and Information | Remarks and references to Appendices |
|---|---|---|---|---|
| LA BOURSE | 29/4/17 | | At last we are able to obtain baths. The men have not had a change of clothing or underclothing since leaving the trenches. The training grounds here are good, and there is an excellent Range. | |
| LA BOURSE | 30/4/17 | | Training Programme started. Work from 8-12 and 2-4. There is an excellent football ground available, and the weather is perfect. | |

M. Shoesmith
Adjutant

to Lieut Colonel
Commanding 8" Battalion The Suffolk

Secret and Confidential   Vol 20

War Diary

of

8th Battalion "The Buffs".

March & May 1917

Volume 21.

Army Form C. 2118.

# WAR DIARY
## or
## INTELLIGENCE SUMMARY
*(Erase heading not required.)*

Instructions regarding War Diaries and Intelligence Summaries are contained in F. S. Regs., Part II. and the Staff Manual respectively. Title Pages will be prepared in manuscript.

| Place | Date | Hour | Summary of Events and Information | Remarks and references to Appendices |
|---|---|---|---|---|
| LA BOURSE | 1.5.17 | | Weather fine. Companies engaged in Training from 8.20 a.m. to 12.30 p.m. and from 2 to 3 p.m. according to Training programme submitted weekly to Brigade Headquarters. 2 men Afternoon rejoined the Battalion from the 3rd Battalion The Buffs. | |
| | 2.5.17 | | Weather continues fine. Training programme adhered to. Men Pdo avoided defaulters made up. Football matches between companies were played during the afternoon | |
| | 3.5.17 | | Fine. Nothing of importance to report | |
| | 4.5.17 | | Usual Training during the morning. The Commanding Officer made a careful inspection of the Battalion by companies on their respective parade grounds. The pattern for the purchase of Company cannon are. A report on the inspection | |
| | 5.5.17 | | Another fine day. N.C.O. L/Cpl + stripes and being taken to withdraw vrules. Clothing from Ord. broyer + all blankets in excess of 4 per man. Three Officers proceeded by bus to Special honours class Being to attend Demi | |

# WAR DIARY
## or
## INTELLIGENCE SUMMARY

*(Erase heading not required.)*

Army Form C. 2118.

| Place | Date | Hour | Summary of Events and Information | Remarks and references to Appendices |
|---|---|---|---|---|
| La Bourse | 5.5.17 | | Officers Course lasting 3 days under the Supervision of the Divisional Staff. This is the Second Course of the kind, the former one is reported to have been excellently arranged. | |
| | 6.5.17 | | Church parades for all denominations. Tattoo Service held that night at La Bourse. Drums played at C of E parade - also Retreat at 5.30 p.m. C.O's paraded over 200 sharp. The R.C.'s went to the local Church. During the afternoon Officers & Sergeants v's Subalterns & Corporals - Football match in the afternoon which resulted in a draw. | |
| | 7.5.17 | | Usual parades during the morning. Inspection by the B.G.C. 7th Infantry Brigade. The Battalion together with the 10th were transport paraded at 4 p.m. on the Range and marched by Companies to the appointed rendezvous. Search continued at 2 p.m. 16 other Ranks joined from Base. Capt A C Maley reported from hospital. | |
| | 8.5.17 | | Raining all day. Proposed scheme of attack in conjunction with Rifle Brigade postponed. Party of 18 Officers & 50 O.R. proceed to 1st Army Rest camp. Autuchier entraining at KILLER's Post 8.5 am. Orders for move received at 3 a.m. | |
| ROBECQ | 9.5.17 | | Scheme Attack scheme cancelled owing to the Battalion moving at 10 a.m. to ROBECQ near ST VENNANT. The Battalion marched off at 10 a.m. & proceeded via BETHUNE. A halt was made on the road for dinner. The Battalion arrived in about 4.30 p.m. Billets are good but very scattered. The Brigade moved to BUSNES. | |

# WAR DIARY
## or
## INTELLIGENCE SUMMARY.
*(Erase heading not required.)*

Army Form C. 2118.

| Place | Date | Hour | Summary of Events and Information | Remarks and references to Appendices |
|---|---|---|---|---|
| ROBECQ | 10/5/17 | | Inspection by G.O.C. Division at 12 noon. The Battalion paraded as though opposite Brigade with Transport and all specialists. The Companies were cleared very far apart - but the billets were excellent being exceptionally clean. The surrounding country is very pretty. In the afternoon walking took place in the canal. | |
| MORBECQUE | 11/5/17 | | The Battalion paraded at 8 am on the main Hazebrouck Road ready to move off. The usual Billeting party left at 7am. The Route was Robecq - St Venant - Haverskerque - MORBECQUE. The Battalion arrived at its destination about 12.30pm. The day was extremely warm making the march more difficult. 17th Div. Postal Headquarters is situated at Hazebrouck. The other Battalions of the Brigade are also situated in Hazebrouck in the southern portion of the town. | |
| STEENVOORDE | 12/5/17 | | Battalion paraded at 6.20 am ready to move off. Was the last on the line of march. The Route was that via Hazebrouck. Battalion arrived in a stale however were billeted at KN'd. S.6. Billets were long distances apart and not very good. | |
| STEENVOORDE | 13/5/17 | | Stormy weather. Remain in Steenvoorde area most of the day spent in cleaning up. Church parade for C of E's at 11am at R.H.Q's. | |

Army Form C. 2118.

# WAR DIARY
## or
## INTELLIGENCE SUMMARY.
*(Erase heading not required.)*

Instructions regarding War Diaries and Intelligence Summaries are contained in F.S. Regs., Part II and the Staff Manual respectively. Title pages will be prepared in manuscript.

| Place | Date | Hour | Summary of Events and Information | Remarks and references to Appendices |
|---|---|---|---|---|
| STEENVOORDE | 13/5/17 | | The Roman Catholics had a service in the church at Steenvoorde. The Battalion rested during the afternoon. The Cotail returns from leave to U.K. | |
| | 14/5/17 | | Leslie Cartwright Tommy, Major Gen & L. Capt. leave the Division on 4 days leave to Paris. Nothing of importance to report. Four returns from up to date unofficial & hospital 33 O.R. refd to duty. Reinforcements 33 O.R. refd to duty. | |
| STEENVOORDE | 15/5/17 | | This Inspection by Army Commander at 11 a.m cancelled as the Officer did not arrive. J.W. B.G.C. saw the Battalion next part. Drawing Programme submitted for 6 days. Rifle very cold wind. Companies busy Training all day. Nothing important happening. | |
| Do. | 17/5/17 | | Weather continues brilliant, having + spots during the afternoon rain. Everyone getting the men in fine form. NCO's parade daily under the 2/in Command for musketry Renunciation drill. All Subalterns Officers parading daily for instruction under the Adjutant. | |

Army Form C. 2118.

# WAR DIARY
## or
## INTELLIGENCE SUMMARY.
*(Erase heading not required.)*

Instructions regarding War Diaries and Intelligence Summaries are contained in F.S. Regs., Part II. and the Staff Manual respectively. Title pages will be prepared in manuscript.

| Place | Date | Hour | Summary of Events and Information | Remarks and references to Appendices |
|---|---|---|---|---|
| STEENVOORDE AREA. | 18/5/17 | | Owing to arrival of fresh drawers the accommodation is limited consequently much of the companies had to give up their present billets. Continues. | |
| | 19/5/17 | | This nothing of importance to report. Baths were arranged for the Battalion at Steenvoorde Baths. | |
| | 20/5/17 | | Church parade for C of E at Battalion Headquarters. The newly appointed Divisional Commander visited the Battalion made the acquaintance of the Senior Officers. Reinforcements 11 O.Ranks arrived from the base; they had all been in the Battalion previously. | |
| | 21/5/17 | | Training under Coy arrangements. The Commanding Officer visiting all Companies in supervision of the work. A boxing Tournament was arranged for the evening. The entries were good & some good performances were put up. Major Guy Lee was the referee. | |
| | 22/5/17 | | Wet all day. Party of Officers taken by motor bus to reconnoitre the lines at Dickibush. | |

2353 Wt. W2514/1454 700,000 5/15 D.D. & L. A.D.S.S./Forms/C. 2118.

# WAR DIARY
## or
## INTELLIGENCE SUMMARY.
(Erase heading not required.)

Army Form C. 2118.

| Place | Date | Hour | Summary of Events and Information | Remarks and references to Appendices |
|---|---|---|---|---|
| STEENVOORDE | 23/5/17 | | Usual Training Programme Carried out. Sports during the evening. | |
| K15.a.3.6 (Sheet 27) | 24/5/17 | | Party of Officers proceeded prior to Steenbreck to reconnoitre the area | |
| | 25/5/17 | | The Army Commander inspected the Battalion on parade at 11.30 am Dress was Drill order Transport - nothing to report | |
| G.19.d.2.8 | 26/5/17 | | The Battalion paraded at 9 am to move to the vicinity of POPERINGHE via ABEELE. The Battalion is accommodated in a field at G.19.d.2.8 in huts. The position to afford one 2 L.G.a billy is arranged the Military Crocs. | |
| G.19.d.2.8 | 27/5/17 | | Whitsun Day Church parade for C of E's Battalion resting the remainder of the day. | |
| | 28/5/17 | | Fine Busy putting the Camp in order, building huts etc. bakery Parties taken up by Coy at 9 pm each evening to Ridge Wood. numbers required 4 + 28 O.R. Ranks. Work commenced tonight in relief of the 9th Royal Sussex Regiment | |

# WAR DIARY
## or
## INTELLIGENCE SUMMARY.

*(Erase heading not required.)*

Army Form C. 2118.

| Place | Date | Hour | Summary of Events and Information | Remarks and references to Appendices |
|---|---|---|---|---|
| G.19.d.2.8. | 29/5/17 | | Usual working parties found. Men left in camp given physical exercises and shot lectures. Little of importance to report. | |
| — | 30/5/17 | | Orders received to the remaining of the Batalion of the Brigade to new trenches to the Skewsvedal Training Area for intensive Training and attack practice over model Trenches. Reinforcements & Officers reported for duty. I.O.R casualty slightly wounded at duty | |
| — | 31/5/17 | | Party proceed by lorry to Dickebusch to reconnoitre the line, working parties contained until 4 am June, also the time the Batalion is withdrawn from trench under the orders of the C.E. X Corps to the Reserve Divisional Area. | |

F.W. Tucker Lieut Colonel
Commanding 8' Battn The Buffs

17/74

Secret and Confidential

War Diary

Vol 21

8th Battalion The Buffs

Month of June 1917

Volume 22.

# WAR DIARY or INTELLIGENCE SUMMARY

Army Form C. 2118.

| Place | Date | Hour | Summary of Events and Information | Remarks and references to Appendices |
|---|---|---|---|---|
| C.Iq.d.2.8. | 1/6/17 | | Lewis Parties concluded 11am today. Battalion rested remainder of day. | |
| STEENVOORDE | 2/6/17 | | Battalion paraded 9.15 a.m. & return to Skeewoode Training area. Arrived in billets about 1 p.m. The billets were in most cases the same as those occupied on the previous occasion when in the area. | |
| | 3/6/17 | | Tactical scheme issued by Brigade was carried at our H.Q. model Trenches. The afternoon was spent in studying and making maps for the attack. | |
| STEENVOORDE | 4/6/17 | | The model Trenches were again used for practising our attack carried out by entire Brigade. | |
| HEKSKEN | 5/6/17 | | Battalion paraded at 2 p.m. & proceeded to HEKSKEN via ABEELE was accommodated in huts in a field. | |
| HEKSKEN | 6/6/17 | | Remain at this Camp during the day - move off at midnight to a camp situated in a wood at M.3.d. Central. Special stores and | |

Army Form C. 2118.

# WAR DIARY
## or
## INTELLIGENCE SUMMARY.
(Erase heading not required.)

| Place | Date | Hour | Summary of Events and Information | Remarks and references to Appendices |
|---|---|---|---|---|
| Ms d Central Sheet 28 | 6/6/17 | | Ammunition was drawn round. The Battalion paraded at 11.30pm in fighting kit and proceeded to the "Assembly positions" in old G.H.Q 2ⁿᵈ line, N°1/the N°9r being echeloned at BURGOMASTER FARM. The Battalion was situated in two deep dugouts, one at ENGLISH WOOD holding about 400 men and one at SCOTTISH WOOD holding about 200 men. | |
| " | 7/6/17 | 3.10 a.m. | At 3.10 a.m. we were awakened by a series of terrific reports as a large number of mines were exploded in front of us, and at the same moment the barrage opened – | |
| | | 11.30 a.m. | We remained in our dugouts until 11.30 a.m. when we received orders to move forward to the OLD FRENCH LINE where we remained | |
| | | 3.10 p.m. | until 3.10 p.m. the new Zero hour for a fresh advance to a new objective. By Zero hour the Battn was formed up under the DAMSTRASSE where it remained until the operations had been successfully completed. | |
| | | 10 p.m. | At 10 p.m. the B⁴ moved up in close support to the newly taken positions relieving units of the 41ˢᵗ Division, the line being held by the 3 B⁴ Rifle Bde 4/1 R. Inn. in front & as & the 12 R. Inn. being behind us in Reserve. | |

**Army Form C. 2118.**

# WAR DIARY
## or
## INTELLIGENCE SUMMARY.
(Erase heading not required.)

Instructions regarding War Diaries and Intelligence Summaries are contained in F. S. Regs., Part II. and the Staff Manual respectively. Title pages will be prepared in manuscript.

| Place | Date | Hour | Summary of Events and Information | Remarks and references to Appendices |
|---|---|---|---|---|
| M S d Wulvet Sect 26 | 8/6/17 | | We remained in the same positions as occupied by us on the 7th. Heavy shelling by the Germans took place at intervals, being most marked between 6am & 7am in the morning & between 7pm & 8pm in the evening. During the latter shelling the S.O.S. was put up by both sides. Lt Sherick was hit at 8pm. A fairly quiet day. We relieved the 3rd RB in the front line commencing at 9pm. A & C Coys went in the front line with B & D in support. Desultory shelling during the night & A Coy sustained a few casualties. | |
| | 9/6/17 | | Both more active with his guns & the artillery fire on both sides increased in intensity as the day wore on. At nightfall the gun fire was still very heavy & caused us considerable trouble since the 9th Warwicks started relieving us at 9pm. The relief was carried out with difficulty being reported complete at 2.30 a.m. | |
| | 10/6/17 | | We sustained several casualties including Capt Gullam (since died of wounds), Lieut Arnold (since died of wounds), Lt Hilary & Capt Curtis & Lt Hilary both wounded. | |

**Army Form C. 2118.**

# WAR DIARY
## or
## INTELLIGENCE SUMMARY.
*(Erase heading not required.)*

| Place | Date | Hour | Summary of Events and Information | Remarks and references to Appendices |
|---|---|---|---|---|
| MIDDLE CAMP WEST | 11/6/17 | | Withdrew from trenches into rest at MIDDLE CAMP WEST - Troops tired out & slept all day - | |
| | 12/6/17 | | Another day of rest except for Officers & NCO's most of whom started by bus at 4 a.m. to reconnoitre the new sector for our next venture. | |
| H.S.d central Sheet 28. | 13/6/17 | | After a quiet day in camp for the men & further reconnaissance by the Officers, the Battn left camp at 5 pm & marched by Companies to our new sector in BATTLE WOOD & took over the line from the 3rd R.B. Relief was carried out without casualties & reported complete at 2 a.m. | |
| | 14/6/17 | | After a quiet day for this part of the line we carried out an attack on the German positions to our front at 7-30 p.m. (See appendix) | |
| | 15/6/17 | | Rather heavy shelling during the day - We were relieved at nightfall by the 2nd Leinsters (see appendix) | |
| | 16/6/17 | | Returned to MICMAC Camp & rested all day - | |

Army Form C. 2118.

# WAR DIARY
## or
## INTELLIGENCE SUMMARY.
(Erase heading not required.)

Instructions regarding War Diaries and Intelligence Summaries are contained in F. S. Regs., Part II. and the Staff Manual respectively. Title pages will be prepared in manuscript.

| Place | Date | Hour | Summary of Events and Information | Remarks and references to Appendices |
|---|---|---|---|---|
| MICRAE CAMP | 17/6/17 | 10.25a | There was a brief inspection of the 16? by the G.O.C (who approved) as shortly into congratulations at the excellent work that had been done in the last two days. | |
| | 18/6/17 | | Battalion noted; a reconnoitring party provided by two to Brestnack at 3am but owing to heavy shelling & roads being closed they immediately returned. RQMS A Vickery of the 2nd Devonshire Regt joined the Battalion as Materiel Quartermaster | |

2353  Wt. W2544/1454  700,000  5/15  D. D. & L.  A.D.S.S. Forms/C 2118.

| Place | Date | Hour | Summary of Events and Information | Remarks and references to Appendices |
|---|---|---|---|---|
| DICKEBUSCH | 19/6/17 | 7.30pm | Bn. moved to BURGOMASTER FARM CAMP. Major J. VAUGHAN M.C. being in command as the Colonel was resting, under M.O's advice, from his wound. | |
| | 20/6/17 | | The Camp was taken over from the 9th East Surreys. Several Officers & N.C.Os go up to visit the trenches: some started at 3.0 a.m. and others at 10 a.m.- the latter were caught by heavy shell fire - no casualties. Small working parties in their Coys. remainder rested. | |
| | 21/6/17 | | In the reconnoitring parties, all went up at 3.0 a.m. At 5.0 a.m. the camp had two heavy shells sent into it - one man was slightly wounded. | |
| | 22/6/17 | | A quiet day until 7 p.m. when the camp was again shelled this time no damage was done - though several horses were hit belonging to some RFA a few yards away. | |

# WAR DIARY
## or
## INTELLIGENCE SUMMARY.
(Erase heading not required.)

Army Form C. 2118.

| Place | Date | Hour | Summary of Events and Information | Remarks and references to Appendices |
|---|---|---|---|---|
| DICKEBUSCH | 23/6/17 | 8pm | The Bn. Recorded offly. Platoons & relieved the 2/20th Rifle Brigade NW of BATTLE WOOD ground to 1 MAOR Trenches. Owing to the heavy shelling of SHRAPNEL CORNER the route was changed so that we moved via CHESTER FARM to 128.C.90.20 where further delay in Cos. went somewhat astray from the point of the Rly. that 2/Lt HANWAR shot two men wounded (one only seriously). Owing to this the companies relief was not complete until 3.45 a.m. | |
| | 24/6/17 | | All ranks worked by day hard restricted the work could hardly be attacked. Their large working parties came up (working) same for 12 Sherwood Forests R.E.s into the position from the 75th B.S. (to the C.I.S. supporting lime). They have been active all day with his artillery. Filling the trenches until | |
| | 25/6/17 | 11.30 | When the opened a very heavy fire on our area which lasted incessantly for one hour. The majority of this missed the front line three weeks no casualties but the working parties in rear suffered very heavily. Our retaliation repeatedly asked for, was not effective. During the Incident the J.O. 2/Lt. J.B. MILLARD was wounded the line with Maj VAUGHAN (Commanding 9/Lt. HANCOCK was killed by a shell), the two latter were completely shaken and a few minutes later both were slightly wounded by another shell ferring at they. | |

# WAR DIARY or INTELLIGENCE SUMMARY

Army Form C. 2118.

| Place | Date | Hour | Summary of Events and Information | Remarks and references to Appendices |
|---|---|---|---|---|
| I30 c 9 & I 36 a 8 0 | 25/6/17 | | 2/4th A.J. SHERWILL assumes the Military Cros. | |
| | 26/6/17 | | Enemy artillery was rather the active during the day & night. Not much damage done. Early morning patrols went out & owing to rain & thick darkness it was hard to get much information. It was decided to push on posts forward that night and the co-ordinates of the 4/7ths at 10 p.m. were such that they could not co-operate with the scheme in whole & a sketch was drawn in early morning of 'B' Coy in left of area & its posts & co-ords. were 136 & 70-60 & Northwards and there consolidated. On the Rgt Lt patrols from 'A' Coy - one under Capt MORRELL found that without heavy covering fire it was impossible to reach the objective & strength & without having covering fire it was impossible to reach the objective. 2/Lt & Coy however & strength relentless of the Hun. At dawn however patrols of the 2/5 L.N. Lancs Regt arrived & reinforced that 13th relieved was & night. The day passes as there in keeping out of sight of working instead of night. | |
| | 29/6/17 | | Relief was not complete until 4.30 a.m. as the relieving B.C. had a very long march from RENINGHELST which took longer than expected. The Hun seemed to get wind of the relief & opened up a heavy fire for a period, but casualties were very small, 2/Lt A.C.NEWCOMB & 3 O.R. being wounded. Coys mags then on way back to NIEMAC CAMP which they arrived at abt 8.0 a.m. During this turn the aerial activity of the Hun was very noticeable. | |

Army Form C. 2118.

# WAR DIARY
## or
## INTELLIGENCE SUMMARY.
(Erase heading not required.)

| Place | Date | Hour | Summary of Events and Information | Remarks and references to Appendices |
|---|---|---|---|---|
| MICMAC CAMP | 29/6/17 | | Bn. paraded at 11.0 a.m. to march to RENINGHELST SIDING to entrain for the training area round LUMBRES district. The train in charge of Lt Col POPE STUDD containing also 2 Bns the Leinsters, 17/KRR, 2nd 1/13, & 17th L.T.MB, left about 2.45pm reached LUMBRES about 6.20pm when we detrained. The night was spent under canvas. | |
| LUMBRES | 30/6/17 | | Camp was struck & we moved off by 7.0 a.m. marching in a heavy bath road to ESCOEUILLES where our advanced party & transport had come by road on 27th & 28th to arrange billets etc. The 14 odd kilometres were covered between | |
| ESCOEUILLES | | | 11.0 a.m. ready to/for the rest earned with the Div. | |

M. McAree Capt.
Adjutant for Lieut Colonel
Commanding 8' Batt. The Buffs

## OPERATIONS 14/16th. JUNE 1917.

In accordance with the pre-arranged plan the Battalion were in the following assembly positions at Zero(7-30.pm.) on the night of June 14th. 1917. (Reference Map Hill 60. Sheet 28.)
A.Company from I.35.c.95.20. to B.35.d.50.30.
C.Company from I.35.d.50.30. to I.36.c.15.55.
D.Company from O.5. a.45.35. to O.5.a.45.60.
B.Company about I.35.d.Central.

A certain amount of sniping occurred whilst Companies were getting to their assembly positions but they were not discovered by the Artillery.

The Battalion attacked on a two Company front, and each Company on a two Platoon front.

The barrage was good though perhaps a little short at first, but the Companies kept well up under it, and casualties were small. The Barrage at Zero was 150 yards in front of our assembly positions, and at Zero plus 4. the Barrage lifted and advanced at the rate of 100 yards every 4. minutes.
Exactly 6. minutes after our Barrage opened, the enemy opened a very heavy Barrage on our assembly positions.
Fortunately, our men had kept well up under our Barrage, and were clear of our assembly positions by this time, otherwise, the casualties would have been very heavy.

The objectives were :-
A.Company The Northern face of the SPOIL BANK. between O.5.b. 35.45. and O.5.b.60.50. and
C.Company the tram- line between O.5.b.85.70. and O.6.a.30.00.

Very little resistance was met with until reaching the SPOIL BANK. Here a good deal of hand to hand fighting occurred but a great many casualties were saved by the prompt action of 2 men (Pte Dunning and Pte.Cornell) who rushed a German Machine Gun in a concrete emplacement, and killed the team and captured the gun.

A. Company on the right killed at least 30 of the enemy and took 3. prisoners.

C. Company on the left had all their officers including the Company Commander hit before reaching their objective, but 2/Lieut. F.D.Wilkinson remained with the Company until all the objectives had been gained and the ground consolidated.

During the Advance C. Company was enfiladed by hostile Artillery from the left.

After C. Company had gained their objective Sergt. Shute took his platoon about 80. yards ahead of the newly won line and cleared a system of dugouts there, killing a great many of the enemy and bringing back 4 prisoners.

About midnight when C. Company had consolidated their position 2/Lieut F.D. Wilkinson withdrew to have his wounds dressed and Sergt. Pells was left in sole charge of the Company.

Touch was established with the Fusiliers on the left, but some difficulty was experienced with the Battalion our right, and not till the following morning were the exact positions discovered

In the meanwhile D. Company had come up behind the TRIANGULAR SPOIL BANK at ZERO. 2 Platoons less 1 bombing section advanced towards the Western edge of the SPOIL BANK and mopped up the Southern side of the bank in conjunction with A. Company, whilst the bombing squad attended to the dugouts on the top of the bank.

Phosphorous bombs and Mills Grenades proved very effective. Most of the dugouts were occupied, there being about 10 or 12 men in each. Several of the enemy attempted to escape across the canal at Lock 6, but these were dealt with by men of D.Company and no one escaped that way.

Further down the SPOIL BANK towards the the enemy put up a much stiffer fight, making considerable use of stick bombs and rifles. 2/Lieut J.B. Paige was killed leading an attack at this point.

Sheet 2.

Many of the enemy then tried to escape round the Eastern edge of the SPOIL BANK but these were also shot, including an officer and a Sergt. Major, and a FELDWEBEL was eventually captured after fighting four of our men single handed.

21 prisoners were taken up to this point by D.Company and a very great many more killed.

D. Company then dug themselves in on the Southern slope of the SPOIL BANK and A. Company in support on the Northern Slope.

2. Machine Guns of the 17th. Machine Gun Company accompanied us, and rendered valuable assistance.

Digging in was rendered more difficult by continuous shelling and sniping which continued all through the night, but it was obvious that the enemy was not certain of our line as he shelled the whole area freely.

During this time B. Company were in support to A. and C. Companies with 1. Platoon under the direct orders of the Commanding Officer. They advanced very close behind the leading Companies owing to the heavy enemy Barrage on our jumping off trenches, and finally dug in at about O.5.B.40.70. - P.5.b.70.80.

Their Lewis Guns engaged an enemy Machine Gun at about O.4.a.40.45. on the railway and silenced it.

The following morning found all the Companies well dug in and in many cases cleverly camouflaged from aerial observation.

A great many enemy aeroplanes came over our lines in the early morning, and tried to discover our positions. Many times they swooped right down and fired their machine guns in to our trenches. About 5.pm. the enemy put up a heavy barrage all along the line, and enemy were seen to be massing on our right.

This information was wired quickly through and our guns at once turned on to them and scattered them.

We were relieved that night by the 2nd. Battalion the LEINSTER REGIMENT.

17th. June 1917.
Lieutenant,
Adjutant 8th. Battalion The Buffs.

No 22

War Diary
of
8th Battalion The Buffs.

Secret and Confidential

Month of July 1917

Volume 23.

# WAR DIARY
## INTELLIGENCE SUMMARY

Army Form C. 2118.

Vol. 23    8th Bn. The Buffs.

| Place | Date | Hour | Summary of Events and Information | Remarks and references to Appendices |
|---|---|---|---|---|
| ESCOEU-ILLES | 1/7/17 | | Day great service held at 10 a.m. & 7 p.m. The 2nd in C who proceeded on leave. The Battn. and neighbourhood being disturbed apart. H.Q. & Coys. bivouacked close together while A & B Coys. are in Billets | |
| ESCOEUILLES | 2/7/17 | | Training programme arranged on the watched from Brigade H.Qrs. from 7.30 to 12.30 p.m. & from 2-3 p.m. The chief object was a central ground with a range for this purpose | |
| " | 3/7/17 | | Much work is needed for making full use of the camps & ranges in improving the billets. Training has been completed. | |
| Do. | 4/7/17 | | Training carried out according to programme and range completed. Instruction in map reading and lectures in musketry for war. | |
| | | | Three given during the afternoon. | |
| ESCOEU-ILLES | 5/7/17 | | Weather continues fine. Passed to Boulogne was full a mg. & parry of Usual Parade. & Repleting & equipping of the Battalion was continued & completed. | |
| | 6/7/17 | | A field day was arranged a simple scheme having been drawn up by the C.O. | |

pkm

# WAR DIARY
## or
## INTELLIGENCE SUMMARY.
(Erase heading not required.)

Army Form C. 2118.

| Place | Date | Hour | Summary of Events and Information | Remarks and references to Appendices |
|---|---|---|---|---|
| ESCOEUILLES | 7/7/17 | | A Roxey Tournament arranged by the 12th Stewood Devotis was amongst held after tea at LOTTINGHEM. Several competitors from the Battalion. | |
| | 8/7/17 | | Battalion was allowed to rest excepting Church parade at 11 a.m. Stretcher bearers by the forming attached to the Battalion. Bay two very fine. | |
| ECAULT | 9/7/17 | | The Battalion paraded in full marching order at 5. am & proceed to Nera-sedn. The proceeding the Brigade was 6th K.R. R. Camp at Sofbuilogue. The march was carried out splendidly. When marching well, we arrived at about 11.30 am. The remainder of the day was spent in putting up accommodation and resting. | |
| ECAULT | 10/7/17 | | There were fatigue parties next day to fill up water to draw rations. The Camp although did all possible to make the time pleasant for the Battalion. A football match was played between the machine Gun Corps. The continue attacking time the score was 3-1 in their favour. | |

[signature]

Army Form C. 2118.

# WAR DIARY
or
## INTELLIGENCE SUMMARY.
(Erase heading not required.)

Instructions regarding War Diaries and Intelligence Summaries are contained in F. S. Regs., Part II. and the Staff Manual respectively. Title pages will be prepared in manuscript.

| Place | Date | Hour | Summary of Events and Information | Remarks and references to Appendices |
|---|---|---|---|---|
| ECAULT | 11/9/17 | | The Battalion paraded at 10.20 a.m. for the return journey. The same route was used and the Battalion arrived in Rest Billets about 5.30 p.m. feeling very tired. | |
| ESCOEUILLES | 12/9/17 | | Battalion Sports were arranged to take place in the morning. Arrived at Tr. 20. G5. (Calais 13). They commenced at 10 a.m. preceded at 7 p.m. by a Divisional Plenary Party. The Brigadier, General Kentish, gave a performance. He came around which was much appreciated. The O/C Battalion & Officers were told a the same day in his place. | |
| Do | 13/9/17 | | Training continued half reputing comp[any]. | |
| Do | 14/9/17 | | 2nd Bn. Sports there class was held. Nothing of importance to report. Proposed review postponed 48 hours | |
| Do | 15/9/17 | | Preparations for departure are being made | |
| LUMBRES | 16/9/17 | | Battalion paraded at 6.20 a.m. marched to LUMBRES along the BOULOGNE - LUMBRES ROAD. Proposed review was not completed. At 10 a.m. motor lorries reported 200 yards in the rear which drove to Battalion. Packs were conveyed by lorry. The Battalion arrived at about 9.45 a.m. feeling much fresher | |

**Army Form C. 2118.**

# WAR DIARY
## or
## INTELLIGENCE SUMMARY.
*(Erase heading not required.)*

Instructions regarding War Diaries and Intelligence Summaries are contained in F.S. Regs., Part II. and the Staff Manual respectively. Title pages will be prepared in manuscript.

| Place | Date | Hour | Summary of Events and Information | Remarks and references to Appendices |
|---|---|---|---|---|
| LUMBRES | 16/6/17 | | 9th R.G.C. 71st Infantry Brigade | |
| RENESCURE 17/7/17 | 17/7/17 | | March is continued to the RENESCURE AREA via ARQUES. The Battalion was the leading Battalion of Composite Brigade. The Battalion paraded at 2.10 a.m. and arrived in at 9 a.m. The march was a long one about 19 Kms. Packs were conveyed. Men and men completed before heat of the day set in. Battalion accommodated in billets ?? for the night. | |
| CAESTRE VII.d.6,4 Sh.27. | 18/7/17 | | Battalion paraded at 5.20 a.m. to proceed to CAESTRE AREA via STAPLE. The march was completed by 9.20 a.m. the Battalion was accommodated in a Bd. Pol camp at VII.d.6.4 Sheet 27 | |
| EECKE AREA | 19/7/17 | | Battalion paraded at 8.30 a.m. & proceed by shortest route to EECKE AREA and was accommodated in a camp at about P.24.a.5.2. (Sheet 27) Just off the CASSEL ROAD. Arrived in camp at 9.30 a.m. | |
| NIEPPE CAMP G.32.c.8.8 | 20/7/17 | | Battalion paraded at 5.30 a.m. & marched via GODEWAERSVELDE and BOESCHEPE to NIEPPE CAMP at G.32.c.8.8 Sheet 28, arriving about 9 a.m. Officers went up to reconnoitre the line | |

*[signature]*

# WAR DIARY
## or
## INTELLIGENCE SUMMARY

Army Form C. 2118.

| Place | Date | Hour | Summary of Events and Information | Remarks and references to Appendices |
|---|---|---|---|---|
| MICMAC CAMP. | 21/7/17 | | Battalion paraded at 6.20 a.m. & proceeded in full marching order to MICMAC CAMP. at about H.31.b.5.6. (shelter). arriving in camp about 9. a.m. | |
| MICMAC CAMP. | 22/7/17 | | Preparations made to take over the line in rear of the Ballahis faced to Ballahis 11th West Yorks Regt. at 7.30 proceeded by platoons to relieve the Suffolk Ballalan Trenches. Battalion H.Q. was situated at Seba Subway I.30.c.4.5.86. A Coy Rudkin House. B Coy CANADA HOUSE. C Coy SEBA SUBWAY. D Coy METROPOLITAN LEFT. To Relief about 120 proceeded at the same time to the Transport lines. Relief concluded at 10.30 p.m. without casualty. | |
| LINE | 23/7/17 | | Relief delayed owing to late shelling of approaches to Battalion Sector. enemy aircraft (planes) were numerous. During daylight hours only normal artillery activity. A Coy was brought up to SEBA SUBWAY as RUDKIN HOUSE was rendered untenable. | |
| " | 24/7/17 | | Early morning "D" Coy moved up from METROPOLITAN LEFT & relieved the front line Coy of 9 Royal Sussex on the Brigade front. This was completed without two casualties although shelling heavy. During the day artillery activity normal. It was impossible owing to hostile observation to reach the front Company by day, unless for any very urgent matter. | |

# WAR DIARY or INTELLIGENCE SUMMARY

Army Form C. 2118.

| Place | Date | Hour | Summary of Events and Information | Remarks and references to Appendices |
|---|---|---|---|---|
| Line | 25/7/17 | | Artillery (enemy) very active between 2.30 & 4.30 a.m. otherwise nothing unusual until about 11.0 a.m. when our heavies fairly busy & Boche replying. Slow shelling (drafts?) & shell bursting on left front post at B.30 & 5590 becoming faster & heavier towards evening. The posts consisting of NCO & 8 men. Several Gas Shells were sent over during the day & Gas alarms were consequently numerous, though no ill effects were found owing to the necessary precautions being taken. Patrols out at night and) rather little information, the ground being wet & being the night dark. | |
| | 26/9/17 26/7/17 | | Enemy artillery again very active in early hours. The day was normal up to 5.15 p.m. when our Artillery opened up & the Corps front enabling 7ᵗʰ a.m. on left to carry out mine activities which resulted in capture of 5 prisoners. Our late evening become unfortunately unable to send out a raiding party. The night was fairly quiet, until early morning again noisy. About 11.30 a.m. a large shell somewhat like a minnenwerfer from pieces found pierced the tunnel killing five men & passing about thirty. This caused a block in the narrow tunnels & caused considerable delay in different carrying parties. | |
| | 27/7/17 | | At 10 p.m. "A" Coy went into the line relieve D Coy carried out quickly + in air. about midnight a patrol under L. Stainforth went out consisting of 1 Officer + NCO H | |

# WAR DIARY
## or
## INTELLIGENCE SUMMARY

Army Form C. 2118.

| Place | Date | Hour | Summary of Events and Information | Remarks and references to Appendices |
|---|---|---|---|---|
| Line | 27/7/17 | | A hostile post reported at J.25.a.89.20. They were fired on & & dispersed. | |
| | 28/7/17 | 8.0 a.m. | Enemy fired at 8.0 a.m. | |
| | | 5.15 a.m. | Enemy practice barrage. This was apparently very satisfactory. | |
| | | | The day was normal until 10.0 p.m. the 2/5th was relieved by 1st Royal Fusiliers. Relief was completed by 12.0 midnight. The enemy's artillery was non active. 'C' Coy had several casualties, especially about I.26.c.70.30. PANARA CANAL. | |
| MICMAC | 29/7/17 | | The Bn arrived in camp about 8.0 a.m. tired after a strenuous 8 days tour. In all we had had 160 casualties. Day was spent in rest, reorganisation. The men rested as much as possible, as we had known of the forthcoming offensive. | |
| | 30/7/17 | | Position ECLUSE TRENCH I.32.a.50.30 during the evening. This reached about 120 officers. Training tactics at J.7.a.25.BUSCH. Artillery up. On critical barrage ration were drawn, one awaited the break of day & the opening of the offensive. ZERO being at 3.50 a.m. 9 officers, lunch & 1 at ZERO + 1 hour the Bn moved up to the position via a little 2 Royal Fusiliers in CANADA Tunnels. No casualties were sustained. Several wounded were met on the way from different Bn's of the Division two others only walked. Account of the attack could be given. | |
| ECLUSE | 31/7/17 | | The Bn lay dormant during the day. Only a few sketches Beavers working about J.9.74 | |

353. Wt. W.2544/4454 700,000 5/15 D. D. & L. A.D.S.S. Forms/C. 2118.

Army Form C. 2118.

# WAR DIARY
## or
## INTELLIGENCE SUMMARY.
(Erase heading not required.)

| Place | Date | Hour | Summary of Events and Information | Remarks and references to Appendices |
|---|---|---|---|---|
| Lux | 31.7.17 | | the tunnels. The heat was stifling in the tunnels and the odour most offensive. | 9.7.7 |

H.C. Malen Capt.
for Lieut Colonel
Commanding 8' Battn The Buffs

17/24
Vol 23

Secret and Confidential

War Diary

of

8th Battalion The Buffs.

Volume 24.

Month of August 1917.

# WAR DIARY
## or
## INTELLIGENCE SUMMARY.

Army Form C. 2118.

| Place | Date | Hour | Summary of Events and Information | Remarks and references to Appendices |
|---|---|---|---|---|
| Line | 1/8/17 | | Until 8.30 pm we remained in those tunnels and then moved up to the front line to relieve the 2nd Bn the Rifle Bde. Owing to unsuitable guides the new line combined with the darkness the relief was not an unqualified success. Several men being left through losing touch - these however reported to Battalion Headquarters in HEDGE ST TUNNELS later on. The line taken over ran from J2.5. 6.50. 20 both South of BODMIN COPSE being the position till morning before by the 1st Royal Fusiliers. It was gradually intended line not-being selected owing to very heavy opposition from shell especially machine gun and rifle fire. | |
| Line | 2/8/17 | | The front line was most uncomfortable especially where 'D' Coy was on the left. It consisted of a series of posts, in shell holes, linked by shallow trenches mostly half full of water. The day was fairly quiet. At night the remainder of 'D' R's Company mostly of 'C' Coy was sent up to relieve a Company of the 10th Royal Fusiliers who were slightly in rear of the front line Coys. A Coys front on the right was extended towards the | |

# WAR DIARY or INTELLIGENCE SUMMARY

Army Form C. 2118.

Instructions regarding War Diaries and Intelligence Summaries are contained in F.S. Regs., Part II. and the Staff Manual respectively. Title pages will be prepared in manuscript.

(Erase heading not required.)

| Place | Date | Hour | Summary of Events and Information | Remarks and references to Appendices |
|---|---|---|---|---|
| Line | 2/8/17 | | centre allowing some of the men of the Rifle Brigade to take back, who had played up to assist in holding the positions occupied. Communication throughout men was very difficult but 2nd Lt Rueston (S.O.) with three runners found all posts under trying conditions & established visual communication. Guns reported to be up by day | |
| Line | 3/8/17 | | Dribbling rain all day with heavy shelling at intervals especially between 2 and 3 AM. Apparently the Huns favourite hour. The neighbourhood was normal. A. & B. Coys were relieved to be relieved by the 9' Bn Royal Sussex and a most successful relief was completed by 11.0 pm. No casualties occurred during actual relief in spite of fair enemy artillery activity - though both the Sussex Bn & ours early on the way up too late actually through down with being Capt. Mansell slightly wounded by shrapnel in the legs. | |
| Micmac | 4/8/17 | | The Battalion reached camp fully about 7.0 am. The Coy being to leave the night before, some platoons having marched until daylight before completing the journey down. In the afternoon Baths were arranged by restora Battalion at DICKEBUSCH | |

# WAR DIARY or INTELLIGENCE SUMMARY

Army Form C. 2118.

| Place | Date | Hour | Summary of Events and Information | Remarks and references to Appendices |
|---|---|---|---|---|
| Meaulte | 5/8/17 | | The Battn. rested & reorganised in Camp. C. In the afternoon the men of the 12" showered fourteens (Power Bath) played to the Bn. 11. | |
| Ruhtuhed line | 6/8/17 7/9/17 | | We moved camp to Dickebusch & the following day we moved up into the line, relieving the 8" Rl. Welsh & 13" Inniskilling Fus. 7th Div. Front. the 8"Bn. Rl. W. Kents & 13" Inniskilling Batt. 5th Bgde. the Div. Front being held by one Bgde. instead of two. Batt. # H.Qs. were in Canada St Tunnels & the Battn. held the line from J.25.B. 30.40 Southwards to Klurian Drive J.25.C.80.10. C. Coy on left, Pt Healy, B Coy on Right. Capt Holloway, A in support - B in Reserve in Tunnels. The relief was incomplete very late — | |
| | 8/8/17 | | the night was too quiet suffering of knowing one way about to this area on a dark night. On the night M/8/9 the S.O.S. was put up by our left Coy, but no attack developed. | |
| | 9/8/17 | | In the night of the 8/9" the Bath were ordered to capture Lower Star Post, a Hun strong point, owing to the inclement | |

| Place | Date | Hour | Summary of Events and Information | Remarks and references to Appendices |
|---|---|---|---|---|
| Kui | 9/9/17 | | weather fine and Troops were out the following day. | |
| | 10/9/17 | | The attack was carried out at 4.35 AM by 47 O.R.s from B. Coy under the command of 2nd Lieut Powers. The party formed up at J.25-B.10.20 at 3.45 AM were subject to very heavy shelling whilst waiting for Zero. At Zero our Artillery Barrage opened & at Zero + 3 the majority of the guns lifted; one battery failed to lift until 12 minutes later; this cost us 12 casualties & greatly encouraged the party. However the party advanced under cut wire to the delay caused by some of the guns not lifting, the party found on arriving at position to be captured, that the enemy were already out of their Dug Outs waiting for them. By this time 2nd Lt Forbes & all the N.C.O.s except one were wounded. The remaining N.C.O. L/Cpl Simpson opened fire with his Lewis Gun | cont'd |

# WAR DIARY or INTELLIGENCE SUMMARY

Army Form C. 2118.

| Place | Date | Hour | Summary of Events and Information | Remarks and references to Appendices |
|---|---|---|---|---|
| line | 19/8/17 | | towards the men in charge. The Lewis gun jammed before the magazine could be fired & the enemy put up a very heavy barrage of rifle bombs. The party having up then two Lewis 2/3 of their men were unable to make any heading against the strong opposition put up by the enemy, & returned to our lines. The total casualties were 5 killed, 23 wounded & 3 missing. The party showed great courage & determination, & their failure was due to no want of keenness & their failure was due to no want of keenness to them. The Bosch was subjected to much heavy shelling during this tour & was considered the S.O.S. to be put up frequently, night remembering along the front. | Ralph |
| | 11/8/17 | | The Battn was relieved by the 2" Lancashires of the night 11/12". Three Coys were relieved easily, but the relief of the left Coy was not effected until after daybreak | |

# WAR DIARY
## INTELLIGENCE SUMMARY

Army Form C. 2118.

| Place | Date | Hour | Summary of Events and Information | Remarks and references to Appendices |
|---|---|---|---|---|
| Nieumacq | 12/8/17 | | The Bath. returned to camp at NieuMacq. and about getting clean & reorganising. Except for a few storms the weather was rather showery any way up. | |
| " | 13/8/17 | | | |
| " | 14/8/17 | | After 4 days in this camp we moved up into | |
| " | 15/8/17 | | our billets at Dickebusch. | |
| Dickebusch | 16/8/17 | | Bourgeois Farm at Dickebusch. On this day we played the Stewards Foresters (Nieuwe Batt) at cricket. The Stewards batted first & scored 38. The Batt. then went in & had 9 wickets down for 30, but the last wicket put on 8 runs so we won on a rather poor by 2 runs. About C.O.H. turned out & kept Roberts for the Stewards. The Stewards afterwards entertained the officers & men to tea & music. | |
| | | 16 – 20 | The four days spent here were uneventful. Except 1 on the 18th where a Tug of war & boxing contest took place between the Batt. & 2nd Leinsters, we easily came to the events. The same afternoon we played a return cricket match with the Stewards. The result this time being a tie, 74 runs all, after four opponents. | |

Army Form C. 2118.

# WAR DIARY
## or
## INTELLIGENCE SUMMARY.
(Erase heading not required.)

Instructions regarding War Diaries and Intelligence Summaries are contained in F.S. Regs., Part II. and the Staff Manual respectively. Title pages will be prepared in manuscript.

| Place | Date | Hour | Summary of Events and Information | Remarks and references to Appendices |
|---|---|---|---|---|
| Rebecourt | 18/9/17 | | Work & life being very normal. Having received 64 for five weeks. | |
| " | 19/9/17 | | On this date the C.O. Lt Col Stroud went on leave to England & Major J.C. Hartley, 12th R.F. took command in his absence. The Batt. moved up to the line in afternoon & took over from the 8th Queens in Lensh worn "Tunnels". D. Coy was attached to the 12th R.F. in Hedge St. Tunnels, & on the morning of the 22nd had to send up 1 Officer & 20 men to hold the line vacated by the 1st R.F. to prevent any such a stunt. The stunt was a great success. | |
| " | 22/9/17 | | The Coys had hard work spent most of their time in carrying & working parties. The Tunnels were overste than usual. The Batt. was relieved in the afternoon by the 9th Royal Sussex & returned to camp at McKay. | |
| Micha | 23/9/17 | 10-25 | The next four days were spent - the usual manner often a tour - the Trenches. Reorganising & training. | Refs |

Army Form C. 2118.

# WAR DIARY
## or
## INTELLIGENCE SUMMARY.
(Erase heading not required.)

| Place | Date | Hour | Summary of Events and Information | Remarks and references to Appendices |
|---|---|---|---|---|
| Merkhe | 26/8/17 | | We had an afternoon Spell in the M. played the 1/RB at Soccer and fortcame off the excellent game by 2 goals to 1 nil. The Battalion (less field & Coy & one side the Lewis M.G. Section) and 2 H. Coys. went to Excellent Trenches. | |
| Stokowel | 27/8/17 | | Bat moved up into Divisional Support and relieves M.G. E Sunrays at Camp K | |
| " | 27.31 | | We stayed in Camp K until the evening of the 31st. nothing of particular interest happened | |
| Lui | 31/8/17 | | On the evening of the 31st we moved up into the Front line, being on the Right Sector. The front line was held by A Coy. Capt Stanforth in command and their position was in Stakhaba in front of Jekrak Trench | i.i.i.m |

F.W. Tomkin Lieut Colonel
Commanding 8/18th The Buffs

№ 24

Fol. No. 25.

Stock and Cash Returns
of the District
-OF-
BALLINA
8TH

Month of September 1917

# WAR DIARY
## or
## INTELLIGENCE SUMMARY

Army Form C. 2118.

(Erase heading not required.)

| Place | Date | Hour | Summary of Events and Information | Remarks and references to Appendices |
|---|---|---|---|---|
| Ins | 1/9/17 | | The Bn. two [?] platoons fell further back. On the night of the 2nd we were relieved by the 6th Bedfords in and support line & Chiswick & Reserve line. | |
| Line | 2/9/17 | | The relief was rather humorous, as both the Reserve & Chaplain's arrived at almost the same time to take over our Batt. H.Qrs. & signals etc. The Chaplain won. | |
| Westoutre | 3rd | | The Bn. H.Q. got out well were conveyed by lorries to a camp at Westoutre for the night, & the following afternoon marched back to ids a la Camp, 1 east of Mic Mac. Owing to the clear sky moonlight nights the Bosche has become particularly effective with his bombs from aeroplanes, & the batteries in consequence very persistent with 3 alarms — the whistles & LIGHTS OUT THERE — the C.O. returned from leave on the 2/9/17. | |
| MICMAC | 4th | | A quiet day spent in training, advantage taken of having the range & assault course which was close at hand. The war games of Football – Badminton etc were played in the afternoon. We then were again busy at night fortunately no bombs were dropped in our city. | [signature] |

**Army Form C. 2118.**

# WAR DIARY
## or
## INTELLIGENCE SUMMARY.
*(Erase heading not required.)*

| Place | Date | Hour | Summary of Events and Information | Remarks and references to Appendices |
|---|---|---|---|---|
| Michem | 5th | | The day passed much as the preceding one; though rain at intervals somewhat interfered with the proposed course of P.T. training. | |
| " | 6th | | Rain in early morning. Usual training programme carried out. 2/Lieut B.T. Young & E. Taylor left to join 1/2/5 Bucks. The night was not disturbed by aeroplanes as by the cries of the people who stood all dressed up & one place to go (England in Cave) fell in a trench full of water. Otherwise uneventful. | |
| Dickebusch | 7th | | P.T. training in morning. At 3.30 pm [parade] former Funeral Camp at DICKEBUSCH which was found much shattered by enemy protection bomb. Huts etc - a precaution apart bombs & such, but not very low together. | |
| " | 8th | | Morning spent in Coy training. In the afternoon Lr Coy Cricket Matches were played; shell also seen in miniature intensive use terrseen was trying. Aeroplanes from E/Aircraft going high into ? Seasonal training carried out 9th afternoon. further Cricket games. | |
| " | 9th | | Late in the evening [words] was some super played. The usual visits from E.A. showed little day might - no damage done. Fought our own A.A. Aircraft was ? (all day) by our own A.A. Aircraft | JVH |

# WAR DIARY
## or
## INTELLIGENCE SUMMARY

Army Form C. 2118.

(Erase heading not required.)

Instructions regarding War Diaries and Intelligence Summaries are contained in F. S. Regs., Part II. and the Staff Manual respectively. Title pages will be prepared in manuscript.

| Place | Date | Hour | Summary of Events and Information | Remarks and references to Appendices |
|---|---|---|---|---|
| Dickebusch | 10 | | Training was interfered with by baths occupying a great deal of the morning. Otherwise usual programme carried out. In the afternoon the Officers v Sergeants played another cricket match which was won by the Officers (who scored about 110 against the Sergeants 49. The Colonel made 39 in capital good form. | |
| Line | 11 | | Morning spent in preparation for relieving the line. We relieved the 8th Bn Queens in a new part to us (our front stretching from just S of Clapham Junction to Ravine Wood). The relief was carried out quickly - but there were casualties on the way up. Two men being killed & one wounded. 2/Lieut Cooper & R.S.M. Dare were both hit & shaken over down temporarily. | |
| Line | 12 | | A quiet time. The Boosh being chiefly active on back areas. Unfortunately hostile artillery caught one working party as they were coming several minor casualties, & one fatal. 2/Lieut Moore being one of the former. Hopl Bosul & P/S Gaskin showed great coolness & bravery for which they were afterwards awarded the military medal. The front line had a quiet time (C&D) but A in reserve was kept very busy with carrying parties - especially those forming dumps for the incoming B.de. | |
| Line | 13 | | The Bosch was no more active than usual, though our own activity increased. Two trench barrages were carried out one in the morning & one in the afternoon. The objectives good & the retaliating barrage not what we had been expecting. During the two RAH |  |

2353 Wt. W3441/1454 700,000 5/15 D. D. & L. A.D.S.S. Forms/C. 2118.

# WAR DIARY or INTELLIGENCE SUMMARY

Army Form C. 2118.

| Place | Date | Hour | Summary of Events and Information | Remarks and references to Appendices |
|---|---|---|---|---|
| Line | 13 | | We were busy in showing officers from relieving Bde round the front & finding accommodation for them. Then parties in the trenches of Hd.Qrs. etc. Two Brigades were carrying on in front of us. Statement of casualties of officers & men. Difficulty in approaching target, partly by day & the darkness of the night. It prevented these sources of parties from obtaining all the information they wanted. The success of the 2 previous outbreaks had stopped at any rate some hostile houses. | |
| Line | 14 | | The day was spent in comparative quiet for NCOs but carrying work was still continuing. Small parties leaving long journeys to & from loads & carry. Not attempt to report enemies with the 9 Yorks, our Bn - the relieving Bn, came up & in the afternoon advanced parties of the 9 Yorks. | |
| Line | 15 | 10.45 pm | The 18th relief was reported complete & we marched down to Cafe independently to DICKEBUSCH through B's old camp. Major F.W. SNEPP of the Norfolk Regt. joined us this day as Acting 2nd in Command. | |
| DICKEBUSCH | 15/16 | | Slept on the night of the 15-16 was curtailed somewhat as the Bn had to parade for entraining at 7.0 a.m. A bright fine morning & men did not look too worn out probably leaving the Salient. The entraining was carried out in conjunction with the rest of the Bde by 10.30 a.m. The Bn reached OUTTERSHENE 3 miles beyond POPERING where they were billeted & the party which had gone on in advance. | 9.94 |

**Army Form C. 2118.**

# WAR DIARY
## or
## INTELLIGENCE SUMMARY.
*(Erase heading not required.)*

Instructions regarding War Diaries and Intelligence Summaries are contained in F. S. Regs., Part II. and the Staff Manual respectively. Title pages will be prepared in manuscript.

| Place | Date | Hour | Summary of Events and Information | Remarks and references to Appendices |
|---|---|---|---|---|
| OUTERSTEENE | 16 | | The day which was quite fine was spent in recuperation, no parades having been ordered. | |
| " | 17 | | The Coys were rather scattered, work was carried out under their own arrangements in the morning. There were good sports arrangements in the afternoon. The Battalion was invited the 12 R.F. when we put [?] of an excellent game - late in the evening on the Brigade HQrs Ground a Brigade contest was staged in which we were first beat 17 in tug of war by the 3rd R.Bs though to our [?] we [?] to us did not know the rules. A large cheaf [?] was in the evening. | |
| " | 18 | | The staff about 75 O.R. was inspected by the Colonel at 11.00 a.m. One of the last drafts we have had lately all [?] of Stone Dragshire having been in the country before. The same programme of sport was carried on as on the 17th. A games were again prominent in the afternoon. The GOC Division ordered me to soccer played with a [?] ball when not employed in the cave. | |
| " | 19 | | At 9.20 a.m. we were inspected by the new G.O.C. Division, Maj Gen'l A.C. Daly, the 17 LTMB paraded at 1.0 - after the inspection the 73 [?] request then proceeded to various training areas in many cases as officers that we The Division was found [?] in many ways the officer work. GAM | |

# WAR DIARY or INTELLIGENCE SUMMARY

Army Form C. 2118.

| Place | Date | Hour | Summary of Events and Information | Remarks and references to Appendices |
|---|---|---|---|---|
| OUDEZEELE | 20 | | Came across several characters mentioned in a book on this war the author of which is probably Locke, known to him through — especially in the 73rd 9th Div.  Everyone was busy Monday with preparations for the move on the following day, which was to be by rail. However the daily programme was carried out including transport on w as to do to by rail. However the daily provisions was carried out including Capt. Cameron as Bulcol. The officers greatly owing to the efforts of Capt. Newall, did our things they were, defeated the toy soldiers Nov 7/8. | |
| | 21 | | The B.P. paraded at 8.45 a.m. marched to BAILLEUL – the transport having gone on wheels. Pq. 10.45 a.m. hardly entrained + at 11.15 westwards to BAPAUME where we arrived after a surprisingly continuous journey about 8.0 p.m. We were told there was then a five mile march which we did. When found that our destination was seven miles further on – it was. The P.O. was reported present in camp about 1.0 a.m. | |
| YPRES | 22 | | When we arose strong flares repeatedly opened over us and above. We found YPRES to be the remains of a pretty little village ruined by explosions not by shells though these had been some of those. The Boche had severely destroyed billets + present on using them. The enemy and wounded were shelled at this place. Good canteens for all. Accommodation too was plentiful. | |

# WAR DIARY or INTELLIGENCE SUMMARY

Army Form C. 2118.

| Place | Date | Hour | Summary of Events and Information | Remarks and references to Appendices |
|---|---|---|---|---|
| Map 62C YPRES | 22 | | The morning was spent by coys in finding places to parade such as ranges which even found to be plentiful. Full use was taken of them. Excellent spots from which evidence views of Hazels. | |
| YPRES | 23 | | Sunday Church parade at 11.0 & a day of rest. Some of us drove to visit scenes too well known — GUILLEMONT – DEVILLE WOOD at the change in these was naturally very noticeable. Several of our officers who fell there from this B⁄n were found. The work on these generally was very good. | |
| " | 24 | | The full programme of work mapped out was unfortunately interfered with carried out owing to working parties having (the tools) but what could be done was carried on. The news that 2/Lt R.N. Hickling had been accidentally killed was received. He was known by a number to Larry near POPERINGHE and was unconscious. | |
| " | 25 | | The B⁄n had further allotted to them the running which included 7½ drill, P.T. being carried The training programme, which included 7½ drill, P.T. being carried at. Funeral was accordingly made of the range. In the afternoon the usual sequence of games took place. | |

J.V.A.

# WAR DIARY or INTELLIGENCE SUMMARY

Army Form C. 2118.

| Place | Date | Hour | Summary of Events and Information | Remarks and references to Appendices |
|---|---|---|---|---|
| Map 62.C YPRES | 26 | | A full morning programme carried out in Camp. In the afternoon several officers went to the hospitality of the 7th R.F. at their ALUA DA sports. An excellent programme was thoroughly enjoyed. Our tug of war team was beaten in the semifinal after being beaten by the 1st R.F. team who beat the 12th Gloucesters in the final. Another event in which we entered was the Officers Mounted Relay Race, also won by the 1st R.F. It was well placed, the infantry diopped the Army Root a party? (Sgt.Griffiths Maj) 94 O.R. proceeded to the Army Rest Camp for a fortnight – excellent idea. | |
| HAUTALAINES | 27 | | A full parade in marching order at 8.0 a.m. At 8.15 a.m. we formed the Bde Column and marched through MOISLAINS & HAUTALAINES arriving here about 10.0 a.m. Shortly the two above mentioned places the G.O.C. 2nd Div. and the Bde met. The Bugade with Coys at 200 yds Interval marched past. The whole Bde was accommodated in a large camp with Officers in huts. | |
| | 28 | | Coy parades in the morning. In the afternoon parade of Football preparation for the Brigadier's inspection of Bde Machine Gunnes which J.H.M. | |

# WAR DIARY
## or
## INTELLIGENCE SUMMARY

Army Form C. 2118.

| Place | Date | Hour | Summary of Events and Information | Remarks and references to Appendices |
|---|---|---|---|---|
| HAUT ALLAINES | 28 | | took place at 5.0 pm. The parade was not too well disciplined to render production of the Regt being the chief source of complaint. The usual foot ball with Reg'tl Band playing was a great sight. I hope went to the above mentioned Sunday, the second to our Cooks for their cleanliness!! | |
| HERVILLY | 29. | | At 8 am the Battalion less ½ Lewis Gun Transport etc proceeded by road to HAUT ALLAINES for HERVILLY about 9 Kilometres distant. The village is a mere hamlet to YTRES. Huts were built of aerodrome. At 2 pm an advance party was sent up to take over with the Indian Divisional Cavalry from whom we were to take over the line. | |
| LINE | 30 | | Companies moved up to take over the line from the Divisional Cavalry Brigade, relief being finished at VENDELLES at 7.30pm. Throughout the relief an was the Left Section drawn at A 2 D 2 relief the Trench being on our right our section remained the relieving section being told by the 3rd Rifle Bde. while W.R's own left in B 2 Subsection was the 10th York Staffs | 9375 |

# WAR DIARY
## INTELLIGENCE SUMMARY.

| Place | Date | Hour | Summary of Events and Information | Remarks and references to Appendices |
|---|---|---|---|---|
| LINE | 30 | | The relief was quickly effected. Our posts ran from DEAN COPSE R5G.0.2 to RED WOOD (exclusive) G.29 Central, and held by an 2 Company. R.h.Rgh - B. a h. Left, the boundary between the companies being ASCENSION FARM. William Av. Rigtiby. C Coy relieved the huts billeting in Dean Trench and D Coy the 12 "Row" in the Reserve. Battalion HQ is at R.u.d.3.1. (Stul6.c) The Coy Comdt spare the above - prevailing unusual wheneven | 94 |

F.W. McLure Lieut Colonel
Commanding 8" Battalion The Buffs

Secret and Confidential

War Diary

of

8th Battalion The Buffs

Month of October 1917

Volume 26

Vol 25

£25.

J.C. Hulward Lieut Colonel
8/Buffs
Commanding 1/11/17

# WAR DIARY
## INTELLIGENCE SUMMARY

| Place | Date | Hour | Summary of Events and Information | Remarks and references to Appendices |
|---|---|---|---|---|
| LINE | 1/3/17 | | The front taken over by the Bn. stretches from L.24.c.5.2 to L.31.c.6.6 (NAROY Est'd) & was held by A Coy on right with 4 posts in the line & 5 posts in the line & B Coy on Left with 4 posts. These are ad[vanced] posts & an entrenched line of work is being done to link them up. C Coy in Right Support in ST ANN TRENCH Sec J.20.d.9 D Coy in North St Est village. Standing patrols which had been out all night & reliefs returned at dawn with nothing to report. Active patrolling impossible owing to bright moonlight. Work by day most advisable except in certain parts of the line in parts of the Support. At night C & D Coys provided working parties to A & B Coys to assist in wiring and making shelters for front posts which are badly needed. The same parties from Support Coys went out & returned at dawn but had nothing to report. | (NAROY Est'd) |
| " | 2/3/17 | | Front our S.I. from RF Bn front which afterwards transferred Shore had a devoted emscauth the 5th R.B. hd with the Borders. Enemy artillery activity gradually ..., two aeroplanes were seen otherwise the day was very quiet. At night the working parties were continued & the patrol. ordered to go out as before shortly before dusk the prophet Ga darken up it having evident the programme was altered. To fighting patrol went out from both Coys fronts. The coy of Patrol (Lt.) in front of Angle Bank up to 2d centre (Pt) | |

# WAR DIARY
## or
## INTELLIGENCE SUMMARY

Army Form C. 2118.

| Place | Date | Hour | Summary of Events and Information | Remarks and references to Appendices |
|---|---|---|---|---|
| LINE | 2/8/17 | | and the left from ASCENSION WOOD round BIG & LITTLE BILL - Hawkesley patrol was out as usual - They returned about 5.0 a.m. but had no news of anything hostile. | |
| " | 3/8/17 | | About 7.30 a.m. five shells fell near were killed & one wounded. Except for a few shells we on left front the enemy's artillery was quite inactive on our front during the rest of the day. A similar programme to that of preceding night was carried out wh patrols & MGs - but no better results obtained with the formation on previous night. | |
| | 4/8/17 | | Quiet Day. Scouting patrol at ascough Court at 1 a.m. returning at 3 a.m. with nothing to report, no enemy movement being noticed. A patrol of 1/Royal W. Surreys OR went out from L.30 a. 26. 20 at PP in returning about dusk along Sussex Road to SE corner of Ascension Road thence to Q 26 a central to SE corner of the enemy wire in Big Bill area. Nothing was seen. No lights were fired. There was a sharp thaw. | |

JMJ

# WAR DIARY
## or
## INTELLIGENCE SUMMARY.
*(Erase heading not required.)*

Army Form C. 2118.

| Place | Date | Hour | Summary of Events and Information | Remarks and references to Appendices |
|---|---|---|---|---|
| LINE | 5.X.17 | | Occasional shelling of the VERQUIER during the morning. Patrol went out from MOLLY post at 7pm & 2 officers & 20 OR to enemy wire. Patrol returned by same point 6.15. about midnight. | |
| LINE | 6.X.17 | | Another Quiet Day. Patrol 2 off. & 20 OR went out from GRAHAM POST at 11.30 pm along SUNKEN ROAD to G.26.a.01.20 then along Eastern Edge of ACHEVILLE WOOD to G.20. G.60.00 to discover Enemy movements or working parties. Nothing was seen. Enemy Trenches 1.30am slightly heard carrying on independent fire G.20.90. & between HULLS SANDER and the railway. Thoroughly of keen Line Broke. Day was usually the usual themumn shells enemy activity. The Battalion was relieved by the 1st Reg. Brochen. The Relief was complete about 11 pm. Nothing to report. | See attached Relief Order |

# WAR DIARY
## or
## INTELLIGENCE SUMMARY

Army Form C. 2118.

| Place | Date | Hour | Summary of Events and Information | Remarks and references to Appendices |
|---|---|---|---|---|
| BERNES | 9.X.17 | | The Battalion was accommodated in huts at BERNES in Divisional Reserve. Rest of the day was spent in cleaning up kit & inspections. The heavy rain during daylight still prevailing was taking place usually two of the men being wet through was a very muddy condition. Training programme was issued & confirmed. | |
| BERNES | 9.X.17 | | Training commenced at 8 & continued until 12.30 p.m. From 2 to 4 pm in the afternoon. A number of aeroplanes including the trophy of the enemy's transport were tests away a considerable amount. | |
| BERNES | 10.X.17 | | Baths were arranged for the Battalion but the Brigade Officer's Bath at the D.R.S. was used at HANCOURT. The idea was that scheme was carried out here. The Sunday was repaired & has been refitting towards the HINDENBURG LINE. The 20'th Division was on fatigue duty to keep in touch with the retiring enemy. The Special idea issued in the general was to take a form held by the enemy into the fore. Two Companies attacked, this was in Reserve. | |
| BERNES | 11.X.17 | | The scheme was carried also again & the plenary day to Illuminate the faults made the previous day. Aux from was attached as to an object of Scheme was carried across enemy and a number of plans to graspers. | |

# WAR DIARY or INTELLIGENCE SUMMARY

Army Form C. 2118.

| Place | Date | Hour | Summary of Events and Information | Remarks and references to Appendices |
|---|---|---|---|---|
| BERMES | 12/10/17 | | The rifle range was used by 'C' Coy in the morning & in the afternoon at O.C.'s A.D.Q. A new scheme in inaugurated for Inter Coy Rivalry (Coy) Lts/Sgts Mess & Sanitary Rooms. Visited the various Coy lines and reviewed per officer branch of the Battalion in Billets. | |
| BERMES | 13/10/17 | | Training Programme carried out. Western Railway P.T. & Squad Drill, Bayonet Fighting. | |
| BERMES | 14/10/17 | | Church parade in the morning. 2nd & 6th Coys played at HOLN in the evening. Whirlpool. | |
| LINE | 15.x.17 | | Entraining a Berge 6.30 morning. Detrained Braid & in turn for Rest Point midday. 5/6 Regent marched to/for Beaumont Battn going to field. Sea Marrons to 11. | |
| LINE | 16.x.17 | | School of Instruction. Standing Patrol at Drunken Road G.25.b 0.10. ANGLE BANK Standing Patrol Annual 10.45 a.m. Observer good all day. Standing Patrols at ASCENSION WOOD and ANGLE BANK. Attachment of the Brigade front line page. The Battalion front Left CR A2 Int Battn Inter was from No 5 Post (ASCENSION FARM) to No 9 Post divided into two Sectors. No 2 Sector inclusive. | |

2353 Wt. W 2544/1454 700,000 5/15 D.D.&L. A.D.S.S./Forms/C.2118.

Army Form C. 2118.

# WAR DIARY
## or
## INTELLIGENCE SUMMARY.
(Erase heading not required.)

Instructions regarding War Diaries and Intelligence Summaries are contained in F. S. Regs., Part II. and the Staff Manual respectively. Title pages will be prepared in manuscript.

| Place | Date | Hour | Summary of Events and Information | Remarks and references to Appendices |
|---|---|---|---|---|
| LINE | 17.XII.17 | | Of~~ ~~3~~ Sector~~ Comprised PPIEL FARM POSTS Nos 3, S1, 1, 2, 4, S2, + 5. Of these only 3 + S1 are approachable in daylight, there being a stationar trench to them. All lie above ground on the forward slope. The exact O.C. Coy in each Sector + section etc. team etc had their own The ANGLE BANK Patrol would to be furnished by this Batt's Staff + signal system. | |
| | | | A Patrol of 1 Officer (2/Lt. ———) + 6 O.R. (2/Lt Halliday %c) proceeded to ASCENSION WOOD at 4 a.m. + remained there all day. Their mission was to search ASCENSION WOOD + watch all movement near BIG BILL. ASCENSION WOOD shewed no signs of recent enemy occupation. Two BOCHES were seen to approach BIG BILL at 5.30 a.m. – much enemy movement at stated points was observed. Patrol rendered a very full + interesting report on returning. | |
| | | | A Patrol on BUISSON RIDGE encountered no enemy. | |
| | | | Enemy artily + artillery activity pretty in excess of normal. E.A. continually sniped by our A.A. G's 8 + GRAHAM POSTS were whizzbanged. From 9 a.m. to 3 p.m. 4.2 s + 5.9 s were fired at JEB + GEORGE. No casualties. Trenches were damaged somewhat. | |
| | | | M.G. fire very active. "I STAND TO" nothing + all very. | |
| LINE | 18.XII.17 | | | |

# WAR DIARY or INTELLIGENCE SUMMARY

Army Form C.2118.

| Place | Date | Hour | Summary of Events and Information | Remarks and references to Appendices |
|---|---|---|---|---|
| LINE | 19.X.17 | | Standing Patrol at ASCENSION WOOD as usual. Fighting Patrol of 1 Off. & 20 O.R. out from 2 a.m. — 4 a.m. without encountering enemy. The Colonel inspected the site from then Bar-Byang Road at MILL SPINNEY. The site in question was being cleared & was had been dumped there. No timber had as yet been obtained & the work was held up on this account. The D.A.A. Q.M.G. accompanied by Capt. CAMPBELL visited Bn. HQ. at 12.30 p.m. Standing Patrol in ASCENSION WOOD under Lt. MARTIN saw no movement near BIG BILL. Enemy casual & artillery activity about N.K. A ration dump on the SUNKEN ROAD at L.34.a.80.70 held a man of ?Coy. This road is under observation in clear weather. | |
| LINE | 20.X.17 | | Standing Patrol at ASCENSION WOOD as usual. A fighting Patrol of 1 Officer & 20 O.R. (2/Lt Hammer) proceeded to a point near S.E. Corner of BIG BILL. Enemy hard in S.E. Corner of BIG BILL & ... ... of 2 men ... about G.26.a.75.60. Our patrol ... leading East from G.26.a to Tortoise Wood in G.26.b. The BUISSON RIDGE Patrol proceeded along track to G.19.b–9.9. found their own track & lying ammn. track. Movement was heard in front but no enemy seen. | |

# WAR DIARY
## or
## INTELLIGENCE SUMMARY.

Army Form C. 2118.

| Place | Date | Hour | Summary of Events and Information | Remarks and references to Appendices |
|---|---|---|---|---|
| LINE | 21.X.17 | | Shell bearing taken from shell holes, the enemy battery shelling GRAND PRIEL FARM, fired from direction of NAUROY. ASCENSION FARM & N°3 Sector feat. intly. barraged during evening. 4.2's were also fired at N°1 & 2 Sector posts. A Bosche Balloon was up all day on a bearing of 58° true from N° 6 Post. | |
| LINE | 22.X.17 | | Standing Patrol posted at ASCENSION WOOD at 6.15 p.m. observed a party of 40-50 Bosches approaching, & withdrew via SUNKEN ROAD to inform O.C. Coy. After ASCENSION WOOD had been shelled by our artillery, our fighting patrol (2/Lt Halliday & 45 O.R.) went out & searched neighbourhood of wood, but found no trace of enemy. After posting a Strong Standing Patrol at N.E. corner of ASCENSION WOOD, Lt. Halliday returned to G.2.c.4.0. without encountering Bosches. Enemy artillery inactive. | See O.O. No 8 |
| LINE | 23.X.17 | | Battn was relieved by 12 R.F. in the evening & proceeded to VADENCOURT — with exception of A. Coy which remained at LE VERGUIER, — being in Bryde Reserve. Relief was completed 9 p.m. | See R.O. No 8 |

Army Form C. 2118.

# WAR DIARY
## or
## INTELLIGENCE SUMMARY.
(Erase heading not required.)

Instructions regarding War Diaries and Intelligence Summaries are contained in F. S. Regs., Part II. and the Staff Manual respectively. Title pages will be prepared in manuscript.

| Place | Date | Hour | Summary of Events and Information | Remarks and references to Appendices |
|---|---|---|---|---|
| VADENCOURT | 24.X.17 | | Day spent in cleaning up + inspecting of kits, equipment, ammunition etc | |
| " | 25.X.17 | | Nothing beyond work up to both Bns in line. | |
| " | 26.X.17 | | An Officers Class formed & puts in 2 hours daily under 2/Lt Pemberton, assisted by 2/Lt L. May | |
| " | 27.X.17 | | The Rifle Bomb firers was reorganised by Capt Hornshaw + the T.O. | |
| " | 28.X.17 | | Trip to LE VERGUIER visited. | |
| " | 29.X.17 | | Enemy aircraft fairly active. He strafed A.A. + our own support them repeatedly. It was noted that a large proportion of enemy A.A. shells are duds. | |
| " | 30.X.17 | | | |
| " | 31.X.17 | | Battalion relieved the 1st R Sussex in the Attlebulst according to attacks orders. The 12 Roy Sussex came into Bde Reserve at VADENCOURT in relief of this Battalion Relief was complete by 7.30 p.m. | See O.O.19. |

K.M.... Lut Colonel
Commanding 9th Bn Buffs

RELIEF ORDERS.
by
Lieut-Colonel F.S.R. Studd,
Commanding 8th Battalion THE BUFFS.

8th OCTOBER 1917.

1. The 8th Battalion THE BUFFS will be relieved by the 1st Battalion ROYAL FUSILIERS on the night 7/8th OCTOBER.

2. A.B.C.&D.Coys. 8th Battalion The Buffs will be relieved by C.D.A.&B. Coys. of the 1st Battalion Royal Fusiliers respectively.

3. Three guides per Company will be at Battalion Headquarters at 6.45 p.m. on the 7th Instant.

4. When relieved, Companies will move to SERRES independently where the Battalion will be in Divisional Reserve.

5. (a) All Trench Stores, Maps, Aeroplane photographs etc., will be carefully handed over and receipts obtained. These to be forwarded to Battalion Headquarters by 12. noon the 8th Instant.

   (b) All points of tactical importance in the line and Front of it must be clearly pointed out.

6. The Transport Officer will arrange for the necessary Transport for Lewis Guns, valises, mess gear, blankets in bundles of ten, etc, to be at Company Headquarters at the following times C & D. 7.30 p.m. A. & B. at 8 p.m. and at Battalion Headquarters at 7 and 8.30 p.m.

7. Completion of Relief will be wired to Battalion Headquarters by the Code word "FISH."

J.F.Hitchcock
Captain & A/Adjutant,
8th Battn. THE BUFFS.

Copy No. 1. To:- C.O.
        2.     1st Battn. Royal Fusiliers.
        3.     O.C. A.Coy.,
        4.     O.C. B.Coy.,
        5.     O.C. C.Coy.,
        6.     O.C. D.Coy.,
        7.     O.C. Details.
        8.     T.O.
        9.     Q.M.
       10.     I.O.
       11.     M.O.
       12.     War Diary.

RELIEF ORDERS.

by

Lieut.- Colonel F.C.R.Studd.

Commanding 8th. Battalion THE BUFFS.

Field. No.11.                                                                14.10.17.

1. The Battalion will relieve the 1st. Battalion ROYAL FUSILIERS in the A.2 Sub Sector to-morrow night the 15th. inst.

2. Dispositions of Companies will be as follows in the Left Sub Sector.
   C.Coy. Right Front        will relieve C.Coy. 1st. ROYAL FUSILIERS.
   D.Coy. Left Front.           "      "  D.Coy.       "        "
   A.Coy. Right Support         "      "  A.Coy.       "        "
   B.Coy. Left Support          "      "  B.Coy.       "        "

3. Three guides per Company will be at Battalion Headquarters at 6.30 p.m. the 15th. inst.

4. All movement E of VENDELLES will be by platoons at 200 yards interval.

5. A. & B.Companies will each send up 1 Officer and 10 O.Rs. to report at Left Battalion Headquarters at 6 p.m. the 14th. inst. to go on patrol to-night with the 1st. ROYAL FUSILIERS. The greatest care will be taken to gain any new information re 'No Man's Land'.

6. Companies will move off at 10 minutes interval in the following order :- Headquarters, D., C., A. & B.Companies. The first Coy. moving off at 4.30 p.m.

7. All trench stores, aeroplane photos, tables of work in hand and proposed, defence schemes and other documents will be carefully taken over and accurate lists forwarded to this office by 10 a.m. the 16th. inst.

8. All Company Stores, Lewis Guns, Valises, Tins of Water, etc., will be ready for loading outside respective Company Headquarters by 4.0 p.m. 1 Limber will be at the disposal of each Company and will accompany it to the line.

9. Completion of relief will be wired to Headquarters by using the Code Words - 'CHARLIE CHAPLIN'.

Captain,

A/Adjutant 8th. Battalion THE BUFFS.

RELIEF ORDERS.
by
Lieut.-Colonel F.J.R.Studd.
Commanding 8th. Battalion THE BUFFS.

Field.
No.8.
Copy No. 13

22.10.17.

1. The Battalion will be relieved by the 1st. Battalion ROYAL FUSILIERS in the A.2 Sub Section to-morrow evening the 23rd. inst. and be in Brigade Reserve at VADENCOURT. excepting A Coy remaining at LE VERGUIER

2. Companies will be relieved as under :-
   C.Coy., 8th. Buffs. Right Front Coy. by C.Coy., 1st. Bn. Royal Fusiliers.
   B.  "     "     "    Left    "    "   "  B.  "     "     "     "     "
   A.  "     "     "    Right Support  "   "  A.  "     "     "     "     "
   D.  "     "     "    Left           "   "  D.  "     "     "     "     "

3. Each Company will provide 2 guides to be at Battalion Headquarters at 3.0 p.m. Relieving Companies will come up in the following order at 10 minutes interval, C., B., D., Headquarters, the first Company moving off at 5 p.m. The Right Support Company will be relieved under arrangements to be made between the Cs.O. Companies concerned.

4. Great care will be taken in handing over all new information gained respecting 'NO MAN'S LAND'. All trench stores, work in hand and proposed, maps, aeroplane photographs, log books, details of working parties, etc. will be handed over. A carefully checked list of all stores handed over will be forwarded to this office by 9.0 a.m. the 24th. inst.

5. Lewis guns, Company stores and valices will be ready for loading at various Company dumps by 3 p.m., blankets rolled in tens by 7 p.m. The T.O. will arrange to collect these with the exception of A.Coy., remaining at LE VERGUIER, and deliver them at VADENCOURT. One limber will report at Battalion Headquarters at 6.30 p.m. and one at 9 p.m. to collect stores and Mess gear. The Maltese Cart will report at the Aid Post at 7 p.m.

6. The Quartermaster will arrange to take over billets at VADENCOURT from 1st. Battalion ROYAL FUSILIERS. Company R.M.Sgts. will meet their respective Companies and show them to their billets. All guards will be found by details for 24 hours under arrangements to be made by 2/Lieut. L.A. LeMay.

7. Completion of relief will be reported to Battalion Headquarters by using the code word 'CABBAGES'.

H.C. Morley
Captain,
A/Adjutant 8th. Battalion THE BUFFS.

Copy No. 1 to The Commanding Officer.
  "    "  2  "  O.C., 1st. ROYAL FUSILIERS.
  "    "  3  "  Second in Command.
  "    "  4  "  O.C., A.Coy.
  "    "  5  "    "   B.Coy.
  "    "  6  "    "   C.Coy.
  "    "  7  "    "   D.Coy.
  "    "  8  "  Transport Officer.
  "    "  9  "  Quartermaster.
  "    " 10  "  Intelligence Officer.
  "    " 11  "  Signal Officer.
  "    " 12  "  Medical Officer.
  "    " 13  "  War Diary.
  "    " 14  "  Office.

RELIEF ORDERS.
by
Lieut.- Colonel F.G.R. Studd.
Field. Commanding 8th. Battalion THE BUFFS.
No.9.  ----oo---ooo----ooo----ooo---oo----           30.10.17.
Copy No. 14

1. The Battalion will relieve the 1st. Battalion ROYAL FUSILIERS in the A.2. Sub Sector to-morrow evening the 31st. inst.

2. A.Coy., 8th. Buffs will relieve C.Coy., 1st. Royal Fusiliers.(Right Front)
   B.  "     "    "    "    "    "   B. "      "       "      (Left Front)
   C.  "     "    "    "    "    "   A. "      "       "      (Right Support)
   D.  "     "    "    "    "    "   D. "      "       "      (Left Support)

3. Three guides per Company will be at Battalion Headquarters, 1st. ROYAL FUSILIERS at 5.0 p.m.

4. All movement will be by platoons at 200 yards interval.

5. The following limbers will be required to collect Lewis Guns, blankets in rolls of ten, valises, etc. at 4.0 p.m. outside respective Headquarters :-
   Two each for Headquarters, A., B., C. and D.Companies.

6. All trench stores, work in hand and proposed, details of working parties and points of tactical importance will be carefully taken over.

7. Completion of relief will be wired to Battalion Headquarters by code word : "WIT".

                                                    J.P.Hitchcock
                                                    Captain,
                              A/Adjutant 8th. Battalion THE BUFFS.


                              DISTRIBUTION.

           Copy No.  1  to  The Commanding Officer.
              "   "  2   "  O.C., 1st. Battalion ROYAL FUSILIERS.
              "   "  3   "    "   12th.    "     ROYAL FUSILIERS.
              "   "  4   "  Second in Command.
              "   "  5   "  O.C., A.Company.
              "   "  6   "    "   B.Company.
              "   "  7   "    "   C.Company.
              "   "  8   "    "   D.Company.
              "   "  9   "  Transport Officer.
              "   " 10   "  Quartermaster.
              "   " 11   "  Intelligence Officer.
              "   " 12   "  Signal Officer.
              "   " 13   "  Bombing Officer.
              "   " 14   "  War Diary.
              "   " 15   "    "
              "   " 16   "  Office.

T.B.114/A

WR 26 17/24

S26.

SECRET

8th Bn. The Buffs Regt.

War Diary for November 1917

Volume 2/

M R Covall
Major
i/c Commanding 8th Bn. The Buffs

a/o
8th Bavin. The Buffs

1.12.17

# WAR DIARY or INTELLIGENCE SUMMARY

Army Form C. 2118.

| Place | Date | Hour | Summary of Events and Information | Remarks and references to Appendices |
|---|---|---|---|---|
| [illegible] Line (Map Ref. NAUROY L29) | 1.XI.17 | | Day quiet – nothing to report. Regular patrol party under 2/Lt MOY Preine went out at night including Pat G & Lt M.E. Bill so traces of enemy patrols. Patrol tried to turn out right while daylight ready to act as soon as warned from standing patrol but recon'd was. | |
| " | 2.XI.17 | | Nothing unusual to report. No enemy activity on our own. Pat S.H.E. went out at 10.30am by Corps Commander. The usual O patrols were carried out. Daylight nothing to report. | |
| " | 3.XI.17 | | A little shelling round GRAND RUIZ FARM reports (no casualties) also APPLE TREE WALK & thermal day normal. Standing patrol & active patrol report enemy seen. No traces found by Lt [illegible] patrol. Which went out & came in to (CARN 4) [illegible] to report to H/Qs informed. | |
| " | 4.XI.17 | | Normal – An American officer attached found in the evening. | |
| " | 5.XI.17 | | Normal day. The night being very dark-patrol went up/at 9pm & stay to 9 did no active work. | |
| " | 6.XI.17 | | ASCENSION FARM had a [illegible] about 11 am no casualties. Maybe the patrol was sent out along ridge S of ASCENSION WOOD when an enemy patrol was noticed – to prevent [illegible] enemy L.G. & 2 troops of men were killed and five wounded. Being otherwise hit little was cautious of fire and the darkness was a great weakness, noise of the enemy could be seen though the patrol went forward [illegible]. | |

Army Form C. 2118.

# WAR DIARY
## or
## INTELLIGENCE SUMMARY.
(Erase heading not required.)

Instructions regarding War Diaries and Intelligence Summaries are contained in F. S. Regs., Part II. and the Staff Manual respectively. Title pages will be prepared in manuscript.

| Place | Date | Hour | Summary of Events and Information | Remarks and references to Appendices |
|---|---|---|---|---|
| LINE Mt Sheet NAUROY Rd. 2 sheet 57a | 7.x.19 | | The day was quiet. No casualties. Patrol at night looked for further signs of enemy patrols - but no trace was found. | |
| | 8.x.19 | | A quiet morning. Bt. HQ moved to new dugout at L34.a.20.80 LE VERGUIER which was built by 190th Tun. Coy R.E. at 5 p.m. The 12th R.F. came up to relieve. Relief was complete by 7.30 p.m. without incident. The American Officers returned to their unit. The Bt. proceeded to BERNES (see Div Reserve) | |
| BERNES | 9.x.19 | | Kit inspections. Lecture to NCOs by 2/i.c. | |
| " | 10.x.19 | | No Training Programme carried out. Baths - | Appendix A. |
| " | 11.x.19 | | Church Parade - Bts paraded full strength. | |
| " | 12.x.19 | | Training Programme - A + B Coys to platoon tactics in view of HARGICOURT & Hargicourt. C coys musketry. the Bt. at training terrain for further Divisional movement. | |
| " | 13.x.19 | | Training Programme - C.O.'s inspection on arrival HARGICOURT. | |
| " | 14.x.19 | | Training Programme - Bts Musketry continued for practical demonstrate. | |
| " | 15.x.19 | | Tactical Scheme. (Observation) | |
| " | 16.x.19 | | Usual morning Coys parade at 2.0 p.m. movement orders to LE VERGUIER rec'd. Bn moved off at 6.15 p.m. Relief complete without incident at 7.25 p.m. | Appendix. |

# WAR DIARY
## or
## INTELLIGENCE SUMMARY.
*(Erase heading not required.)*

Army Form C. 2118.

| Place | Date | Hour | Summary of Events and Information | Remarks and references to Appendices |
|---|---|---|---|---|
| Khue | 17.XI.19 | | Nothing unusual was doing that day was normal. Patrol and carried as night. No nothing to report. | |
| " | 18.XI.19 | | Quiet - Visibility 7 a.m. to 9 a.m. 2 rockets received not-result 1200 from Pot Ruh. 9pt 2 Peninsula offensive Agricultrice Captains Rice. | |
| " | 19.XI.19 | | Day normal at night a convoy consisting of 2 Officers & 50 OR went out to protect Party of R.E.'s (104 Coy) party in forcus attack on the road. At ZERO emphaslin with operations on our North. An enemy patrol interfered. It was given off & 7 for, later refr. 1 prisoner and the work was resumed. | Appendix 'B' |
| " | 20.XI.19 | 6.20 a.m. ZERO hour | Unfortunately the Engineer was employed easily & so failed to arrive at the opening of barrage to the North. These operations were successful in down the enemy flank. A considerable uplift towards true. It was impossible at this time to advance on an inside light. Patrols were sent out at night to advance & find out if he was still in the line. Reports received to the effect that enemy had away from the area to the nearest opposite no retirement. | |
| " | 21.XI.19 | | Normal on Pot's front. Patrols similarly employed as previous night - our our & no enemy front. | |
| " | 22.XI.19 | | Day Quiet. Patrols out with same object as night last patrol reported enemy being heard about 11.30 p.m. - a few shots were fired but no casualties received respectively inflicted. | |
| " | 23.XI.19 | 2.00 a.m. | Apparently some enemy patrol advanced between 30 & 40 strong & headed once our Left posts ( No 2) Fire was R'Co. & Lewis Gun Events there the enemy Officer Pty & 1 N.C.O. killed on our wire & six wounded. Morning W.S. Sin wounded. Recorded wire .... B.H. | |

# WAR DIARY or INTELLIGENCE SUMMARY

Army Form C. 2118.

| Place | Date | Hour | Summary of Events and Information | Remarks and references to Appendices |
|---|---|---|---|---|
| LINE | 24-XI-17 | | Day normal. About 5.0.5. falling of Valley of Coste and was adm - some minutes from enemy trench mortar. At night the Bgde was relieved by 1st R.F. and went into Bgde Reserve at VADENCOURT arriving there about 9.0 p.m. B Coy with Bn. HQ. found a Coy in close support to the VERQUIER. | |
| VADENCOURT | 25-XI-17 | | Practically no training could be carried out in the PM's being to parade been working parties in front line 12/13 4 of R.F. A NCO's class was formed with the RSM. + while a number of NCOs who had passed a similar class during the tour of R.F. in the line, passed out. | |
| " | 26-XI-17 | | Quiet. NCOs drill. working parties as before. | |
| " | 27-XI-17 | | Nothing unusual to report. | |
| " | 28-XI-17 | | Quiet day. Enemy artillery active on No 2 front + a few shells fell near the village at about 10 p.m. from rifle and trench mortars. | |
| " | 29-XI-17 | | Hostile artillery again active now on the Division front immediately on our left. It opened with a heavy bombardment about 11 p.m. + kept up firing of various intensity in violence till about dawn. | |
| " | 30-XI-17 | | Desultory gun fire from same direction again today beginning all day, later news came through that Itavenary had broken through on the front of the Division on the left. but the situation was not very clear. | |

The average Trench Strength of companies during this month was 84.

[signed]
Lt Col
Commanding 8th Bn The Buffs

## 8th Bn "The Buffs"
### Training Programme from 9th Nov. to 16th Nov 1917

| Date | 7.30am-8.0am | 9.0am-10.0am | 10.30am-11.30am | 12.0 Noon-12.45pm | 2.0pm-3.0pm | 3.30pm-4.30pm | 5.30pm-6.30pm | Remarks |
|---|---|---|---|---|---|---|---|---|
| Friday 9th | | Baths and Kit Inspection for Battalion 7.0 AM until finished. | | | Lecture to All Officers by 2nd in Command | | | |
| Saturday 10th | Physical Drill. Dress:- Lecture Order | Saluting Drill, Section & Platoon Drill, Rifle Exercises. Dress:- Drill Order. Platoon & Coy Drill under Drill Sgt for Junior NCOs | Company Drill Junior NCOs under Drill Sgt | Musketry and Lewis Gun Instruction | Lecture to all Officers by 2nd in Command. Subject:- "Organisation of Company etc." | Lecture to all NCOs by 2nd in Command. Subject:- "Duties of Platoon Sgt and Section Commander" | Lecture to A. Coy. Place:- 'A' Coy's Hut. | |
| Sunday 11th | | | 10.0am-11.0am Church Parade. 12.0 Noon-1.0pm Lecture to all available Officers "Discipline" Lecture to all NCOs "Discipline" | | | | | |
| Monday 12th | Physical Drill. Dress:- Lecture Order | Saluting Drill, Section & Platoon Drill, Rifle Exercises. Dress:- Drill Order. Platoon & Coy Drill under Drill Sgt for Junior NCOs | Company Drill Junior NCOs under Drill Sgt | Musketry and Lewis Gun Instruction | Lecture to all Officers and NCOs by 2nd in Command. Subject:- Company Drill. | | Lecture to B. Coy. Place:- 'A' Coy's Hut. | |
| Tuesday 13th | Physical Drill. Dress:- Lecture Order | Saluting Drill, Section & Platoon Drill, Rifle Exercises. Dress:- Drill Order. Platoon & Coy Drill under Drill Sgt for Junior NCOs | Battalion Drill | Musketry and Lewis Gun Instruction | Lecture to all Officers and NCOs by Selected Officer. Subject:- Patrols and Patrol Reports. | | Lecture to C. Coy. Place:- 'A' Coy's Hut. | |

## Training Programme "C" Coy

| Date | 7.30 AM – 8 AM | 9.0 AM – 10.0 AM | 10.30 AM – 11.30 AM | 12.0 NOON – 12.45 PM | 2.0 PM – 3.0 PM | 3.30 PM – 4.30 PM | 5.30 PM – 6.30 PM |
|---|---|---|---|---|---|---|---|
| Wednesday 14th | Physical Drill Dress: Loose Order | Saluting Drill Section & Platoon Drill Rifle Exercises Dress: Drill Order Platoon vly. Drill under Drill Sgt. for Senior N.C.O.s | Battalion Drill | Musketry and Fuse Saw Instruction | Lecture to all Officers and N.C.O.s by Capt. Mainforth Subject: Map-reading | | Lecture to "D" Coy Place: "A" Coy's Hut |
| Thursday 15th | | | | Tactical Exercise | | | |
| Friday 16th | Physical Drill Dress: Loose Order | Rifle and Equipment Inspection | | | Lecture by Company Commanders | | |

1. This Programme is subject to alterations owing to Working Parties and weather
2. Games every afternoon from ... pm to ... pm

Nov 1917

M. Cavill Major
8th Batt. The Buffs

INSTRUCTIONS FOR COVERING PARTY furnished by 8th Battalion THE BUFFS.
on Y/Z night.

Ref. Map. Special Sheet edition 2. B. Scale $\frac{1}{20.000}$.

Copy 13.

## 1. OBJECT of COVERING PARTY.
To form a complete screen to cover Party working at N.E. corner of BIG BILL. To be in position by 1. a.m. on Z day.

## 2. DISPOSITIONS.
Covering Party is divided into 2 Groups. "A" & "B". "A" Group commanded by 2nd Lieut. Froome. "B" Group by Lieut. Spence. 2nd Lieut. Froome will also be O.C. Covering Party.

(a) "A" Group Strength 1 Officer and 50 O.R. This Group will form a crescent-shaped screen 5 paces between men. The Officer will be in the centre. Screen to be as far forward from Working Party as possible. The minimum distance to be 100 yards.
(b) "B" Group Strength 1 Officer and 50 O.R. This Group is divided into 4 Sections numbering 1 to 4 constituted and disposed as follows:-
NO.1 SECTION. 1 N.C.O. and 6 men on track at G.26.a.80.50.
NO.2 SECTION 1 N.C.O. and 6 men on S. side of road at G.26.c.30.95.
NO.3 SECTION 1 Officer and 9 O.R. in pairs at ten paces interval forming a line running North and South Right resting on G.25.b.50.70. The officer will be in the centre.
NO.4 SECTION. 1 N.C.O. and 6 men in valley at G.19.d.90.80.

## 3. MISCELLANEOUS INSTRUCTIONS.
Covering Party will assemble at GRAHAM POST at 10.30P.M. on Y night and will proceed to their allotted positions via MOLLY POST and SUNKEN ROAD S. of ASCENSION WOOD.
A guide known as No.1 Guide will be dropped at MOLLY POST to conduct Working Party to N.E. corner of ASCENSION WOOD. This Guide will also conduct Working Party back on completion of their task.
On arrival in position O.C. "A" Group will dispatch a Guide known as No. 2 Guide to O.C. Working Party assembled at N.E. corner of ASCENSION WOOD to report "All clear", then conduct the Party to N.E. corner of BIG BILL. He will report to O.C. "A" Group when work is completed, returning to BIG BILL to act as Guide to Sapper left to fire charges.

## 4. WITHDRAWALS.
"A" Group will withdraw down track running S.W. of BIG BILL to point of rendezvous on SUNKEN ROAD at G.25.b.40.30. collecting No. 1 and 2 Sections on the way. O.C. "A" Group will then dispatch Runner to No.3 Section Commander with Orders to withdraw to point of rendezvous.
No.3 Section Commander will send similar orders to No.4 Section Commander. Covering Party on being complete will return to MOLLY POST.
O.C. Covering Party will then telephone the Code Word "FROOME" to Battalion Headquarters.

## 5. Acknowledge.

W.R. Corrall, Major.
Lieut. Colonel,
Commanding 8th Battalion THE BUFFS.

19:11:17.

Copy No. 1. O.C. Covering Party.       No. 2. O.C. Working Party.
        3. 17th Infantry Brigade.          4. O.C. 3rd Rifle Brigade.
        5. O.C. 8th Queens.                6. O.C. A. Coy.
        7. O.C. B. Coy.                    8. O.C. C. Coy.
        9. O.C. D. Coy.                   10. I.O.
       11. 17th M.G. Coy.                 12. O.C. Right Group, R.F.A.
       13. War Diary.                     14. File.

# Tactical Scheme No 6

8 Buffs

(1). A tactical scheme (narrative attack) will be carried out by 8th Buffs on Thursday 15th inst, in conjunction with a contact aeroplane.

(2). The 8th Buffs will be assembled at about Q4A 20.60 on BERNES – HAMELET Rd at 9-30 am on the above date where orders will be issued to O/C Battalion.

(3). The contact aeroplane (Armstrong Whitworth with black line on right underwing continued in a black streamer) will fly over the attacking troops from time to time, should the attack be held up at any point, the aeroplane will sound a series of A's on a klaxon horn or fire a white very light) on hearing or seeing which the foremost troops will light RED ground flares to show their position. On reaching their objective the infantry will again light RED ground flares, when the aeroplane calls for them in a similar manner.

(4). O/C 8 Buffs will establish a signal station at his Battn. HQ which will be marked in the usual manner, and which must be prepared to receive from & send messages to the aeroplane, and also be in readiness to collect message bags dropped from the aeroplane, (when a message is about to be dropped near Bn. HQ. the aeroplane will sound a klaxon horn). In a similar manner Divisional HQ will establish a collecting station (near the existing HQ) to obtain aerial communication with Bn. HQ.

(5.) The enemy (a skeleton force) will carry flags, whose meaning is as follows:—  Man = Sniper Scout &c
　　White Signalling Flag = Section
　　Blue　　　"　　　"　 = Platoon
　　Maroon　"　　　"　 = Machine Gun

They will be provided with blank ammunition, rattles &c & will wear caps.

(6). Dress for the above Scheme will be in fighting order as laid down in S.S. 145 (Section XXXI.

Note:— Should the weather be very foggy the aeroplane will not be present.

Awtingh Lieut Col.
Commanding 24th Divisional Reserve

Secret and confidential

"Volume to O"
S E Kent R¹
Vol 27

War Diary

for month of December 11/17

G Hitchcock a/Capt
 & Major
Commanding 8 Battn The Buffs

3:1:18

Army Form C. 2118.

# WAR DIARY
## or
## INTELLIGENCE SUMMARY.
*(Erase heading not required.)*

Instructions regarding War Diaries and Intelligence Summaries are contained in F. S. Regs., Part II. and the Staff Manual respectively. Title pages will be prepared in manuscript.

| Place | Date | Hour | Summary of Events and Information | Remarks and references to Appendices |
|---|---|---|---|---|
| VADENCOURT | 1-12-17 | | Owing to enemy's advance on the Corps left pursual that moves for the move which was to have been made from this sector were postponed & the Bn stood in readiness to move & hold a any direction required. | |
| | 2-12-17 | | [illegible handwritten entries] | |
| | 3-12-17 | | [illegible handwritten entries] A | A |
| LINE Mapsheet NAUROY 62c N.11.b.6.6. | 4-12-17 | | [illegible handwritten entries] | |
| | 5-12-17 | | [illegible handwritten entries] | B |

# WAR DIARY
## or
## INTELLIGENCE SUMMARY.

*(Erase heading not required.)*

Army Form C.-2118.

| Place | Date | Hour | Summary of Events and Information | Remarks and references to Appendices |
|---|---|---|---|---|
| LINE | 7-12-17 | 12.30pm | No action followed. Shelling was rather indiscriminate & the enemy's part of it was not in any way concentrated. Bn. was relieved in evening by 7th Bn., Sea. Bns. into Cat Bde. (Appendix "C") Relief completed by 8pm. Bn. proceeded to billets at HANCOURT, arrived in at 11.30pm. | "C" |
| HANCOURT | 8-12-17 | | Day spent in kit inspections, cleaning up and improving billets which were very poor. | |
| HANCOURT | 9-12-17 | | Informs billets. Church parade 12.0 noon - Service by our Chaplain Rev. Trufan. | |
| HANCOURT | 10-12-17 | | C & D Coys proceeded to TEMPLEUX-LE-GUERARD (Map 62c NE. L.2) (Appendix D) At noon, remainder of battn. were ordered to be clear of billets at HANCOURT by 2.30pm, and marched to MONTIGNY FARM (62c NE K 35d.) | D |
| MONTIGNY | 11-12-17 | | Training programme No. 1 issued. Concert by Batten in DALY'S THEATRE. Lecture by Maj. Coulthie to Officers & Senior NCOs of 17th BDE. at 3.30pm in DALY'S THEATRE. | |
| MONTIGNY | 12-12-17 | | Training programme No. 2 issued. C & D Coys returned from TEMPLEUX-LE-GUERARD. | |
| MONTIGNY | 13-12-17 | | Training programme No. 3 issued. Officers & other NCOs recnnoitred in BERNES C & D Coys marched from BERNES escorted by C.O., B.M. & other officers & N.C.O.'s Concert in ARS Coys Gts Mess 8pm. | |
| MONTIGNY | 14-12-17 | | Training programme No. 4. New line F. of TEMPLEUX-LE-GUERARD reconnoitred by Officers & N.C.O.s from each Coy. | |
| MONTIGNY | 15-12-17 | | Coys performance. March-past with white ?letter. B.G.C. inspected Bn. Parade in C&D Coys Gte new Bt BERNES. Sports in afternoon. | 9/a EVANS |
| MONTIGNY | 16-12-17 | | Training programme. Reconnoitring of new area. Hue & Rat to hospital. Church parade 12.0 noon in DALY'S THEATRE | |
| MONTIGNY | 17-12-17 | | Training programme not carried out owing to heavy fall of snow during night. Men employed clearing away & building up huts. Dry mounts and huts. CB of Coy Commaders reconnitred new Line E & B | |

HARCOURT (62c NE L.6)

JAH

Army Form C.2118.

# WAR DIARY
# or
# INTELLIGENCE SUMMARY.
(Erase heading not required.)

Instructions regarding War Diaries and Intelligence Summaries are contained in F.S. Regs., Part II. and the Staff Manual respectively. Title pages will be prepared in manuscript.

| Place | Date | Hour | Summary of Events and Information | Remarks and references to Appendices |
|---|---|---|---|---|
| MONTIGNY | 18.12.17 | | Reconnoitring continued by officers from each coy. Snow till prevalent. | |
| MONTIGNY | 19.12.17 | | Reconnoitring continued. Hun front. Quiet in Day's Theatre by Regts. A + B Coys. | |
| MONTIGNY | 20.12.17 | | Recce into coy. areas and preparing to go into line. Hun front. | |
| MONTIGNY | 21.12.17 | | Bn. relieved 8th R.W. KENT REGT. (less 1 Coy.) and 1 Coy. 2nd LEINSTER REGT. (62C N.E.) (Appendix "F"). Relief completed at 12.15p.m. Disposition as per appendix F. Visibility very poor Hostile Artillery very quiet. Front extended from G.1.d.25.45 to G.7.b.50.70. A Coy — 1 Platoon B Coy at Quarry Wood 19th K.R.R. on LEFT and Nauroy HUSSARS at RIGHT. Quiet in morning. Good sniping by Huns but front again — active at night. E.A. very active all day, flying low. Shelling near Bn. Hqrs. about 2.30 p.m. (New) Much movement behind German lines chiefly at QUARRY WOOD and around BELLICOURT. A German MINENWERFER was observed. Complete intact of rail T 50 rounds ammunition in the German dugout at G.7.b.60.95. Signalled read from a red scarf station in neighbourhood of DIAMOND COPSE. Int. coy chiefly German artillery rather more active than usual, in neighbourhood of VILLERET, otherwise quiet. Hun front continued. | F |
| LINE Map Sheet NAUROY Ed.2B L.10, 6, 11 + G.1 | 22.12.17 | | Hun front continued – VILLERET received constant attention from German Artillery. A considerable amount of movement around BELLICOURT. E.A. flew over our lines very lit up. | |
| | 24.12.17 | | | |
| | 25.12.17 | 7.30 | During the day ONION LANE was shelled & 2 men seriously wounded + 2 men slightly wounded. At night 2 men killed + the Brigade Signals were first [illegible] Hq. to premises of minor O.H. [illegible]. Enemy presented a serious line. Little damage was done. The Bn. [illegible] to Hq. had hopes of spending that which for H.Q. same time. Movement was seen in BELLICOURT, [illegible] the morning and after mid-day barometer became unfavourable owing to the frost. | |

# WAR DIARY or INTELLIGENCE SUMMARY

Army Form C. 2118.

| Place | Date | Hour | Summary of Events and Information | Remarks and references to Appendices |
|---|---|---|---|---|
| | 26.9.17 | | ONION LANE shelled 3 direct hits on the trench. Movement was observed in BELLICOURT. E.A. were inactive. | |
| | 27.9.17 | | Enemy batteries ONION LANE & PONO SUPPORT were shelled in the morning and some direct hits obtained. Considerable movement in BELLICOURT - R.F. Dragons were seen going towards MAUROY. During the day our snipers killed two Germans. A German messenger found in German trench was shot. German batteries fired on a quantity of ammunition. Aeroplanes C.7.a.35.85. also a quantity of ammunition. | |
| | 28.9.17 | | Bn. relieved by 2 Leinsters Bn. Enemy shelled MARKET Valley & held up relief for some time. The Bn was relieved at 2 p.m. with exception of C platoon which relieved after dark. Arrived at MONTIGNY. | |
| MONTIGNY | 29.9.17 | | Day spent in improving the mens huts. Material obtained from Dump & Bath commenced. | |
| | 30.9.17 | | Church Parade. Men washed in Rue & toilets made for Xmas Dinner. | |
| | 9.10.17 | | Wet day for men. Sporting trucks but on the whole in the evening Dinner started at 2 p.m. Everyone thoroughly happy & contented. Ended in Daly's Theatre. | |

G. Whitehead
Capt. Adjt. 7/R. Inn Fus.

C. Conway
Lt Col. Commanding 8th Bn R. Innis. Fus.

"F"

RELIEF ORDERS.
by
Major W.R.Carroll.D.S.O.
Commanding 8th. Battalion The Buffs.
-----oOo-----oOo-----oOo-----oOo-----oOo-----

Field.
No. 94.
Copy No. 13

Reference Map: Sheet 62.c.N.E.

1. The Battalion will relieve the 8th. Battalion ROYAL EAST KENT Regt.(less one Coy.) and one Company 2nd. Battalion LEINSTER Regt. on the 21st. inst.

2. DISPOSITIONS.---- The following will be the dispositions:-
   "C" Coy.   3 platoons.                        POND TRENCH.
              1    "                             POND SUPPORT.
   "D" Coy.   2    "      and Coy. H.Q.          LEICESTER LODGE.
              1    "                                 "        "
   "B" Coy.   2    "      and Coy. H.Q.          Quarries. L.10.a.
                                                     "        "
   "A" Coy.

3. GUIDES.---- One guide per platoon of the 8th. ROYAL EAST KENT Regt. will be at L.26.c.70.20. at 9 a.m.

4. ORDER OF MARCH.---- Companies will move off in the following order:- Headquarters, C., D., B., A. 200 yards distance will be kept between platoons until reaching HARBIDCOURT when a similar distance will be kept between half platoons.

5. STORES.---- Lewis guns, Mess kit, Blankets, etc. will be stacked outside respective Headquarters at 7 a.m. by C. & D.Companies and 7.30 a.m. by Headquarters, A. & B.Companies.

6. TRANSPORT.---- Transport arrangements will be issued later.

7. TRENCH STORES.---- All trench stores, etc. will be carefully taken over and lists forwarded to Battalion Headquarters by 9 a.m. the 22nd. inst.

8. DETAILS.---- Details from Headquarters, A. & B.Companies will parade under the R.S.M. at 7.45 a.m. and proceed to the Recreation Room BRUNOY. Details from C. & D.Companies will report to the R.S.M. at this place at 8.15 a.m.

9. Completion of relief will be sent to Battalion Headquarters by code word "BILLIE".

                                            Captain & Adjutant,
                                            8th. Battalion The Buffs.

DISTRIBUTION.

Copy No.  1  to  The Commanding Officer.
  "   "   2   "  O.C., 8th. Battalion ROYAL WEST KENT Regt.
  "   "   3   "    "   2nd. Battalion LEINSTER Regt.
  "   "   4   "    "   A.Company.
  "   "   5   "    "   B.Company.
  "   "   6   "    "   C.Company.
  "   "   7   "    "   D.Company.
  "   "   8   "  Transport Officer.
  "   "   9   "  Quartermaster.
  "   "  10   "  O.C., Signals.
  "   "  11   "  R.S.M.
  "   "  12   "  War Diary.
  "   "  13   "
  "   "  14   "  Office.

8th Bn. The Buffs.

Training Programme from 10th Dec: to 15th Dec: 1917.

| Date | 7.30am - 8.0am | 9.0am - 10.0am | 10.30am - 11.30am | 12.0noon - 12.45pm | 2.0pm - 4.0pm | 5.30pm - 6.30pm |
|---|---|---|---|---|---|---|
| Monday 10th | Physical Drill. Dress:- Loose Order. | Saluting Drill Section & Platoon Drill Rifle Exercises Dress:- Drill Order. Platoon & Coy Drill under Drill Sgt. for Senior N.C.Os. | Company Drill Junior N.C.Os. under Drill Sgt. | Musketry and Lewis Gun Instruction. 'A' Coy. Range from 11.30am - 2.0pm. (Dinners on return) | Games | Lecture to 'A' Coy. N.C.Os. |
| Tuesday 11th | Physical Drill. Dress:- Loose Order. | Saluting Drill Section & Platoon Drill Rifle Exercises Dress:- Drill Order. Platoon & Coy Drill under Drill Sgt. for Senior N.C.Os. | Company Drill Junior N.C.Os. under Drill Sgt. | Musketry and Lewis Gun Instruction. 'B' Coy. Range from 11.30am - 2.0pm. (Dinners on return) | Games | Lecture to All Officers |
| Wednesday 12th | Physical Drill. Dress:- Loose Order. | Saluting Drill Section & Platoon Drill Rifle Exercises Dress:- Drill Order. Platoon & Coy Drill under Drill Sgt. for Senior N.C.Os. | Battalion Drill | Musketry and Lewis Gun Instruction. 'C' Coy. Range from 11.30am - 2.0pm. (Dinners on return) | Games | Lecture to 'B' Coy. N.C.Os. |
| Thursday 13th | Physical Drill. Dress:- Loose Order. | Saluting Drill Section & Platoon Drill Rifle Exercises Dress:- Drill Order. Platoon & Coy Drill under Drill Sgt. for Senior N.C.Os. | Battalion Drill | Musketry and Lewis Gun Instruction. 'D' Coy. Range from 11.30am - 2.0pm. (Dinners on return) | Games | Lecture to 'C' Coy. N.C.Os. |

## Training Programme. (cont)

| Date. | 7.30am – 8.0am | 9.0am – 10.0am | 10.30am – 11.30am | 12.0 noon – 12.45pm | 2.0pm – 4.0pm | 5.30pm – 6.30pm |
|---|---|---|---|---|---|---|
| Friday 14th. | Physical Drill. Dress:– Loose Order. | Saluting Drill Section & Platoon Drill Rifle Exercises Dress:– Drill order. Platoon & Cy Drill under Drill Sgt. for Senior N.C.O's. | Battalion Drill | Musketry and Lewis Gun Instruction | Games. | Lecture to All Officers. |
| Saturday 15th. | Physical Drill. Dress:– Loose Order. | Saluting Drill Section & Platoon Drill Rifle Exercises Dress:– Drill order Platoon & Cy Drill under Drill Sgt. for Senior N.C.O's. | Battalion Drill | Musketry and Lewis Gun Instruction. | Games. | Lecture to D. Cys. N.C.O's. |

This Programme is subject to alterations owing to Working Parties and weather conditions.

9th Dec. 1917.

C. H. Winston Capt & ? ? Major
Commanding 8th Bn. The Buffs.

A

## RELIEF ORDER.

by
Major W.R.ODEHALL. D.S.O.
Commanding 8th. Battalion THE BUFFS.

Field.
Copy No. 13.                                                              3.12.17.

1. The Battalion will relieve the 1st. Battalion ROYAL FUSILIERS in A.2 Sub Sector, to-night December 3rd.

2. DISPOSITIONS.—
   A. Company.    Right Front Company.    C. Company.    Right Support.
   B.    "        Left    "       "       D. Company.    Left    "

3. TIME OF PARADE.—— Companies will move off by platoons at 200 yards distance in the following order from VADENCOURT :- A., B., C. & H.Q.
   First Company to move off at 4.30 p.m. D.Company will move off from LE VERGUIER as soon as light will permit.

4. BAGGAGE.—— All Company Stores, Lewis Guns, Valises, etc. will be ready for loading outside respective Headquarters by 4 p.m. 2 limbers will report for Headquarters Stores at 4.30 p.m.

5. TRENCH STORES, ETC.—— All trench stores, aeroplane photos, tables of work in hand and proposed, defence schemes and other documents will be carefully taken over and accurate lists forwarded to this office by 10 a.m. the 4th. inst. Particular attention is to be paid to the taking over of all information concerning "NO MAN'S LAND".

6. Completion of relief will be wired to Headquarters by code word "URQUHART".

7. DETAILS.—— Details will parade at 5 p.m. under R.S.M. and report to the Quartermaster at RONSSOY.

8. O.C. Companies will report to Battalion Headquarters before moving off that their Company billets are left clean. C.Q.M.S. of each Company is responsible for handing over billets, stores, etc. held on their Company charge. One Sergeant will be detailed to hand over Headquarter billets, stores, etc.

                                              [signature]
                                              Captain & Adjutant,
                                              8th. Battalion THE BUFFS.

DISTRIBUTION.

Copy No.  1. B.G., 17th. INFANTRY BRIGADE.
  "   "   2. The Commanding Officer.
  "   "   3. O.C., 1st. Battn. ROYAL FUSILIERS.
  "   "   4.  "    19th.
  "   "   5.  "    A. Company.
  "   "   6.  "    B.    "
  "   "   7.  "    C.    "
  "   "   8.  "    D.    "
  "   "   9. Transport Officer.
  "   "  10. Quartermaster.
  "   "  11. O.C., Signals.
  "   "  12. Medical Officer.
  "   "  13. R.S.M.
  "   "  14. War Diary.
  "   "  15.
  "   "  16. Office.

SECRET. B

# OPERATION ORDER.
by
Major W. H. Corrall. M.C.
Commanding 8th. Battalion The Buffs.

Field.
No.U.O.S.
Copy No. 11

5.12.17.

Reference Map : HAUCOURT Edition 2.b.

1. The Battalion will furnish a party of 2 officers and 60 O.Rs. for covering a R.E. party laying Bomb Throwers at the N.E. Corner of BIG HILL on the night of 6/7th. December.

2. The covering party will assemble at GRAHAM POSTS at 5.30 p.m. moving off at 6 p.m. It will be divided into two groups numbered 1 and 2. The strength of No. 1 group will be 1 officer and 40 O.Rs., that of No. 2, 1 officer and 20 O.R.

3. No. 1 group will move S.E of BIG HILL along road running N.E. and form a screen on the N.E. Corner of BIG HILL. The screen to be sufficiently forward to keep any enemy out of bombing range of R.E. party. 1 N.C.O. and 10 men will be left on the road at O.26.d.90.50 to protect the right flank. The R.E. party will accompany this group, remaining at N.E. corner of ASCENSION WOOD until the all clear has been sent back by O.C., Covering party.

   No. 2 Group will move along road running N.E. through ASCENSION WOOD and form a screen in front of LITTLE HILL to protect the left flank. O.C. No. 2 group will send word to O.C., Covering party, who will be with No. 1 group, when he is in position.

4. When both groups are in position, O.C. Covering party will send a runner back to the R.E. party at N.E. Corner of ASCENSION WOOD. This runner will remain with the R.E. party and inform O.C., Covering party when the work is completed. Both groups will then withdraw by their respective routes, No. 1 group collecting the Section left to guard right flank.

5. Should the enemy be encountered whilst work is in progress, they must be driven off by rifle fire.

Captain & Adjutant,
8th. Battalion The Buffs.

## DISTRIBUTION.

Copy No. 1. to H.Q., 17th. INFANTRY BRIGADE.
"   "   2. "  O.C., 3rd. Battn. THE RIFLE BRIGADE.
"   "   3. "   "    R.E. Working Party.
"   "   4. "   "    17th. M.G.C.
"   "   5. "   "    Right Group, R.F.A.
"   "   6. "   "    A.Company.
"   "   7. "   "    B.Company.
"   "   8. "   "    C.Company.
"   "   9. "   "    D.Company.
"   "  10. "   "    Covering Party.
"   "  11. "  War Diary.
"   "  12. "   "
"   "  13. "  Office.

"D"

OPERATION ORDERS 23
— by —
Major E.R. O'Brien D.S.O.
Commanding 8th Battalion The Buffs.

Field                                                           9.12.17.
Copy No... 10.

1. "C" and "D" Companies will relieve tomorrow 10th instant 2 Coys 10th Royal Fusiliers at present in Left Flank Support of the 73rd Infantry Brigade (H.Qrs. L.1. b.10.40.)

2. Completion of relief will be reported to these Headquarters at once.

3. All other details will be arranged direct between OsC. Companies concerned.

4. Companies will be clear of HARCOURT by 10 a.m. tomorrow 10th inst.

5. The Transport Officer will detail 4 limbers. 2 for each Company concerned to be at respective Company Headquarters at 9 a.m. tomorrow 10th inst.

6. Headquarter Signallers and the 2 Signallers per Company under instruction will not proceed but will report to these Headquarters 9 a.m. tomorrow 10th inst.

7. Captain A.MCGUIRE will detail one mounted officer to proceed in advance to reconnoitre the route and Headquarters.

                                                    [signature]
                                                    Captain,
                                    Adjutant 8th Battalion The Buffs.

Copy No.1. to O.C. "C" Company.
"    2.    O.C. "D"    "
"    3.    O.C. "A"    "
"    4.    O.C. "B"    "
"    5.    Transport Officer.
"    6.    Quartermaster.
"    7.    I.O.
"    8.    M.O.
"    9.    R.S.M.
"    10.   War Diary.
"    11.   File.

To :- 17th Infantry Brigade.
-----------------------

In sending you all my best wishes for Christmas and the best of Good luck in the New Year, I would like to convey to all ranks of the 17th Brigade my unbounded admiration for all the splendid work they have done throughout the Year.

It has been a very hard year, and great demands have been made on all of you, and the magnificent way in which those demands have been met and accomplished, not only in your many battles, but also during all the most trying times you have been holding the Line, is worthy of the highest traditions of the British Army, and could not have been equalled.

You have established a record which I am confident, no matter what may be in front of us, you will always uphold. Remember that the great traditions of the 17th Brigade, left to us by those gallant men who died to make them, must ever be in our safe keeping, and above all we must ever preserve the memory of those great men who gladly gave their lives for the greatest cause in Christendom and for the Honour of their Regiments and Brigade.

The capture of LIEVIN in April - the Battle of MESSINES in June- followed within a week by the Attack on the strongly fortified Enemy positions East of BATTLE WOOD- holding the sector East of YPRES until the end of June - the Third Battle of YPRES on July 31st - holding the YPRES Sector until September 16th - and holding the Line from September to the present time. is a fine record, and in looking back on 1917 it will always be to me a record of fine work well done - and I thank you from my heart for your great efforts.

I have never yet heard a grumble- never had to deal with a serious case of Lack of Discipline - and the loyal support which has been given me by all ranks has made my period of Command an easy one. To have had the Honour to Command such men as these will ever be the proudest period of my life.

This high standard could never have been achieved without that spirit of Camaraderie and mutual confidence which pervades all Ranks. With this spirit we will start the New Year, full of Hope for the future, and assured of Victory.

24/12/17

Brig. General.

Commanding 17th Infantry Brigade.

## RELIEF ORDERS.

by

Major W.R.Corrall.M.C.
Commanding 8th. Battalion The Buffs.

Field:
No.25.
28.12.17.

1. The Battalion will be relieved by 2nd. Battalion LEINSTER Regt. on 28th. and on relief will proceed to MONTIGNY.

2. ROUTE.---- Light Railway - Ration Dump - Valley(L.10.a.-L.9.b.-L.8.c.)- Crucifix on TEMPLEUX Road - TEMPLEUX - NESBECOURT - NERVILLY - MONTIGNY. 200 yards distance will be maintained between platoons.

3. GUIDES.---- Each Company will send 2 guides to be at the junction of TEMPLEUX-HARGICOURT and JEANCOURT-HARGICOURT Roads (L.4.75.35) at 12.30 p.m. The relief will be carried out by day except that the platoon in BAIT TRENCH will not be relieved until dark unless weather permits.

4. STORES.---- All trench stores, aeroplane photos, gun prints and sketches and Defence Schemes will be carefully handed over and receipts obtained.

5. TRANSPORT.---- The Transport officer will arrange for two limbers per Coy. and 2 for Headquarters to be at the ration dump at 5 p.m. Companies will arrange for guards to be left for their Company stores.

6. Completion of relief will be sent to Battalion Headquarters by code word 'CHAT'.

Ref.Map : Sheet. 62.c.N.E.

J.Hitchcock
Captain &/Adjutant,
8th. Battalion The Buffs.

## DISTRIBUTION

Copy No. 1. to The Commanding officer.
"   "   2. "  O.C., 2nd. Battalion LEINSTER Regt.
"   "   3. "   "    A.Coy.
"   "   4. "   "    B.Coy.
"   "   5. "   "    C.Coy.
"   "   6. "   "    D.Coy.
"   "   7. "  Transport Officer.
"   "   8. "  Quartermaster.
"   "   9. "  R.S.M.
"   "  10. "  R.S.M.i/w.
"   "  11. "  War Diary.
"   "  12. "   "   "
"   "  13. "  Office.

Serik + Confidential

8 E Kent Regt
Vol 28

War Diary

for month of January 1918

No. 5
INFANTRY SECTION,
G.H.Q.,
3rd ECHELON.
No. ........
Date 5 FEB 1918

Commdg Officer's day.
Lieut Colonel
8th Bn The Buffs
Commanding 8th Bn The Buffs

2nd Feb 1918

Army Form C. 2118.

# WAR DIARY
## or
## INTELLIGENCE SUMMARY.
(Erase heading not required.)

Instructions regarding War Diaries and Intelligence Summaries are contained in F. S. Regs., Part II. and the Staff Manual respectively. Title pages will be prepared in manuscript.

| Place | Date | Hour | Summary of Events and Information | Remarks and references to Appendices |
|---|---|---|---|---|
| THATIGNY | 2/1/18 | | Received news from Divn. that 10 Officers & 10 other ranks could proceed on leave to the United Kingdom. | |
| | 3/1/18 | | An advance party of 2 Officers & 50 other ranks proceeded on leave to the United Kingdom. Baths available in Daly's Theatre. | |
| | | | Battn. Dept. Paid. Ride for Officers & N.C.O.s at 10 a.m. Concert in the "Y" Hut in the evening. | |
| | | | Boxing Competition. Excellent results considering it was the first practice. Running took place by Companies in the afternoon. Owing to the hardness of the ground no games were played. | |
| | 4/1/18 | | Training for Brigade Review continued. Owing to the intense cold a Running Parade for the Battn. took place from 9-10 a.m. Lecture was held at MONTIGNY at 3 p.m. subject "Geography of the War". Officers & N.C.O.s attended. Colonel Stadd returned from leave in the afternoon. A Coy. played Brigade Reserve and practice in the morning. In the afternoon, short stick ball. | |
| | 5/1/18 | | at football v.last. The ground was very hard. Heavy transport came over during the night through bye-paths. Bogen planes came over during the night also. The Battn. played Stanwood at Hockey. The game was Cinema Parade 12-mid day. Played at RO1SEL. We lost 3-1. Raw commenced at night. It rained hard during the night. | |
| | 7/1/18 | | Rain pouring in the morning. Brigade Review cancelled. Companies carried on with musketry in their Huts. | |
| | | | Battn. turned out to Royal Sussex kept. Commanded to MONTIGNY on | |

Army Form C. 2118.

# WAR DIARY
## or
## INTELLIGENCE SUMMARY.
*(Erase heading not required.)*

Instructions regarding War Diaries and Intelligence Summaries are contained in F. S. Regs., Part II. and the Staff Manual respectively. Title pages will be prepared in manuscript.

| Place | Date | Hour | Summary of Events and Information | Remarks and references to Appendices |
|---|---|---|---|---|

Army Form C. 2118.

# WAR DIARY
## or
## INTELLIGENCE SUMMARY.
*(Erase heading not required.)*

Instructions regarding War Diaries and Intelligence Summaries are contained in F. S. Regs., Part II. and the Staff Manual respectively. Title pages will be prepared in manuscript.

| Place | Date | Hour | Summary of Events and Information | Remarks and references to Appendices |
|---|---|---|---|---|
| LILLE | 21.1.18 | | We inspected N.W. Harbour & 3 sheds east Bruce are sent down to investigate. W/S received information that enemy had been using Bruce as a hospital. | |
| | 22.1.18 | | Party left Hancourt for LILLE to endeavour to find out truth. Proceeded to huts at HANCOURT. Party notification received not with by light railway from a point 1ML of Peroine. | |
| HANCOURT | 22.1.18 | | Men put to dig baths & cleaning up to OC to proceed to England. | |
| | 23.1.18 | | Baths. Men worked on mud walls round huts. | |
| | 24.1.18 | | Working parties. | |
| | 25.1.18 | | Whole batta paraded to work on new defence line. Inspector Major before country took, were inspected by Maj.Gen. Daly, who informed us his intention of authorising standard huts & Maj. Cobalts appointed 2nd in Command. | |
| | 26.1.18 | | Work on new defence line. C.O. returned from England. 2Lt. R.W. Kent Regt & 2Lt STAINFORTH joined from India, reinforced hospital. | |
| | 27.1.18 | | Work on new defence line. 2Lt STAINFORTH fell from horse near recruited hospital. | |
| | 28.1.18 | | Work on defence line. Enemy planes flew over Camp about 8pm, but no bombs dropped near here. | |
| | | | Four MONTIGNY. | |
| | 29.1.18 | | Work on defence line ROISEL bombs in morning. Enemy planes busy during evening & bombs dropped near VRAIGNES and district. | |
| | 30.1.18 | | Work on defence line. Aircraft very active during the night, but no bombs dropped in vicinity. Range used in morning afternoon. | |
| | 31.1.18 | | Work on defence line. | |

C.R.B. Lee Colonel

# ROUTINE ORDERS.

by

Major T.R.Borrall, M.C.
Commanding 8th. Battalion The Buffs.

Field.
No. 28.
Copy No. 11.

1.1.19.

1. The Battalion will be relieved by 1st. Battalion NORTH STAFFORDSHIRE Regt. on January 2nd. 1919 and on relief will move to Camp at VRAIGNES in Reserve.

2. The following distances will be maintained - 200 yards between platoons and 200 yards between each 2 Transport vehicles.

3. ORDER OF MARCH.---- Battn. H.Q., Adv. Gd., C. & D.Companies.

4. TIME.---- Battalion H.Q. will be ready to move at 2.4" p.m. but will not move off until Battalion H.Q. and 1 Company of the 1st. NORTH STAFFORDSHIRE Regt. has arrived at MONTIGNY.

5. STORES.---- All stores for conveyance by transport must be ready for loading outside respective Headquarters at 2 p.m.

6. Os.C. Companies will notify Battalion H.Q.
    (a) That their billets are clean before moving off.
    (b) When their Companies have arrived at VRAIGNES.

7. One Officer per Company, 1 Sgt. for Headquarters and one N.C.O. per platoon will go on in advance to take over billets. They must report at VRAIGNES by 12 noon.

J.Hitchcock
Captain & Adjutant,
8th. Battalion The Buffs.

D I S T R I B U T I O N.

| Copy No. | 1 | to | The Commanding Officer. |
| " | " | 2 | " O.C., 1st. Battalion NORTH STAFFORDSHIRE Regt. |
| " | " | 3 | " " A.Coy. |
| " | " | 4 | " " B.Coy. |
| " | " | 5 | " " C.Coy. |
| " | " | 6 | " " D.Coy. |
| " | " | 7 | " Transport Officer. |
| " | " | 8 | " Quartermaster. |
| " | " | 9 | " R.S.M. |
| " | " | 10 | " War Diary. |
| " | " | 11 | " " " |
| " | " | 12 | " Office. |

GENERAL,

Reference Relief Order No. 88 attached, all blankets, spare kits, and stores not necessary for blankets etc will be stacked ready for loading at 9 a.m.

7.1.16.

*[signature]*
Captain A/Adjutant,
7th. Battalion The Buffs.

TB 3/7

8th. Battalion The Buffs.

Training Programme from 3rd. January to 7th. January 1918.

| Date. | 7.30 a.m.- 8 a.m. | 9.15 a.m.- 10.15 a.m. | 10.30 a.m.- 11.30 a.m. | 11.45 a.m.- 12.45 p.m. | 2 p.m.- 4 p.m. | 5.30 p.m.- 6.30 p.m. |
|---|---|---|---|---|---|---|
| Thur. 3rd. | Physical Training | Squad & Platoon Drill | Battalion Drill. Saluting & Rifle Exercises. | Musketry. | Games. | Lecture to all N.C.Os. |
| Fri. 4th. | Physical Training | Squad & Platoon Drill | Battalion Drill. Saluting & Rifle Exs. | Musketry. | Games. | Lecture all Officers. " A.Coy. N.C.Os. by R.S.M. |
| Sat. 5th. | Physical Training | Squad & Platoon Drill | Battalion Drill. Saluting & Rifle Exs. | Musketry. | Games. | Lecture B.Coy. N.C.Os. by R.S.M. |
| Sun. 6th. | | | | | | Lecture all Officers. " C.Coys. N.C.Os. by R.S.M. |
| Mon. 7th. | Physical Training. | 9 a.m. Battalion will parade for Brigade Ceremonial Parade. Further details will be notified later. | M U S K E T R Y. | | | Lecture D.Coy. N.C.Os. by R.S.M. |

N.C.Os. Class will parade under the R.S.M. daily.
Signalling Class will parade under Signalling Instructor, daily.

2.1.18.

J Hitchcock Capt &/Major
Commanding 8th. Battalion The Buffs.

# RELIEF ORDERS.

by

Lieut.-Colonel F.C.R.Studd.
Commanding 8th. Battalion The Buffs.

Field.  
No. 25.  
Copy No. 11

6.1.18.

1. The Battalion will relieve the 9th. Battalion ROYAL SUSSEX REGT. at MONTIGNY on the 8th. inst.

2. ORDER OF MARCH.---- Headquarters will move off at 1.0 p.m. followed by D., C., B. and A.Companies at distances of 200 yards between platoons.

3. TRANSPORT.---- All blankets and stores not for immediate use will be ready for loading by 9.0 a.m. The remainder by 1.0 p.m. The Transport Officer will arrange accordingly. 200 yards distance between each six Transport vehicles must be maintained.

4. The Quartermaster will arrange to take over billets etc. at MONTIGNY by 1.0 p.m. the 8th. inst.

5. Companies will render reports (a) That billets have been left clean. (b) When they have arrived in their new billets.

Captain & Adjutant,
8th. Battalion The Buffs.

## DISTRIBUTION.

| Copy No. | 1 | to The Commanding Officer. |
| " | " | 2 | " O.C., 9th. Battalion ROYAL SUSSEX REGT. |
| " | " | 3 | " " A.Coy. |
| " | " | 4 | " " B.Coy. |
| " | " | 5 | " " C.Coy. |
| " | " | 6 | " " D.Coy. |
| " | " | 7 | " Transport Officer. |
| " | " | 8 | " Quartermaster. |
| " | " | 9 | " R.S.M. |
| " | " | 10 | " War Diary. |
| " | " | 11 | " " |
| " | " | 12 | " Office. |

## RELIEF ORDERS.
### by
### Lieut.- Colonel F.C.R.Studd, D.S.O.
### Commanding 8th. Battalion The Buffs.

Field:
No.26.
Copy No. 10.

11.1.18.

1. The Battalion will relieve the 8th. Battalion ROYAL WEST KENT Regt. in the Right Sub-Sector on the 13th. January.

2. DISPOSITIONS.---
    'B' Coy., 1 Platoon and 1 L.G.Section of 'A' Coy.     Front Line.
    Remainder of 'A' Coy.     1 Support.
    'C' Coy. less 1 Platoon.     2 Support.
    'D' Coy. and 1 Platoon 'C' Coy.     Reserve.

3. ORDER OF MARCH.--- Companies will move off at 12 noon in the following order:- Headquarters, Front Line, 1 Support, 2 Support, Reserve.
200 yards distance will be maintained between platoons.

4. ROUTE.--- HERVILLY - HESBECOURT - TEMPLEUX - Valley South of HARGICOURT Road - Light Railway - LEICESTER LOUNGE.

5. TRANSPORT.--- All blankets and stores will be ready for loading at 11 a.m. The Transport Officer will arrange for 2 limbers per Company and 2 for H.Q. to be at respective H.Q. at 11 a.m.

6. Look-out Post and A.A. Lewis Gun Positions will be handed over. The Quartermaster will arrange to hand over Camp.

7. TRENCH STORES.--- All trench stores, Maps, Defence Schemes, etc. will be carefully taken over and receipts forwarded to Battalion H.Q. by 12 noon the 14th. inst.

8. DETAILS.--- Details remaining behind will parade under the R.S.M. at 12 noon.

9. Companies will render a report that billets have been left clean before marching off.

10. Completion of relief will be wired to Battalion H.Q. by the Code Word 'BOBBY'.

*(signed)*
Captain & Adjutant,
8th. Battalion The Buffs.

### DISTRIBUTION.

Copy No. 1 to The Commanding Officer.
" " 2 " O.C., 8th. Battn. ROYAL WEST KENT Regt.
" " 3 " " A.Coy.
" " 4 " " B.Coy.
" " 5 " " C.Coy.
" " 6 " " D.Coy.
" " 7 " Transport Officer.
" " 8 " Quartermaster.
" " 9 " R.S.M.
" " 10 " War Diary.
" " 11 " " "
" " 12 " Office.

## RELIEF ORDERS.

by

Lieut.-Colonel F.C.R.Studd,D.S.O.
Commanding 8th. Battalion The Buffs.

─oo─ooo─ooo─ooo─oo─

Field.
No. 27.                                                                  17.1.18.
Copy No. 12

1. The Battalion will be relieved on the 21st. inst. by the 2nd. Battalion LEINSTER Regt. and on relief will move to Camp at HANCOURT in Corps Reserve.

2. On relief Companies will move by platoons at 200 yards distance to ROISEL where the Battalion will entrain at O.Y.205(K.12.a.55.9.) at 8 p.m.

3. Lieut. C.C.Allen will proceed to reconnoitre the entraining point on the 21st. inst.

4. All gum boots of Companies in No. 2 Support and Reserve and all spare gum boots from Companies in front line and No. 1 Support will be handed in at 9 a.m. the 21st. inst., wet gum boots to HARGICOURT Drying Room and the remainder to Gum Boot Store(L.10.a.) The remaining gum boots of the front line Company and No. 1 Support Company will be changed and handed into Brigade Gum Boot store as platoons move out of the trenches. Receipts will be obtained for all gum boots handed in.

5. All trench stores, aeroplane photos, defence schemes, maps, etc. will be carefully handed over and receipts forwarded to Battalion Orderly Room by 12 noon the 22nd. inst.

6. All blankets, mess gear, Company Stores, Lewis Guns, etc. will be carefully taken on the Battalion Dump ready for loading at 6 p.m. The Transport Officer will arrange for 2 limbers per Company and 2 for Headquarters to collect same.

7. All Look-Out Posts, A.A. Lewis Gun Positions, etc. will be carefully taken over. The Quartermaster will arrange to take over the Camp at HANCOURT.

8. Companies will report:-
   (a) Completion of relief by code word 'BOMB'.
   (b) Arrival in billets in HANCOURT.

                                                    Captain & Adjutant,
                                                    8th. Battalion The Buffs.

### DISTRIBUTION.

| | | |
|---|---|---|
| Copy No. 1 to The Cmdg. Officer. | Copy No. 8 to | Transport Officer. |
| 2   O.C. 2nd. Leinster R. | 9 | Quartermaster. |
| 3   Second in Command. | 10 | R.S.M. |
| 4   O.C. A.Coy. | 11 | C.S.M. i/c. |
| 5   "   B.Coy. | 12 | War Diary. |
| 6   "   C.Coy. | 13 | "   " |
| 7   "   D.Coy. | 14 | File. |

S E C R E T.

OPERATION ORDER NO. 1.
by
Lieut.-Colonel F.C.R.Studd.D.S.O.
Commanding 8th. Battalion The Buffs.
——oo—ooo—ooo—ooo—oo——

Field.
Copy No. 13.

Reference Map: HARGICOURT Special Sheet 1.a.

1. The Battalion on our left will raid the enemy trenches on the morning of 20.1.18.

2. Zero hour will be notified later.

3. In conjunction with this raid the 8th. Battalion The Buffs will carry out the following programme commencing at Zero :-
(a) A party of 1 Officer and 11 O.R. of 'B' Company will manipulate 3 groups of figures in 'NO MAN'S LAND', representing advancing infantry, at about C.1.c.60.05.
(b) A party of 1 N.C.O. and 12 men of 'D' Company will, if the wind is favourable, light a number of smoke candles in CURTAIN LANE at C.7.c.60.95.
(Both these parties will parade outside Company H.Q. in POND SUPPORT one hour before Zero with all necessary material. They will be under the command of 2/Lieut. F.C.Frost who will be responsible for the operation. This Officer will see that the groups of figures are placed in position during the night, and he will use his own discretion as to whether the wind is in the right quarter at Zero for the use of smoke candles.)
(c) Three Lewis Guns will be mounted in POND TRENCH under orders of the Lewis Gun Officer and will keep up a continuous fire on points selected by him until our artillery barrage stops, when they will cease fire.

4. All other troops will be kept under cover, in dugouts if possible, till the raid is over and enemy activity has ceased.

5. A representative from each Company will report at these Headquarters at 12 midnight 19.1.18 to synchronise watches.

18.1.18.

Captain & Adjutant,
8th. Battalion The Buffs.

D I S T R I B U T I O N.
————————————

| Copy No. | 1 | to Commdg. Officer. | Copy No. | 8 | to O.C. B.Coy. |
|---|---|---|---|---|---|
| | 2 | H.Q. 17th. Inf. Bde. | | 9 | " C.Coy. |
| | 3 | O.C. 1st. Roy. Fus. | | 10 | " D.Coy. |
| | 4 | " 12th. Roy. Fus. | | 11 | 2/Lt. F.C.Frost. |
| | 5 | " 3rd. Rifle Bde. | | 12 | War Diary. |
| | 6 | " 3rd. D. Cav. Bn. | | 13 | " " |
| | 7 | " A.Coy. | | 14 | File. |

# RELIEF ORDERS.

by

Lieut.- Colonel F.C.R.Studd, D.S.O.
Commanding 8th. Battalion The Buffs.

Field.
No.27.
Copy No. 13.

19.1.18.

1. The Battalion will be relieved on the 21st. inst. by the 2nd. Battalion LEINSTER Regt. and on relief will move to Camp at HANCOURT in Corps Reserve.

2. On relief Companies will move by platoons at 200 yards distance to ROISEL where the Battalion will entrain at O.Y.205(K.12.a.66.9.) at 9 p.m.

3. Lieut. C.C.Allen will proceed to reconnoitre the entraining point on the 21st. inst.

4. All gum boots of Companies in No. 2 Support and Reserve and all spare gum boots from Companies in front line and No. 1 Support will be handed in at 9 a.m. the 21st. inst., wet gum boots to HANCOURT Drying Room and the remainder to Brigade Gum Boot Store(L.10.a.) The remaining gum boots of the front line Company and No. 1 Support Company will be changed and handed into Brigade Gum Boot Store as platoons move out of the trenches. Receipts will be obtained for all gum boots handed in.

5. All trench stores, aeroplane photos, defence schemes, maps, etc. will be carefully handed over and receipts forwarded to Battalion Orderly Room by 12 noon the 22nd. inst.

6. All blankets, mens gear, Company stores, Lewis Guns, etc. will be on the Battalion Dump ready for loading at 8 p.m. The Transport Officer will arrange for 2 limbers per Company and 2 for Headquarters to collect same.

7. All Look-out Posts, A.A. Lewis Gun Positions, etc. will be carefully taken over. The Quartermaster will arrange to take over the Camp at HANCOURT.

8. Companies will report:-
    (a) Completion of relief by code word 'BOMB'.
    (b) Arrival in billets at HANCOURT.

*[signature]*
Captain & Adjutant,
8th. Battalion The Buffs.

## DISTRIBUTION.

| | | |
|---|---|---|
| Copy No. 1 to The Commdg. Officer. | Copy No. 8 to | Transport Officer. |
| 2   O.C. 2nd. Leinster R. | 9 | Quartermaster. |
| 3   Second in Command. | 10 | R.S.M. |
| 4   O.C. A.Coy. | 11 | C.S.M. i/c. |
| 5   "   B.Coy. | 12 | War Diary. |
| 6   "   C.Coy. | 13 | "   " |
| 7   "   D.Coy. | 14 | File. |

## Training Programme Jan 22nd to Jan 27th 1915

| Date | 7 - 7.30 am | 9.15 - 10.15 am | 10.30 - 11.30 am | 12 noon - 12.45 pm | 2 - 4 pm | 5.30 - 6.30 pm |
|---|---|---|---|---|---|---|
| Fri 22nd Jan. | Parades | Squads | Company arrangement | Kit inspection etc | | |
| Sat 23rd | Physical Training | Rifle Exercises, Saluting, Platoon & Company Drill | Battalion Drill | Musketry & Specialist training | Games | Lecture to all N.C.O.'s by O.C. Command |
| Mon 24th | Physical Training | Rifle Exercises, Saluting, Platoon & Company Drill | Battalion Drill | Musketry & Specialist training | Games | Lecture to N.C.O. Officers by O.C. Command |
| Tues 25th | Physical Training | Rifle Exercises, Saluting, Platoon & Company Drill | Battalion Drill | Musketry & Specialist training | Games | 5.30 - 6 pm Lecture to O.C. Catechetical N.C.M. |
| Wed 26th | Physical Training | Rifle Exercises, Saluting, Platoon & Company Drill | Battalion Drill | Musketry & Specialist training | Games | Lecture N.C.O.'s Catechetical on R.S.M. |
| Thurs 27th | | Church Parade as ordered | | | | |

N.C.O. Classes, Lectures run class a signal Class daily. Their classes will attend 10.30 - 11.30 am daily.

Pemberton
Major O.C.
8th Battalion The Buffs

www.ingramcontent.com/pod-product-compliance
Lightning Source LLC
Chambersburg PA
CBHW080923230426
43668CB00014B/2182